I0810257

# Mainstream Culture Refocused

# Mainstream Culture Refocused

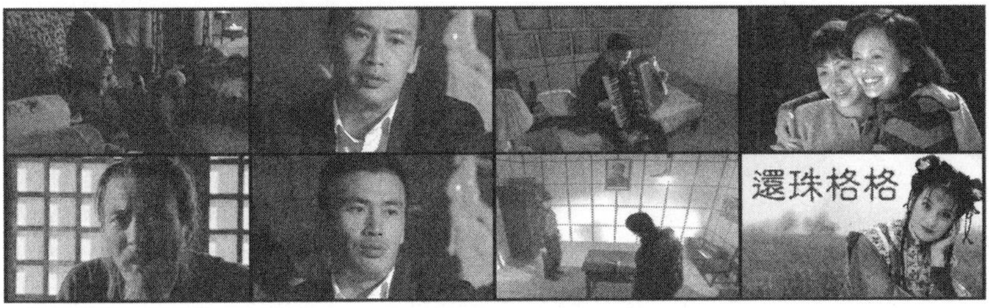


## Television Drama, Society, and the Production of Meaning in Reform-Era China

ZHONG XUEPING

University of Hawai'i Press
Honolulu

Printed in the United States of America
15 14 13 12 11 10 6 5 4 3 2 1

**Library of Congress Cataloging-in-Publication Data**

Zhong, Xueping.

Mainstream culture refocused : television drama, society, and the production of meaning in reform-era China / Zhong Xueping.

p. cm.

Includes bibliographical references and index.

ISBN 978-0-8248-3417-3 (hardcover : alk. paper)

ISBN 978-0-8248-3469-2 (pbk. : alk. paper)

1. Television plays, Chinese—History and criticism. 2. Television—Social aspects—China. 3. Popular culture—China. I. Title.

PL2368.T44Z46 2010

791.45'70951—dc22

2010010583

University of Hawai'i Press books are printed on acid-free paper and meet the guidelines for permanence and durability of the Council on Library Resources.

Designed by University of Hawai'i Press production staff
Printed by The Maple-Vail Book Manufacturing Group

*To the memory of*
*Charles Nelson (1925–2008):*
*mentor and friend*

# Contents

# Acknowledgments

The idea of writing a book on Chinese television drama began to take root in the year 2000, when a Chinese-television-related conference was held at Tufts University. I thank a former colleague, Wang Qingping, for proposing and organizing the conference. I would also like to thank my colleagues, especially Vida Johnson and Christiane Romero, of the Department of German, Russian, and Asian Languages and Literatures of Tufts University for making the conference possible and for actively participating in welcoming the Chinese delegation at the conference.

I am also grateful to my colleague Mingquan Wang for his untiring willingness to help me troubleshoot computer-related problems.

An American Council of Learned Societies research grant as well as a summer faculty research grant and other research grants from Tufts University made it possible for me to make several trips to China. Invited talks and presentations were good opportunities for me to flesh out ideas and questions about how to approach what proved to be a challenging project. I thank Yomi Braester for inviting me to a conference on visuality at the University of Washington, Hong Zhang for asking me to give a talk on the phenomenon of Chinese television drama at Colby College, Zhang Zhen for having me give a talk on "history drama" at New York University, Chris Berry for inviting me to join a panel at the Association for Asian Studies on Chinese television drama, Paul Festa for the opportunity to present the chapter on television songs at a workshop on popular culture in Asia at Harvard University, and Wang Ban and Ching Kwan Lee for inviting me to present the chapter on anticorruption drama at a conference held at University of Michigan.

Many colleagues and friends have been, in various ways, inspirational over the years in confirming the importance of this project. Thanks are therefore due to Cai Rong, Cao Tianyu, Chen Huifen, Claire Conceison, Huang Zhen, Haiyan Lee, Lin Chun, Liao Kebin, Lu Yan, Wang Ban, and Ye Weili. I must also thank the two anonymous readers of the manuscript for this book for their constructive comments and suggestions. I am particularly grateful to Pamela

Kelley at the University of Hawai'i Press for her recognition of the significance of the book's subject matter and for her professionalism, which made the revision process smooth and efficient. Special thanks go to Lili Ch'en, whose upbeat spirit, sense of humor, and wisdom have sustained me throughout years of a sometimes drudging way of life. My heartfelt gratitude goes to Susan Greenberg, whose excellent editorial skills unfailingly help clean up a nonnative-language writer's various mistakes, big and small. I would not have developed a critical sense of my own writing if not for Malcolm Griffith, who has been the most critical, sharp, and demanding reader of what I write in English. Indeed, I will never be able to thank Susan and Malcolm enough for the help they have given me over the years and for the special friendship I have with each of them. My final thanks are reserved for the late Charles Nelson, my mentor at Tufts University, whose friendship was essential during the years I have been at Tufts. He was a *liangshi yiyou* to me, a most kind, considerate, supportive, and funny mentor and friend. I dedicate this book in memory of Charlie.

INTRODUCTION

# Mainstream Culture Refocused

## Toward an Understanding of Chinese Television Drama

It seems only yesterday that scholars of Chinese literature and culture were all in an uproar about the "second renaissance" of modern Chinese literature and the new generations of Chinese filmmakers who burst onto the cultural scene of the 1980s. Since the early 1990s, however, this cultural landscape has evolved, and literature and film no longer occupy the central position they held during the 1980s. Among other things, they have had to contend with television and other forms of commercialized mass media and the Internet for public attention. One of the major storytelling forms in China today exists on television as *dianshiju* (television drama) or *dianshi lianxuju* (television serial). In the last three decades, especially since *Kewang* (Yearnings, 1990), television dramas have generated widespread public attention and serious debate on a range of issues.[1] Television drama has come to constitute a major part of contemporary China's cultural landscape, and critics are hard-pressed to disregard its presence and larger sociocultural implications. Yet many still do (despite burgeoning scholarly attention).[2] The propagandistic and commercial dimensions of television culture and the mainstream and quotidian nature of television drama in particular have continued to ensure a minor status for Chinese television drama in the hierarchy of cultural forms studied by the humanities.[3]

Many critics have casually used the term "soap opera" to identify Chinese television drama. Indeed, even though the term "soap opera" originated in the United States, making visible the connection between corporate sponsorship and the production of daytime television dramas, today its connotation mainly pertains to the representational characteristics of television drama in general, referring to the melodramatic "codes" of its narrative construction.[4] I will return to the notion of "melodrama" later in this Introduction, but as a cultural form and practice, has Chinese television drama, *dianshiju*, always been American soap opera's double? If we hesitate to answer "yes," it is chiefly because a ready application of the term to Chinese television drama collapses one set of cultural production with another without fully recognizing their very different social, cultural, and historical conditions and contexts of meaning production. The casual application of "soap opera" in the Chinese case is therefore more indicative of an ongoing low-level intellectual interest in the topic of (Chinese) television drama rather than a clearly delineated understanding of the phenomenon. More than that, it is also indicative of an ongoing intellectual uncertainty about how to engage this cultural phenomenon.

Along with some recent studies of Chinese television drama, mostly by media studies scholars, this book aims at changing these dynamics.[5] Instead of merely lamenting and dismissing the rise of television culture and the impact of televisual dramas in China—a perspective largely informed by (Western) intellectual criticisms of "mass culture" and "mainstream popular culture"—I argue for a need to recognize that, along with the powerful rise of the television medium (which is now competing with the rise of yet another technology-aided medium, the Internet), Chinese "mainstream culture," including both state and market forces, has become a site of ideological and discursive struggles. According to Wang Hui, if a "depoliticization" (which means "depoliticized politics") process characterizes the postrevolution Chinese economic reforms, the politics and the tensions within this process, nevertheless, await fuller analysis and understanding.[6] Contemporary Chinese mainstream culture is in flux, in part owing to structural changes spurred on by changes in the dominant ideology and in the state's economic and cultural policies and also by a corresponding rise of market forces. Critics have rightly questioned the nature of these changes and the relationship between the state and the market within the larger context of the latest round of globalizing capitalism. But at the same time, the state-market-dichotomy perspective assumes a monolithic view of the two entities and ignores the fact that Chinese mainstream culture consists of multiple social, cultural, and historical forces whose coexistence, and the tensions and contradictions among them, constitute the seen and, to echo Haiping Yan, "unseen rhythms" that shape and inform cultural production.[7] Mainstream culture thus produced inevitably manifests social changes, corresponding problems, and ideological struggles. In other words, although surely subject to the forces of the state and the market, cultural production within this context continues to be influenced by different and sometimes conflicting cultural and ideological legacies related to the complexity of one and a half centuries of modern Chinese history. Television drama as a quintessential mainstream cultural phenomenon, I argue, offers a diverse collection of televisual textual materials with which to study the implications of these influences.[8]

In introducing this study, I first highlight the "fate" of mainstream culture and the debates about it in the West, with a brief observation about their own sociocultural particularities. In the Chinese context, I then argue for a need to move beyond the existing mode of state-market dichotomy in order to arrive at a historically informed understanding of the production of contemporary Chinese mainstream culture in general and television drama in particular. In China, mainstream (popular) culture continues to be unabashedly tied to social concerns, and this tie is rich with contradictions indicative of ideological tensions. Questions that interest me here include the following: What kind of social concerns are at issue? What gave rise to them? What informs their cultural representations? And, above all, how are we to understand televisual representational implications in the context of the rapidly changing social and economic conditions in the last three decades of economic reforms, with the inevitable corresponding ideological and discursive struggles, and the major cultural and historical legacies, from previous historical periods, that coexist in contemporary China? In conjunction with situating the production of television drama within the historical context of the last three decades, I believe there is a need to understand "melodrama," the dominant mode of narrative representations in television drama, in historical terms. Indeed, while most dominant intellectual anxiety toward "mainstream culture" stems in part from a (continuing) discomfort with the latter's "melodramatic" characteristics, little clearly delineated discussion exists regarding how to understand "melodrama" in relation to cultural production such as television drama and, by extension, in relation to the historical contexts and experiences of "Chinese modernity." While the Introduction may seem somewhat abstract, the chapters in the rest of the book focus on some of the major subgenres of television drama, highlighting representative dramas in relation to the central questions raised above.

## "Mainstream Culture" Refocused

In today's (Western-influenced) academic discourses, "mainstream (popular) culture" is largely equivalent to "low" culture, unworthy of serious critical attention. Indeed, despite the Western Marxian critique of ideology in recent decades that argues for the importance of examining how the hegemony of the dominant class' ideology works through mainstream popular culture, and despite the fact that there are different ideological persuasions and stances within criticisms of mainstream popular culture, part of the shared result is a critical distancing from and a general reluctance to acknowledge that "mainstream popular culture" also requires serious analysis and interpretation.[9] And yet, to echo Zizek and Carla Freccero, such acknowledgment is important not because mainstream culture is simplistic and ideologically manipulative and therefore deserves ready criticism, but because, ironically, it appears to be obviously the case and therefore easily dismissible.[10] A ready dismissal of mainstream popular culture, I might add, is indicative of the tenacious elite-popular divide whose own social particularities, including critics' own social positions, tend to remain invisible in existing critical discourses.[11] The result of a ready dismissal, as Freccero maintains, is a weakened intellectual position from which to engage mainstream popular culture critically.

In arguing why it is important to take mainstream popular culture seriously, Freccero points out:

> As long as popular culture remains a degraded cultural form in the minds of liberal educators and students themselves, it will be available for use without analysis, much the way religion and morality are invoked in U.S. public culture as givens without meanings that are subject to contestation. Liberal arts education will will itself into anachronism—as it is already being accused of doing—by focusing exclusively on forms of cultural production that are not widely shared in public culture. The domain of popular representation will pass as fact, unavailable for argument, debate, and analysis, or it will become an arena of technocratic competence where the focus will be on how to manipulate or manage it, but not analyze and interpret it.[12]

Here Freccero echoes Zizek's questioning when the latter identifies a shift in Western Marxist criticism of ideology "from Critique of Political Economy to Critique of Instrumental Reason: from Lukacs's *History and Class Consciousness* to the early Frankfurt School, where ideological distortion is derived from the 'commodity form,' to the notion of Instrumental Reason which is no longer grounded in a concrete social reality but is, rather, conceived as a kind of anthropological, even quasi-transcendental, primordial constant that enables us to explain the social reality of domination and exploitation."[13] The problem, Zizek continues, is that "such an approach, although it is adequate at its own level, can easily ensnare us in historicist relativism that suspends the inherent cognitive value of the term 'ideology' and makes it into a mere expression of social circumstances."[14]

To expand on Zizek's point, one can argue that the dismissive approach to mainstream popular culture in the West does not necessarily lead to a better understanding of—indeed it has shifted much-needed attention away from—the social and class characteristics of the cultural criticism itself that has evolved in the West since the counterculture movement—or, in the words of some Chinese critics, the bourgeois "cultural revolution"—of the 1960s.[15] Indeed, the rise of the technology-aided mainstream popular culture in the

West is itself a social, economic, and ideological phenomenon historically closely related to the dominance of the bourgeois class whose values, beliefs, ideals, and aesthetics would be transmitted and normalized via mass media and later ensconced in the name of the euphemistically termed middle class. Intellectual criticisms in academia—developed into the form of cultural studies—are themselves part of this "cultural revolution" and have helped effect changes in cultural criticism vis-à-vis (the production of) mainstream popular culture.[16] And yet today the condemnatory approach to mainstream popular culture, as a critical practice, persists in ways that blur the social characteristics of the last half century of cultural struggles in the West. As such, it also remains blind to the social particularities of the development of the critical discourse about mainstream popular culture in the West. Such blindness is at least partially responsible for taking "critical thinking" into what some critics refer to as "the dead end of paradoxes." One can even suggest that, while Gramsci's theory of "hegemony" effectively exposes the ideological dominance of mainstream culture in "democratic" Western societies, subsequent applications of his theory have virtually depleted an equally if not more important attention to modes of production, social relations, the political economy of structural problems, and their socioeconomic particularities. And the widespread and unreflective application of the theory has led to a dogmatic approach toward anything that is labeled "mainstream," leaving the social specificities of such theorization itself largely out of sight and continuing to subject studies of mainstream culture to a critical practice that remains hierarchically oriented and is itself little questioned.[17]

The point of moving beyond the elitist tendency of seeing mainstream popular culture as monolithic and unchanging, as always lowly, conservative, and hegemonic, is to understand that (mainstream) culture in any given society functions, to echo Zygmunt Bauman, as structure and praxis, and therefore always is subject to and can effect change.[18] Production of culture is inevitably informed by and subject to, among other things, major social relations and contradictions within them, but culture as structure and praxis can also effect an unstable and dialectic relationship between cultural practices. One such dialectic may be between practices that are deemed either "apologetic" (mainstream) or "critical" (avant-garde). Within this dialectic, if I may stay on an abstract level, what is considered "apologetic" inevitably generates "critical" responses, and what is "critical" can be ideologically either "conservative," "progressive," or "avant-garde," and can always be co-opted by and absorbed into the less critical part of the mainstream culture. The interaction between the two roles, in other words, can lead what is "critical" to being simultaneously absorbed into, while also effecting changes in, the "mainstream culture." Depending on the social specificities within a particular society and the power structure of its culture and discursive struggles for beliefs, ideals, and values, changes can either give rise to opposition and critical forces, or they can co-opt the critical component, which may in turn result in the weakening of the avant-garde nature of cultural criticism (which, incidentally, often takes the form of placing "avant-garde" on the pedestal of the elite culture). Such a process indicates not only that "mainstream culture" is constantly subject to challenge and change, but also, and more importantly, the dialectic relationship between the apologetic and critical dimensions of culture as praxis allows room for exploring and seeking cultural and social alternatives. The interaction between the two makes it possible to explore the role of mainstream (popular) culture in a society and the extent to which it manifests various social tensions while also effecting changes.

With regard to television culture, few influential Western cultural theorists or critics have paid as much specific attention to television culture in general and television drama in particular as Raymond Williams. Williams hoped to effect change via a new technology-aided popular cultural form, namely, television drama. Grounded in a specific sociocultural context, Williams' discussion of television in 1974 stemmed in part from his expectations for developing a popular culture capable of questioning and resisting the hegemony of dominant culture—in the case of Britain, the blatantly class-oriented elite. The globalizing power of American culture dressed up as "popular culture" has subsequently dimmed such hopes and has also made Williams' positive view of television appear too idealistic. Still, the structural implications of television drama he describes can help ground discussion of representational issues in relation to the political economy of technology-aided modern cultural practices.[19]

Williams sees in television drama "[a] new mobility in time and space, and a new flexibility in movement between kinds of dramatic speech—especially between the conventions of 'spoken' and 'unspoken' thought and feeling.... What could be seen from an orthodox theatrical position as the limitations of the broadcasting medium became opportunities for different kinds of dramatic creation."[20] He recognizes that "for more than half a century there had been an especially interesting complex relation between dramatic structures and the new technological means of production"[21] and that "the comparatively low-cost original television play, which could quite quickly be shown to a very large audience, represented a new dimension of cultural possibility."[22] Williams relates such technology-aided possibilities to the notion of "structure of feeling" and finds that "it is not surprising that many television plays reproduced... [an] assumption of the nature of representative reality."[23] There is, in other words, a dialectic structural relationship between television as a technological system and television drama as a new cultural form. Williams fleshes out this relationship by noting the social and cultural effects such a new development could bring when he remarks that both in Britain and the United States, "it is not uncommon for the majority of viewers to see, regularly, as much as two or three hours of drama, of various kinds, every day. The implications of this have scarcely begun to be considered."[24] It is clear, he states, that "one of the unique characteristics of advanced industrial societies is that drama as an experience is now an intrinsic part of everyday life, at a *quantitative level* which is so very much greater than any precedent as to seem a fundamental *qualitative change.* Whatever the social and cultural reasons may finally be, it is clear that watching dramatic simulation of a wide range of experiences is now an essential part of our modern cultural pattern" (emphasis mine).[25]

Williams' discussion recognizes the dialectic between culture as structure and as praxis and also the complex roles of "mainstream popular culture." In terms of the quantitative and qualitative dialectic, one wonders in what ways the Internet and cyberculture have contributed to significant changes in meaning production in this post-Williams age both in the West and in other parts of the world, an issue I mention here in passing both to situate Williams' remarks within their own time and also to indicate their continuing applicability in other historical contexts.

Today, almost four decades since his remarks, Williams' expectations for an alternative television culture may indeed have proven too idealistic (although attempts at creating such a culture continue to exist), but the fact that his ideals appear too idealistic today may be one of the best examples of the social, or class, characteristic of the Western "cultural revolution" of the 1960s, which ensured the rise to power of a different kind of popular culture than he had imagined. As such, it also helps demonstrate the need to explore the political economy of (Western) mainstream popular culture and the need to treat it "seriously," as argued by the critics quoted above. What, then, would "fundamental qualitative change" be in China (a postsocialist industrial capitalist society? or socialism with Chinese characteristics?) in relation to the quantitative surge in the production and broadcasting of Chinese television dramas? Given the specific historical context of contemporary China, where does a popular culture form such as television drama fall, socially and structurally, in relation to the official ideology and mainstream culture compared with the historical contexts of meaning production in popular culture either in Britain of the 1960s and 1970s or today's United States? How do we identify and understand the "different kinds of dramatic speech" and "different kinds of dramatic creation" on television in the context of China's last three decades of economic reforms?

Even though the "state" plays a complex and powerful role in cultural production in Western societies—values, ideals, beliefs (including prejudices and biases)—Western cultural studies critics tend not to draw attention to the role of the state in their studies.[26] When it comes to China, no discussion of contemporary Chinese culture can get around noting the role of the state. Given the limited scope of this study, I will not elaborate on the implications of this difference. Suffice it to say that one should not conclude that the state does not also play a role in cultural production in the West. Recognizing the role of the "state" and the "market," some discussions have correctly argued that, in order to better understand Chinese popular culture (including television culture), the relationship between the "official" and the "unofficial," and between the "state" and the "market" must be fully recognized and critically examined.[27] Ruoyun Bai's analysis is one example.[28] Focusing on three major forces at work, the author suggests that "the ascendancy of television entertainment in China from the 1990s onward is mainly the result of media restructuring and the subsequent deepened media commercialization, to which the party-state's proactive participation is central."[29] Media restructuring, she argues, includes three developments—reconsolidation of television stations, establishment of private companies for content production, and China's entry into the World Trade Organization—all of which have been made possible by the changes in state policies. Such changes have one goal: changing the television medium from being mainly the outlet of Chinese Communist Party (CCP) directives and propaganda to becoming a means for commercial gain. The author points out a paradox underlying these changes, namely, "if television is the Communist Party's property and mouthpiece, or at least the Party's 'Publicity Inc.,' then what does the trivialization of Chinese television mean to the discursive monopoly desired by the Party? What is entertainment doing to the Chinese people?" She wonders, "How can we therefore characterize China's media and political environment, an Orwellian one or a Huxleyean [*sic*] one, or a mixture of both?"[30] These questions point to some of the complexities and paradoxes that exist in today's China, but the Eurocentric—Orwellian versus Huxleyan—frame of reference here makes it impossible for the discussion to move beyond placing Chinese television culture at the dead end of trivialization and paradoxes.[31]

Yin Hong, a scholar who works in China, offers his insights in a recent article (part of which has been translated and published in English, using television drama as his focus).[32] "The development of Chinese television drama," he states, "must be viewed within the context of the double-track movement (*shuanggui yunxing*) of marketization with Chinese characteristics (*zhongguo tese de shichang hua*) and [the media] being state-owned (*guoyou xing*). On the one hand, [the production of] television drama is subject to the control, intervention, and guidance of the state. On the other hand, it is also under the strong impact of the market economy and consumer culture. Together, this phenomenon epitomizes the changes in the role played by the media in the various larger power struggles in contemporary China. The development of Chinese television drama not only reflects the realignment and conflicts within contemporary Chinese politics, economy, and culture, but has also exerted a complex and profound influence on the ethos, value formation, and cultural trends [of the society]."[33] Here, Yin not only points out the complex dynamics that occur between the state and the market in the production of television drama, but he also recognizes the impact of television drama on other aspects of the society at large such as "the ethos, value formation, and cultural trends." Whether one likes television drama as a cultural form or not, Yin's discussion helps move issues regarding television drama beyond the narrow domain of (aesthetic) "taste," recognizing the role of a popular cultural form as cultural practice and the need to explore its implications. Such a shift in focus also helps move the definition of television drama beyond the dichotomy of "high" or "low" culture. Still, the very notions of the state and the market need to be further fleshed out, and Yin's discussion (here and in some of his other writings in Chinese) tend to assume but do not fully examine what the "realignment and conflicts" are, what sociocultural forces are involved, and in what ways and to what extent the latter function to affect "the ethos, value formation, and cultural trends."

Jing Wang has questioned situating the study of Chinese popular culture within a framework of "official" or "unofficial" or, for that matter, "high culture" or "low culture."[34] Wang argues that "popular culture" in China does not easily fall into either category—official or unofficial—in the way they are generally assumed and presented—the general assumption being that, since "popular" implies "people," popular culture must belong to the "unofficial" culture. She maintains that only by moving beyond the official-unofficial dichotomy and its problematic assumptions to the link between cultural polices of the state and the production of popular culture can one begin to recognize and attend to popular culture's more complex relationship with, among other things, the state and the market. Wang's discussion points out that a simple (and simplistic) designation of a cultural phenomenon as one thing or the other suffers from a limited and limiting conceptual model and understanding. In her more recent discussion of related issues, Wang further cautions "against treating all organized and planned spaces in contemporary China as devoid of transformative potentials" and points to possible blind spots in existing studies of Chinese popular culture with the Chinese saying *deng xia hei,* or "the most invisible place is the spot right underneath a light."[35] What remains to be illuminated, besides the state and the market, is what, if any, other forces with "transformative potentials"—possibly in "the most invisible place right underneath a light"—exist that mediate official cultural policies and the production of popular culture, what role they play, and, for that matter, to what extent the seemingly "organized and planned spaces" are in fact more than just "organized" and "planned."

The questions raised by these critics are important for investigating the relationships between policies and commercial interests in the development of communication industries nationally and internationally. Structural understanding is crucial in making visible the complex relationships between different interest groups and their power relations. Together, the aforementioned studies help delineate a historical trajectory in which the social, economic, and political logic of changes in television culture is touched upon. At the same time, however, the conceptual framework of these and other existing discussions tends to assume the "state" and the "market" to be two self-explanatory entities. Once these two terms are invoked, what they mean is assumed to be self-evident, leaving society, cultural practices, the complex history of the "state," and many related issues (such as the role of various cultural legacies, historical memories, and cultural politics motivated by changing social relations) at the margins of their critical vision. Underneath the very "light" of the dichotomized state-market framework, much that informs contemporary Chinese mainstream popular culture remains invisible and unrecognized.

An important point of departure must therefore be made here: the specific historical context in which China witnessed the rise of television culture and television drama is neither akin to that of Williams' Britain nor to that of the Adorno-critiqued mass culture in the United States. In contemporary China the quantitatively measurable process can be qualitatively characterized as one of commercialization at the behest of the "state," in the postsocialist and postrevolution era in which several major cultural legacies coexist. The formation of contemporary Chinese "popular culture" has been accompanied by what can be identified as a state-sponsored postrevolution economic reform as China opened its doors and has actively tried to "join the international tracks" (*yu guoji jiegui*), and the last three decades of reform have been full of internal ideological tensions and struggles that are reflected in changes in policies and in social and everyday lived experiences. A corresponding (in Wang Hui's words) depoliticization and also, I must add, a different kind of repoliticization have resulted in an "everyday life" whose imaginary has been increasingly governed by materialist desires and their discontent, defined and informed by the globalizing consumer capitalist logic.[36] At the same time, "everyday life" manifested in contemporary Chinese popular culture such as television drama and in its "everyday" reception is filled with an array of socially, economically, and politically specific problems, tensions, and contradictions. How these specific issues are identified, discussed, debated, and represented is itself tension-filled and not explainable by the existing monolithic view of a state-market dichotomy. If part of what characterizes the Chinese televisual representational characteristics is their "unabashed social concerns," such concerns are informed by different but coexisting cultural and historical legacies, which formulate a strong tension-filled undercurrent that informs this "unabashed tie" in the production of contemporary mainstream culture.

As I will discuss later in the Introduction, the proliferation of subgenres in television drama—one major characteristic of the quantitative and qualitative dialectic in the production of television drama—corresponds to structural changes and commercial interests, to be sure, but also to growing social and economic problems and tensions and to the different historical, cultural, and ideological legacies that inform and shape televisual representations of these issues. Along with that proliferation, the quantitative-qualitative relationship vis-à-vis the production (and reception) of Chinese television drama is also characterized by a corresponding shift of ideological and discursive struggles into the domains of mainstream popular culture, in this case specifically popular televisual representations that have become a dominant form of dramatic representation.

Although I do not suggest that cultural texts and social reality have a direct cause-effect correlation, I do want to emphasize the link between the two. I will explore its implications "symptomatically," via the notion of melodrama within the Chinese context. The development of television drama as a cultural form is explosive, unruly, and full of contradictions that, despite having generated much discomfort on the part of critics, still defy simple conclusion and generalization. Indeed, as mainstream popular cultural products, Chinese televisual representations, along with their production and reception, are no less emblematic of the issues and contradictions within China's latest round of social transformation than issues and contradictions represented in other forms of cultural and narrative representation. As in studies of other cultural forms, therefore, the relationship between social, economic, and political contexts, (televisual) texts, and historical subtexts constitutes the central concern of this study and motivates its approach. Above all, it is my insistence on recognizing the production of television drama as a sociocultural engagement—as cultural practice with complex ideological implications—that anchors the significance of this study.

In the sections that follow, I turn to the difficult task of fleshing out the complex aspects of television drama as a mainstream popular cultural production and cultural phenomenon. I focus on four "mainstream" aspects including the state and the market, the institutional and social characteristics of the practitioners in the production of this cultural form, the representational characteristics—especially those of melodrama—of television drama, and social concerns (and what informs them) as they are manifested in the development of "subgenres." I explore the ways in which the state, the market, Chinese intellectuals, and different social groups are all implicated in the rapid development of this mainstream cultural phenomenon, on the one hand, and how the tensions and contradictions within their interactions manifested televisually, help complicate our understanding of contemporary Chinese society, on the other. The emergence of and rapid growth in the production of television drama can be seen as having functioned as a cultural site where contemporary social-economic issues are addressed and different cultural legacies and ideological views transmitted and contested. By highlighting some of the major points of contention in recent debates and discussions of the notion of melodrama in literature and film studies in the West, I discuss how the continuing tensions within these discussions help both complicate the notion of melodrama and make it a useful point of entry into studies of Chinese television drama. In addition to recognizing its melodramatic mode, I argue for the need to approach television drama via its "subgenre manifestations." While the development, including the rise and fall, of (certain) subgenres is in some ways "planned and organized" officially and commercially, that indicates precisely the fact that subgenres represent clusters of different ideas, values, and points of view, and the tensions and struggles within and the rise and fall in popularity of subgenres constitute active cultural engagement and manifest ideological renegotiations.

## Between State and Society: Understanding the Political Economy in the Development of Chinese Television Culture and Televisual Drama

If the last three decades of reforms are characterized by a determined quest for "modernization"—as in the famous slogan "development is an unnegotiable principle" (*fazhan shi ying daoli*)—in postrevolution China, the promotion of the idea of *fazhan* (development) and policies oriented around this principle manifest a complex history of changes in the official ideology, in the role of the state and its various policies, and in social relations. The development of television as a technology-aided culture within this context consists of a complex mix of forces whose changes and interactions are both symbolic and symptomatic of the process of this quest.[37] The slogan indicates the role of the state—in terms of initiating the idea of development, of qualifying it as a central and key concept, and of imagining what it entails with a slew of policies—in this recent round of economic reforms. *Fazhan,* or development, as an idea has since played a complex and problematic role ideologically and has been and will continue to be subject to different critical assessments and evaluations. Indeed, within the last three decades in China, nothing has been more "mainstream" than the idea of "development," but the fact that it has simultaneously been subject to various interpretations and (implicit and explicit) criticisms manifests the complex relationship between the role of the state—including various social, cultural, political forces and persuasions—and that of the various critical engagements in response.

There was positive response from the very beginning to the call for state-sponsored social and economic reforms. Socially and culturally, that is, the idea of "development" was a state-initiated idea that enjoyed widespread appeal and social support and, by extension, political legitimacy. At the same time, from the very beginning there were different views and positions within the "state," indeed within the CCP itself, debating what it meant to "reform" and what kind of social, economic, and political structure should be envisioned. While in a vocabulary derived from Western mainstream culture, such struggles were termed (and have continued to be termed) struggles between "reformers" and "hardliners," the real issue was and is far more complex than this simple binary characterization. The presence of the debates and differences also indicates that from the beginning of the postrevolution "economic reforms," the Chinese "state" was itself to be subject to multiple lines of persuasion, or, in terms of political economy, subject to ideological struggles within. And the struggles within were not only real but would also lead to real social, economic, and political consequences that would generate further debates over different ideas, values, and points of views expressed by different interest groups including intellectuals. To study Chinese television drama as part of contemporary Chinese mainstream culture is to recognize fully the central contradictions within this "mainstream" phenomenon, namely, the state, the market, and their complex relationship with various cultural practitioners including intellectuals, the cultural industry, and viewers.

Recent examinations of modern Chinese social and historical changes vis-à-vis the notion of the Chinese state have posited that we should more fully recognize and understand China's revolutionary and socialist "temporalities," that is, experiences, legacies, lessons, and even more important their historical legitimacies, in assessing contemporary Chinese social and economic conditions and their larger implications. Lin Chun's recent study of the "transformation of Chinese socialism," for example, reminds us of the larger complex and specifically modern challenges that have informed modern China's historical choices and sociocultural and political practices—especially during the Chinese socialist period—and have also affected the last thirty years of reform.[38] Indeed, Lin Chun's provocative study calls for a basic historical understanding that many current studies of China's post-Mao economic transformation appear to find inconvenient to deal with or brush aside with simplistic labels. Wang Hui's critical discussions of the "new Chinese order," additionally, delineate the intellectual debates in China in a similarly provocative way.[39] These discussions help make palpable the ideological tensions that exist in relation to the transformation of both the Chinese state and society as different groups of intellectuals debate with one another both in and outside of China.[40]

In the next several sections I bring forward four seemingly straightforward terms—television set (*dianshi ji*), television industry (*dianshi chanye*), television culture (*dianshi wenhua*), and television drama (*dianshiju*)—in order to both focus and expand the discussion regarding the relationship between state and market forces and cultural production. These four terms are indicative of television's role among "global" and globalizing technology-aided cultural phenomena, but they are also socially and historically particular to modern and contemporary Chinese history, rich with specific implications. They help illuminate the complex relationship between the state and the collective imaginary of "modernization" shared by different social groups and between the state and different players who have participated in the development of television culture as mainstream popular culture in ways specific to the social characteristics in contemporary China. Manifested and implied in these terms are the changing state policies that have aided the marketization of the television medium and culture, which, in turn, has shaped and effected changes in the roles of intellectuals whose participation as writers and critics (or whose disdain toward television) further manifests the shift of ideological/discursive struggles into such popular storytelling forms as television drama. Each of the four terms, additionally, bears with it numerical figures that reveal a complex interplay between the state, the market, and various sociocultural forces that participate in the production and reception of television drama and, by extension, in the production of meaning and ideological tensions.

## *DIANSHI JI*, OR TELEVISION SET: THE FIRST COLLECTIVELY DESIRED COMMODITY IN THE "MODERNIZATION" IMAGINARY OF POSTREVOLUTIONARY CHINA

Even though the People's Republic of China began to experiment with television technology and established a few television stations in the 1950s and the 1960s, television remained a highly exclusive and limited medium until the late 1970s. It was not until the beginning of the open-door and reform era in the late 1970s and early 1980s that television, both in the material and cultural sense, quickly became one of the early commodity symbols of "modernization" and functioned essentially to inaugurate the arrival of postrevolution, technology-aided mass culture in the reform process. Coming to China later than to many other parts of the world as a modern technology product and as a modern commodity, the television set nevertheless quickly captured the imagination of a society that was ready to devour anything bearing the sign of "modernization." Owning a television set became one of the earliest collective obsessions on the part of urban Chinese. Indeed, if ownership of a television set symbolized an initial collective modernization imaginary of the post-Mao era, as it turns out, it also signified the beginning of the postrevolutionary age of commodity worship in contemporary China. That eventuality is indicative of the early ideological shift in the Chinese dominant official discourse.

The actual participation in the purchasing and widespread ownership of television sets, by people from all walks of life, helped set the stage for a further collective embrace of a "modernization" imaginary oriented around material ownership and, by extension, for the emergence of a cultural industry and its related cultural products celebrating such an imaginary. At the beginning of 1976, there were altogether only 463,000 television sets nationwide in China, with only 4,000 color sets among them (most of which were owned by "work units").[41] A little over ten years later, in 1987, there were 1.2 hundred million television sets nationwide with 47.8 percent of households owning a television set (in 1978, it was 2 percent).[42] By the end of 2002, there was more than 91 percent television coverage, or more than 1.1 billion television viewers in China,[43] along with (at least by 2000) 374 provincial-level television stations, 1,273 county-level television stations, 234 cable television stations, and other related facilities set in place nationwide.[44] By the turn of the twenty-first century, watching television became so routine and so everyday, and the television industry and television culture became so ubiquitous a mainstream popular culture force and social reality that the collective obsession over owning a television set seems to belong to a distant memory.[45]

In brief, both materially and symbolically, the rapid growth and spread of television-set ownership ushered China into an age of development-worship-cum-commodity-worship, quickly linking an industrial modernization imaginary with a commercial one, with the state authorities anxious to find a way both to utilize and to control the television industry and television culture. The exponential growth of television-set ownership can be seen as symptomatic of the following: the relationship between the open-door and reform policies, the subsequent rise to dominance of a commodity-worshiping-and-materialism-oriented modernization imaginary and discourse, a collective embrace of the ideological turn by the elite and the populace alike, consequent social tensions and problems, and the more recent intellectual debates on how to understand the past three decades of economic reforms in relation to sociocultural development and the direction of China's ongoing social transformations. Put differently, although a ubiquitous and mundane object today, the history of television-set ownership in China is symptomatic of the complex relationship between the state, society, the elite, and the populace in relation to China's post-socialist transformation and related discursive and ideological struggles.

In less than three decades, China managed to complete the journey to establish a structural network for television broadcasting, setting the stage for the economic and ideological interests of such players as the "state" and the "market," but also for the contradictions between and within them and for other related social problems and concerns to play out. Today, with hundreds of millions of television sets beaming with the ever-increasing lure of a materialistic "modernization" imaginary in people's everyday life, televisual stories thus transmitted also manifest complex changes in social relations, contradictory social conditions, ideological tensions, all of which affect cultural and meaning production. Television culture in general and television drama in particular are not only related to the current state of affairs in China, but are also related to the contested views of historical experiences, political choices, and promises throughout modern Chinese history.

### *DIANSHI CHANYE,* OR TELEVISION INDUSTRY, AND THE STATE

With the exponential growth in television ownership came the rapid expansion in television networks and coverage, which generated the need for programming and content production (including commercials). The state—by issuing various guidelines and policies—would play a major role in the structural formation of a Chinese-style television industry as well as in its evolution from four levels of government-owned television stations to a mixture of corporate-like media entities that play a dual role in directly conveying the official line in ideas, perspectives, and points of view and in creating programs to fill hundreds of channels while being responsible for their own financial interests. It is this dual role that characterizes the Chinese television industry, and it has been the major focus of criticism of Chinese television culture (including that by some of the critics mentioned earlier).

These changes indicate, as mentioned by Ruoyun Bai and Yin Hong, the structurally guaranteed dual role of the state and the market in the formation and control of the television industry, television culture, and, by extension, the production of television drama. In terms of commercial interests, their post-revolutionary return can be traced to January of 1979, when viewers saw the first advertisement on television in Shanghai.[46] By the mid-1990s, commercials cost staggering amounts of money for a five-second slot during the prime-time news on Chinese Central Television (hereafter CCTV).[47] The year 1994 witnessed the creation of the first "private" television company (even though its appearance was at first met with official disapproval).[48]

Structurally speaking, the quantitative and qualitative dialectic in China has been a direct result of policy changes in the (aforementioned) reorganization of the television industry, which further led to something called *zhibo fenli*, or the separation of broadcasting and content production. *Zhibo fenli* means that, other than most of the news items, television stations were no longer the sole program-making entities as they had been.[49] Content production was thus poised to become a new (technology-aided) cultural industry for "creative possibilities." One of the quantitatively measurable effects has been the exponential increase in the output of television dramas since the early 1990s.[50] In 2003, for example, after about ten years (1994–2003) of little official support, private "culture" companies were officially allowed to compete with other entities for content production.[51] Providing "opportunities for different kinds of dramatic creation," the specific modern-Chinese-history-related quantitative and qualitative dialectic within the development of this mainstream cultural phenomenon tells socially and historically messy and specific "stories" from reform-era China. The rise and fall of many private television drama production companies and the expansion in subgenres in Chinese television drama all testify to the complexity of this history.[52]

### *DIANSHI WENHUA*, OR TELEVISION CULTURE, AND THE STATE

While the state has always played a controlling role in the development of television as a cultural industry and in its content production, it was not until the 1990s that new official cultural policies made it possible for television drama to be "stretched" and expanded into a dominant storytelling form and cultural phenomenon. These new official cultural policies not only enabled the structural changes mentioned above, but also encouraged content production in the direction of so-called *zhuxuan lü* (main melody) plus *duoyang hua* (multiplicity).[53] This official guideline is indicative of the coexistence of arbitrary censorial control and fluidity in what a "guideline" can be made to mean. Narratively, *zhuxuan lü* and *duoyang hua* can simultaneously evoke "social realism," "critical realism," "socialist realism," "revolutionary romanticism," or melodrama, all of which also evoke different historical references, ideological implications, and cultural/political meanings. Additionally, while "realism" may be combined with melodrama, this may or may not be based on a clear ideological perspective, owing, in part, to the "depoliticization" politics of postrevolutionary China and to the fact that the reform era's "reality" itself has been tension-filled and interpreted differently by different sociocultural forces.

Indeed, ideologically, the new guideline differed from both early-twentieth-century left-wing intellectuals' attempts at constructing a "proletariat literature" *(puluo wenxue)* and Mao's idea that "art" must serve the workers, peasants, and soldiers (*wenyi wei gongnongbing fuwu*).[54] It manifests the postrevolutionary depoliticized populist nature of the mainstream and official ideology that has moved in the direction of decoupling culture from what is deemed "politics." This official populist maneuver, I might add, is ironically (or not so ironically) reminiscent of post–Cultural Revolution intellectuals' declaration of *gaobie geming*, or farewell to revolution, widely expressed throughout the 1990s.[55] Indeed, if contemporary Chinese academic critics sneer at this official "catch-all" set of *zhuxuan lü* plus *duoyang hua* slogans, the irony is that they seem to have overlooked their own role in imagining and constructing a depoliticized society in which the "modernization" imaginary rules. Incidentally, the notion of *duoyang hua*, or multiplicity, is not that dissimilar from the notion of "multiculturalism," a catchword in recent U.S. cultural politics in which class-oriented social and power relations and contradictions are deemphasized and even concealed in favor of celebrating ethnic and gender diversities (in an everyday sense). It is precisely in this sense that serious analysis and interpretation of mainstream popular culture is necessary.

Despite the stated official guideline on making television drama, given the "depoliticization" and "repoliticization" in everyday life in contemporary China, what constitutes "reality" is no longer defined by a single force, be it the state, the market, or even a combination of the two. In this sense "realism" itself has become less definable.[56] I will not elaborate on the notion of realism; suffice it to suggest here that, today, in the name of "modernization," "development," "joining the international tracks" (*yu guoji jiegui*), "moving with the times" (*yu shi jujin*), and establishing a "harmonious society" (*hexie shehui*), attempts to normalize a seemingly depoliticized culture in a socially troubled society are precisely what is questioned in the subtext of many "realist" television dramas.[57] Indeed, as I will demonstrate in the next section and the rest of the book, more often than not television drama has proven to be not that "harmonious" a cultural site after all, but, to reiterate an earlier point, a site where a range of "mainstream" problems and issues are constantly politicized under the guise of entertainment and where different ideological positions and cultural legacies coexist and are contested.[58] Thus, as a cultural phenomenon, television drama has also become, to use Mikhail Bakhtin's words, more "polyphonic."

Furthermore, there is a wide spectrum of practitioners in the production of television drama, including well-known and not-so-well-known writers, filmmakers, actors, and other "culture workers." Their active participation inevitably turns television drama into a contested cultural site where different social, political, and ideological persuasions contest and negotiate. The importance of script writers compared with directors in the production of television drama is often viewed as a shortcoming of this narrative form, but putting aside the hierarchical reflex may enable us to better explore the implications of such specificities of this visual narrative form.[59] Indeed, the crossover between literature, theater, film, and television drama has always been a unique characteristic in the development of Chinese television drama as a narrative and cultural form, and from time to time certain subgenres have become (temporary) bastions of creative energy, the result of which is an expansion of the bulk of television dramas. While the market plays an important role in making such a crossover attractive, the creative energy thus released cannot be explained by market interests alone. The seemingly most clichéd places may well be where unexpected maneuvers are attempted, controversies generated, and "unseen rhythms" exist, all because there are real political implications at stake.[60]

The widespread success of the first large-scale (fifty-episode) Chinese-made serial, *Yearnings*, in 1990 signaled and in effect inaugurated the beginning of the crossover of literature writers into creating and writing for television drama. The script writers of *Yearnings* included such then well-known writers as Wang Shuo and Zheng Wanlong (both of whom had been known for having produced "oppositional" literature). Their active participation in the production of what to many critics was a problematic melodrama gave writers a new role in the production of television drama.[61] Today, debates continue regarding the role of well-known writers in the production of television drama, manifesting an ongoing intellectual anxiety over the (changed and changing) role of "intellectuals" in contemporary China.[62] The success of *Yearnings* brought about the practice in television drama of dealing with issues believed to relate to ordinary people's lives, thereby reintroducing "everydayness" as a legitimate subject of representation in storytelling and creating a critical anxiety regarding "realism" and melodrama.[63]

It is worth noting that some Chinese critics in the humanities and communication studies, during the 1980s and parts of the 1990s, saw television drama as a new art form with potential artistic possibilities for both elite and popular taste (*yasu gongshang*).[64] Like Williams, most of these critics did not immediately associate the medium of television with commercial interests but as yet another addition to the existing narrative forms in literature, film, and theater, only more promising in terms of transmission and reception. I identify this as another layer in the quantitative and qualitative dialectic regarding the evolution of television drama in China. Like Williams, before the onset of the television industry in China, Chinese critics did not realize the degree to which commercial interests could impact television culture as a whole. As a result, ironically, there existed, also from the start, a fluidity between the views toward television drama and those toward other forms of storytelling. The fact that early television dramas in China, especially those made in the 1980s, were mostly based on literary classics attests to this early orientation.[65]

There are dozens of television-related magazines, newspapers, and journals, funded and published by television guilds, television stations, and universities, and many are circulated nationwide. In the last decade, additionally, the Internet has proven to be an active and influential space for the public to engage with various contemporary cultural productions including television dramas. There people read and share (often heated) comments and reviews, on the one hand, and stories about the making of television drama, about their favorite actors, and thinly disguised gossipy pieces, on the other.[66] Many of the debates on the Internet find their way into the mainstream print media, thereby further foregrounding both the dominant influence of television dramas and public reactions to some of the issues (or nonissues) generated by their televisual dramatic representations. The electronic media, the print media, and the Internet are inseparable components that have helped turn television drama into a dominant cultural form with a double-edged function—"mainstream" and therefore seemingly apologetic, but also often explicitly and implicitly provocative and therefore manifesting tensions within this dominant mainstream cultural form. The significance of these different dimensions of Chinese television culture in general and the production and consumption of television drama in particular signify what Raymond Williams identifies as "the quantitative and qualitative connection" within.

## Understanding "Melodrama" as a Mode of Representation in Television Drama

Televisual storytelling as a form first emerged in 1958 in China, but television drama was not popularly available until 1978, when television was poised on the verge of entering every household and everyday life. Like the early development of film, television drama in China went through a stage in which different formats coexisted, starting mainly with domestic-made single plays and short serials and longer imported dramas.[67] Today, a Chinese television drama serial usually runs for twenty to fifty episodes.[68] Once a serial is on the air, it will run daily until completed. Generally, there are both new shows and reruns showing daily.[69] Most shows last less than a month and are immediately followed by new ones.[70] While only eight episodic televisual dramas were made in 1978, in the year 2000 alone, 1,271 titles with 22,231 episodes were approved by the State Administration of Radio and Television (Guojia Guangbo Dianshi Ju), and 458 titles with 7,535 episodes were actually produced.[71] An unofficial count puts television drama production companies nationwide at more than one thousand, with Beijing having almost half of them.[72] In the 1990s alone, the total number of television drama titles produced easily reached the thousands, although fewer were actually shown.[73] In short, during the last three decades, China has witnessed an exponential expansion in the production of television drama.

How are we best to understand the television dramas thus produced? Indeed, given the numerous subgenres that deal with seemingly very different (but also overlapping) subject matter, what narrative characteristics do they share? And how do these characteristics relate to the various socioeconomic, cultural, ideological, and historical forces that inform the production of contemporary Chinese mainstream popular culture in general and television drama in particular? Regardless of the exponential growth in the number of television dramas and the proliferation and mutation of different subgenres, the one characteristic they all share is, simply, that these dramas are unfailingly represented melodramatically. At the same time, a habitual negative reflex toward "mainstream popular culture" and its melodramatic mode of representation, on the part of many critics, has maintained a *deng xia hei* situation, indeed a blind spot right underneath the light, when it comes to how to understand melodrama as a shared narrative mode of television drama.[74]

The debates on melodrama over the last several decades, mainly in the field of film studies in the United States, shed light on this issue. In these debates, scholars have argued for understanding melodrama as more than a genre and considering the historical linkage between "melodrama" and "modernity."[75] Such a linkage is illuminating in the Chinese case because much of modern Chinese history has comprised a series of struggles as China has attempted to come to terms with its "modern" encounters with the West and with the "modern" experiences conditioned by such encounters.[76] If, as I have argued, television drama as China's dominant form of storytelling is informed by various social and cultural forces, legacies, and tensions within them, how can a better understanding of the notion of "melodrama" help illuminate this seemingly familiar but little explored cultural mode within the Chinese context?

Although debates on melodrama emerged in American academia in the mid-twentieth century, Peter Brooks, a scholar of literature, is generally credited with arguing for taking melodrama seriously.[77] He contends that, given that melodrama continues to enjoy a strong presence in both popular and elite cultures, only by taking it seriously can we begin to explore why this is the case and how to understand such cultural tenacity. His discussions were picked up by film studies scholars, mainly in the United States, whose studies of Hollywood cinema have taken the debates much further. Today, although the term "melodrama" still tends to be used pejoratively, scholars have taken the term seriously and defined it variously as "a mode of conception and expressions . . . a certain fictional system for making sense of experience,"[78] "a product of modernity," or a "code" that is permeated in various (other) forms.[79] While some question the conservative bent and ideological manipulation of melodrama as a cultural form, others argue that melodrama, being a product of "modernity," can be subversive in either gender or class terms. Some argue that these mixed possibilities are inherent in such characteristics of melodrama as "excessive," "situational," "overly emotional," "morally polarizing," and "sentimental," all of which can elicit "strong pathos."[80] These and other attempts at defining melodrama make the point that melodrama should be understood historically as opposed to generically.

These theoretical debates on melodrama help illuminate why Raymond Williams saw in television drama "[a] new mobility in time and space, and a new flexibility in movement between kinds of dramatic speech—especially between the conventions of 'spoken' and 'unspoken' thought and feeling . . . What could be seen from an orthodox theatrical position as the limitations of the broadcasting medium became opportunities for different kinds of dramatic creation." Along the same lines, in the context of contemporary China, these debates can help illuminate the need to recognize the connection, via the notion of melodrama, between different kinds of televisual dramatic speech and creation and the legacies of the different historical experiences, cultural resources, and ideological persuasions that inform them. In what ways, we can ask, for example, does melodrama, as a "fictional system for making sense of experience," function in "different kinds of dramatic creation" on television? How, via strong pathos, emotions, sentimentalism, and other narrative codes, are melodramatic representations both informed by and able to manifest social changes and different cultural, historical, and ideological legacies in modern Chinese history? And how do we identify and understand such manifestations?

Subgenres in television drama, as "different kinds of dramatic creation" with slippery narrative boundaries, are indicative of the "inherently" context-contingent nature of the specific meanings of "melodrama." The proliferation of televisual subgenres is not only conditioned by the "accomplices of the state and the market" but is also informed by different social, cultural, and ideological tensions and contradictions.

To complete this brief consideration of melodrama as a shared narrative mode in television drama, I must also point out the "word-centered" (as opposed to visual-centered) characteristic of television drama. Indeed, I consider "word centrism" to be part of the melodramatic mode of Chinese television drama. In the existing scholarly discourse, visual texts and their verbal components tend to be critically scrutinized with the assumption that the latter work to limit the meaning of the visual texts. In his discussion of the "rhetoric of the image," for example, Barthes explores the relationship between word and image (despite poststructuralist critical interventions, the combination of word and image continues to play an essential role in the technology-aided globalized late-capitalist economy and has become so invasively ubiquitous that it is both widely visible and conspicuously unnoticed, not to mention far from being understood). Barthes observes that "knowing that a system which takes over the signs of another system in order to make them its signifiers is a system of connotation, we may say immediately that the literal image is *denoted* and the symbolic image *connoted*" (emphasis original).[81] He goes on to explore the relationship between the "denoted" and the "connoted," and observes that "today, at the level of mass communications, it appears that the linguistic message is indeed present in every image.... In every society various techniques are developed intended to *fix* the floating chain of signifieds in such a way as to counter the terror of uncertain signs; the linguistic message is one of these techniques" (emphasis original).[82] Differentiating photography from other types of visual expression, including paintings, drawings, advertisements, and films, which tend to be aided linguistically, Barthes concludes that "it can thus be seen that in the total system of the image the structural functions are polarized: on the one hand there is a sort of paradigmatic condensation at the level of connotators (that is, broadly speaking, of the symbols), which are strong signs, scattered, 'reified'; on the other a syntagmatic 'flow' at the level of the denotation—it will not be forgotten that the syntagm is always very close to speech, and it is indeed the iconic 'discourse' which naturalizes its symbols."[83] Although Barthes goes on to articulate a desire to resist the aforementioned structural tendency (by insisting on the need to "read" symbols in the image without being controlled by the word), we must pay attention to the dialectics of the relationship between word and image in various forms of narratives told visually.

One of the characteristics of Chinese television drama is a heavy linguistic presence that "connotes" but also "denotes" and "naturalizes" symbols or images. Given this characteristic, television drama's narrative structure is more dominated by dialogue than film is. The serial nature of most Chinese television dramas also means that their storyline is arranged with the intention of organizing people's daily routine so that the viewers want to (and can) follow the events in the story. To study such narratives, one must pay attention to the ways in which words function to direct the meanings of the imagery, characters, plot, storyline, and overall narrative structure. "Word" in television narratives, in this sense, means more than just what is spoken. It is also the plots, events, storyline, narrative structure, characters and their relationships with one another, diegetic implications, and the spoken and unspoken thoughts and feelings conveyed within. The visual, which often tends to be passive and formulaic on television, in essence becomes part of the dialogic/polyphonic components adding meaning to the more determining narrative elements.[84] And yet the presence of all of these elements constitutes the unstable nature of the relationship between the visual and the verbal and, by extension, the "kinds of dramatic speech" conditioned by the "dialogue"-cum-"dialogic"-cum-"polyphonic" specificities of this particular narrative form.

## Subgenres as a Useful Analytical Category

The official production guideline that encourages dramas that "promote the main melody" and those that address a range of different topics is not based on an interest in encouraging television drama to deal with difficult social issues, but it is vague enough for a range of subject matter to be tackled.[85] The result is a relatively rich array of "subgenres." Even though "subgenres" in Chinese television drama are often only casually noted and most critics do not seem to be particular about how to identify them,[86] the emergence and development of these subgenres is the site at which the relationship between representations and changing state policies, market interests, and cultural and ideological logic in contemporary China that informs "dramatic creation" can be located and examined. Why, how, and which subgenres appeared on the cultural scene are emblematic of changes and tensions in various "mainstream" preoccupations, problems, and problematics.[87] While the production of numerous dramas has been motivated by the potentiality (i.e., marketability) of a particular subgenre, it is those that either try to push boundaries in both a visual and a verbal sense, or happen to respond to a public mood or generate controversy that manage to attract public attention and generate debate. Even though "boundary breaking" may not function in an avant-garde fashion, it can still function to offer different ways of representing and therefore thinking about seemingly familiar social and cultural issues, ideas, values, and problems.

Related to this particular kind of "boundary breaking" is the previously mentioned crossover on the part of many well-known writers who play a role in television drama production either as sources for materials to be adapted, as direct participants in script writing, or both. Although literary works had been adapted into television dramas in the 1980s, the direct participation of two well-known writers from the 1980s, Wang Shuo and Zheng Wanlong, in the conception and script writing of *Yearnings* changed the dynamics between televisual and literary production. There are writers, filmmakers, and actors who pride themselves on not participating in televisual production, but that does not prevent others from crossing over and producing interesting, provocative, controversial, and thought-provoking television dramas. The participation of these writers in television drama production has contributed to the formation of certain subgenres as well as to the lack of clear-cut boundaries between subgenres. Zhou Meisen's novels, for example, have been adapted into popular dramas that tend to be identified as "anticorruption" dramas. At the same time, however, his novels as well as their adaptations can be identified, as Jeffery Kinkley does, as political novels or political dramas.[88] Writings by women writers such as Chi Li and Wang Hailing have been adapted into television dramas and identified as *jiating hunyin ju* (family-marriage drama), *nüxing jiating hunyin ju* (women family-marriage drama), or *jiating lunli ju* (family ethics drama). Regardless of whether they choose to participate in adaptations of their works and whether critics find such crossover problematic, these writers nevertheless leave strong marks on popular culture.

In this sense, through the prism of (the rise and fall of) "subgenres," television drama can be seen as having functioned as a "contested cultural site" where a range of "mainstream" problems and problematics have been implicitly and explicitly considered and represented melodramatically.[89] The rise and fall of specific subgenres in television drama is related to state and market interests, to be sure, but it is also emblematic of sociocultural politics closely related to the rapid (and in many ways troubled) changes and transformations in social relations and to the larger context of globalizing capitalism and the impact of its cultural logic and imaginary in China. The relatively wide array of subgenres that have emerged in the last thirty years of television drama production has left us with more questions than answers regarding, among other things, China's latest round of rapid social transformation.

In the two decades since *Yearnings* (1990), a slew of subgenres have come into existence rapidly, signifying both the rise in dominance of popular culture, in which television drama exists as a major form of storytelling, and a corresponding rise in the number of sociocultural issues being addressed publicly via television drama. The subgenres include, on the one hand, crime, corruption, rising social injustice, and changing social positions of individuals and social groups due to access (or the lack thereof) to money and power, and, on the other hand, historical topics ranging from the Chinese revolution and its participants, politics in various ancient courts, (imagined) life stories of (in)famous historical figures, and legends from "classical" stories and modern martial arts novels. Mixed within these issues and topics are related ideological ones regarding changes in social relations, values, notions of sexuality, gender identity, and romantic love; cultural ones such as loyalty, filial piety, and familial relationships; and psychoanalytical issues such as desire, fantasy, despair, and hope. The result is an expansion in subgenres, with an unstable nature, that cluster around different sets of issues and tensions.

Some of the commonly known subgenres that have appeared on the television screen are identified as *fanfu ju* (anticorruption drama), *jingfei ju/pian* (police-crime drama), *jiating hunyin ju* (marriage-family drama), *jiating lunli ju* (family ethics drama), *diwang ju* or *huangdi ju* (emperor drama), *wuxia ju* (martial arts drama), *guzhuang ju* (costume drama), *fenghua xueyue ju* ([Republican era] petty-bourgeois love drama), *geming lishi ju* (revolutionary history drama), *qingchun ouxiang ju* (youth-idol drama), plus imported dramas such as *Ri ju* (Japanese drama), and *Han ju* (Korean drama) (the importation of foreign dramas has exerted a constant impact on the development of subgenres and has also generated the reaction from Chinese creators and producers of developing Chinese equivalents, the result of which is more subgenres). As there is no standard for "naming" subgenres, many of them continue to be called by different names, reflecting a lack of clear boundaries between the different subgenres.[90] The lack of boundaries is indicative of the presence of multiple meanings that can generate different angles and different questions when critics engage with the same dramas.

The development and expansion of subgenres is not simply a matter of popular culture running amok. Jing Wang's point about questioning the notion of "popular culture" as "unofficial" comes to mind once again. However, when the coexistence of the "main melody" (*zhuxuanlü*) and the Republican era romance (*fenghua xueyue*) subgenres indicates a collective postrevolution depoliticized historical consciousness, it does not follow that new social problems and social tensions will not become part of the storytelling content. Indeed, the development and expansion of subgenres are inevitably motivated by viewers' interest in contemporary issues and problems. Whether or not such interests are profit-driven or cater to an escapist tendency, they do not prevent real and serious social issues from being addressed and various related issues from being evoked—indeed as the most *visible* place in the spot right underneath the light. It is for this reason that I suggest that television drama has functioned, and therefore needs to be understood, as a mainstream but contested cultural site.

In the end, we come back, full circle but on a different level, to my point regarding studying Chinese television drama as a mainstream-culture form represented in a melodramatic mode. In subgenres we recognize the relationship between the making of television dramas and some of the driving ideas, values, and tensions within contemporary Chinese society. Oriented around specific subject matter in a subgenre, different ideas, values, and contradictions contest, manifested melodramatically via specific types of characters often with overwrought but also conflicting emotions; a strong sense of (in)justice; the desire for power, material gain, vengeance; and more. Focusing on and exploring the implications of these narrative characteristics by way of subgenres helps make visible coexisting but different cultural resources and historical and ideological legacies that conflict and negotiate with one another in a society going through rapid social transformation.

Because of the limited scope of one book, this study does not examine all of the major subgenres. I am regrettably unable to include the so-called red classics (*hongse jingdian*), *zhuxuanlü* dramas (in this case those specifically about Communist revolutionary leaders), *rushang ju* (Confucian merchants drama), *fenghua xueyue ju* (love drama set in the Republican era), *jingfei ju/pian* (police-crime drama), and several others. These subgenres, along with those studied in this book, constitute rich sources for future studies.

CHAPTER ONE

# Looking through the Negatives

## Filmic-Televisual Intertextuality and Ideological Renegotiations

❑ ❑ ❑ ❑ ❑

Television and film tend not to mesh in current established academic disciplines. The "disciplined" film-television divide in academia has effected more than just a disproportionate division of labor in the studies of these two cultural forms. It has also limited the role of the critic when it comes to analyzing, interpreting, and critiquing popular culture including television, which continues to be viewed as being too "extreme mainstream" to merit analysis and interpretation.[1] As indicated in the Introduction, recent publications on television culture in China in general and television drama in particular, by scholars mostly in media studies and some in film studies, are beginning to change these dynamics. However, there is more to explore with regard to the overlapping of the two cultural forms, including the phenomenon I explore in this chapter, namely, television as a meaningful motif found in recent Chinese films. By shedding light on this motif, I hope to further situate Chinese television culture and television drama in particular not in a hierarchically conditioned dumping ground but within a specific historical moment in China in which multiple cultural forms converge, contest, and negotiate. Indeed, while many Chinese (academic) critics in China have adapted themselves to Western disciplinary divisions, conceptual perspectives, and ideological positions, cultural production in China has nevertheless been attuned to a differerent set of demands, contextual specificities, and (albeit conflicting) cultural and historical legacies. To understand Chinese cultural production and its textual representations requires moving beyond the dominant negative views on television. In this way we will be able to refocus and gain additional perspectives that will contribute to a more complex understanding of Chinese television drama as today's dominant form of storytelling.

In the world of film culture, which includes so-called mainstream and art-house cinema, filmmakers in the latter category are often recognized as having made a conscious choice to comment and critique via an experimental style. Their style, in turn, has allowed the filmic form itself to be viewed as capable of performing the role of culture critic. For this reason I turn to films first, specifically a few Chinese films that use television as a motif. As my reading below will demonstrate, film-television dynamics (and intertextuality between the two) in these films helps bring television into the foreground as an important sociocultural phenomenon and a cultural text for direct analysis and interpretation. More important, the use of television as a motif in these films represents the extent to which television exists in a rapidly changing physical and social landscape either as an object of desire (to possess), as background noise that nevertheless reveals part of everyday life, or as a source of complex self-identification. In seemingly small ways, these representational characteristics help situate television in the context of social relations in contemporary China, while making visible the complex cultural and ideological implications within this context. In these filmic representations, television as a cultural phenomenon is made meaningful in a number of ways.

In the following pages, I discuss three films intentionally using television as a motif. They are *Ermo* (*Ermo,* dir. Zhou Xiaowen, 1994), *Unknown Pleasures* (*Ren xiaoyao,* dir. Jia Zhangke, 2002), and *Still Life* (*Sanxia haoren,* dir. Jia Zhangke, 2006). After discussing the filmic representations and their implications, I consider the extent to which the filmic-televisual intertextuality invites additional analysis and interpretation of the most dominant form of storytelling in contemporary China.

## Ermo's Desire: Television Possessed but Not Quite Consumed

When *Ermo* was released in 1994, critics took notice.[2] Not only was it the first "rural" film by Zhou Xiaowen, who had been known for his urban orientation, but it departed from the "fifth-generation" filmmakers' pattern of representing the past allegorically and focused, instead, on issues of sociocultural transformation in the contemporary reform era in rural China.[3] It did so by representing the peasant woman Ermo's desire and efforts to own "the biggest television set in the county." Ensuing studies have examined the gender dimensions of the film or questioned the elite filmmaker's urban-oriented perspective on rural social mores, or hailed the film's take on globalized consumer culture permeating rural China. My discussion here extends existing discussions on the "televisuality" of the film identified by Anne T. Ciecko and Sheldon H. Lu and by Ping Fu, and focuses more closely on the film's use of television as a motif involving the main character and how the film portrays the social issues related to the cultural dialectics manifested in the rise of television culture.

Narratively, the film is about its title character, Ermo, a hard-working peasant woman from a small village in northern rural China, who is caught up in the rapid social and economic changes that have affected her, her family's, and her fellow villagers' lives. Looming in the background of the story is the "household responsibility" system—a system engineered in the early 1980s to replace the commune system—that had changed the social and economic relations within villages and rural families. In Ermo's case, the system has changed her role in the family and her relationship with her husband. With her former-village-chief husband now physically frail, Ermo takes on many of the familial responsibilities to both earn income and take care of the household. In addition to trying to earn extra income by weaving large baskets for fruit packaging, she also makes dry noodles and sells them in the township. Ermo, in this respect, is represented as a strong woman in her own right. Specifically, the film focuses on one manifestation of her strong will, namely, competing with her neighbor's wife to earn for her family a television set, the biggest in the county at that. Traveling to the county seat to sell her noodles, she discovers the biggest television set in a department store, which she is told even the county head cannot afford. Her desire to own such a television set drives her into situations that she has never experienced before. She takes a job making noodles in a restaurant in the county seat and, living away from home, realizes that she can also make money by selling her own blood. She has a short-lived affair with the neighbor's husband, Xiazi (a nickname that literally means "blind man"), whose beat-up truck has made it possible for her to travel and to experience all of these new things. Toward the latter part of the film, Ermo stops the affair when she discovers that Xiazi has been subsidizing her income through her boss in the restaurant. She refuses to accept the setup and abruptly ends the relationship because, as she states, "I'm not in the business of selling myself" (*wo bushi mai kang de,* literally: she does not sell her bed). She goes back to selling noodles in the township until she accumulates enough money to buy the biggest television set in the county. After purchasing the set and bringing it home, however, she realizes that the biggest set in the county is actually too big for the family's one-room house—it has to be moved inside the house through the window, and the only spot for it is on the brick bed. When villagers congregate in her house to watch television, Ermo is shown sitting next to, rather than in front of, the set, looking pale and weak.

Once the object of her desire is obtained, Ermo appears to have no interest in what shows up on the screen of this thing called *dianshi ji.* Indeed, while she is motivated by her determination to *mai tai dianshi ji* (buy a television set), the film shows that throughout the entire process of obtaining and owning the set, Ermo is largely disassociated from what television brings, namely, the content that is shown. In addition to the scene just mentioned, the very last scene in the film highlights this disconnect. At this point some time has passed after the purchase of the television, and arrangements have been made to make this "biggest set in the county" available to her fellow villagers. At the start of the scene, the frame is completely filled by a television screen, showing one episode of *Dynasty* (the well-known American prime-time soap opera that ran between 1981 and 1989). Two lovers, their conversations dubbed in Chinese, are in an intimate moment. Meanwhile, an off-screen space is indicated through the sound of breathing and snoring. With a reverse cut, we see the three members of Ermo's family—husband, son, and Ermo—still sitting on stools against a wall, sound asleep. Their collective breathing is amplified while the camera lingers on their faces and then, zooming out, on the rows of stools in front of them (indicating that the whole village has been here, but they have now all left). The camera then cuts back to the television, which, having just finished the *Dynasty* episode, is now showing weather forecasts, about Moscow, Cairo, London, and so forth. Shortly after, the television screen goes blank, leaving behind a static pattern and noise that then fills the entire film screen accompanied, still, by the sound of the sleeping family. A few seconds later, with the static image still filling the entire frame, we hear Ermo's noodle-selling chant *mai mahua lou*. With that, the film ends.

This last scene is clearly designed to symbolize the disconnect between television culture in terms of its content and the real issues and concerns in peasants' everyday life. Whether or not the director runs the risk of being accused of urban elitism in suggesting that peasants are unable to "get" the content, this disconnect is part of the film's central theme. And the film's selective use of content on television closely related to the West and modernization—programs that use the English language, American television dramas, American football games, and weather forecasts for international cities, all of which are presented in scenes in which peasant viewers respond in ignorance—suggests where the disconnect lies. The comical effect is at the expense of the peasants. To put it in academic terms, the film helps make visible the incompatible temporalities and, as Ciecko and Lu put it, the "uneven and overlapping modes of production in Deng's China" that, thanks to the spread and increasingly ubiquitous existence of television, nevertheless now coexist in the lives of Ermo and her fellow villagers.

This particular kind of disconnect is accentuated in other moments in the film in which Ermo is vicariously associated with (the idea of) television—through her son, who frequently goes to the next-door neighbor's to watch television despite her objection to his going, through her burning the midnight oil counting money, and through her selling blood in order to quicken the accumulation of money needed for the biggest television set in the county. It is also demonstrated through two moments when Ermo comes face to face with a number of television sets that are turned on, both times in the department store in the county seat. The first time she "discovers" the biggest television set, and the second time she returns to check on it. Her introduction to the biggest television set in the county is accidental—when she walks into a department store, it is among several rows of TV sets all turned on to the same program. But Ermo's desire to possess a bigger TV set than her neighbor's is generated when a shop assistant tells her that even the county head cannot afford the biggest one. Her relationship to television, in this sense, is mediated via changes that take place in her own life, changes whose meanings stem from a mixture of existing mores and newly generated desires. At the same time, these changes and their meanings are represented in a way that indicates the problematics within them. Even though the film's emphasis during her face-to-face encounter with a television program is on her intention to own the set itself, the film nevertheless also zooms in on Ermo, whose gaze is one of wonder, incomprehension, curiosity, and determination, but not recognition. Looking at Ermo's wide-eyed gaze, the viewer is also made aware of the "gaze" behind the camera and its intended interpretation and commentary.[4]

During the first face-to-face encounter with a television program, Ermo is looking at an English-speaking program in which a Chinese "expert" is speaking to a non-Chinese on how to celebrate the Chinese New Year. Even though Chinese New Year would have personal meaning to Ermo as a Chinese peasant, at that moment, ironically, it falls completely outside her purview of recognition. Instead, she wonders aloud why they do not speak Chinese and whether people on TV always speak foreign languages. On this TV program, the Chinese New Year is represented as a cultural symbol of "Chineseness" to the non-Chinese when in actuality there has never been one uniform way of celebrating the New Year in China. On television, the spatial and temporal complexities of "Chinese culture" along with rich regional diversities are reduced to a one-dimensional representation. On television, furthermore, the Chinese New Year becomes disconnected from the lives of ordinary people like Ermo, who have to make sense of what they watch and what they see by resorting to their own cultural resources. As viewers, they remain, one might say, actively misinformed. In Ermo's second face-to-face encounter with what is on television, she walks in on a show of synchronized swimming. Staring at the camera (which assumes the position of the television sets), she marvels at the blond hair on the foreign athletes' arms. As in the first encounter, the film cuts to a close-up shot of Ermo, showing a wonder-filled face that is staring at something intensely but without due recognition. The series of close-up shots are again reflective of the gaze behind the camera, which invisibly zooms in and captures a seemingly spontaneous—therefore peasantlike?—gaze. This captured gaze, realized in a rather conventional method of editing is, once again, one of incomprehension, which underscores the disconnect between the content on television and peasants like Ermo.

By thus representing Ermo, the film offers a commentary on the disconnect between Chinese peasants and the globalizing consumer culture. On the one hand, there is a degree of urban elitist condescension toward peasants who are ignorant of "new" culture codes. The invisible gaze upon Ermo's uncomprehending stare at the television is a manifestation of such condescension. On the other hand, we also recognize sociocultural problematics symbolically represented through Ermo's story. Whether or not these implications are intended by the filmmaker, the film reveals (1) a disconnect between what is seen on television and the everyday life of peasants and, (2) at the same time, a disjointed connection between the two, manifesting what Jason McGrath calls "the gap between the imaginary of popular culture and the intractable reality that the characters actually inhabit."[5] Both are symptomatic of a sociocultural impact informed, shaped, and contained by changes in social and economic relations. Ermo embodies this disjointed connection and its costly (to her health, for example, and to her sense of self), fragmented, and confusing nature—indeed, the object of her desire is at the same time something almost alien to her. Ermo, in other words, is represented as an unlikely "consumer" whose alienation from the object of her desire betrays a sociocultural alienation. By showing this disjointed connection, the film *Ermo,* with its urban elitist biases, motivates a critical representation of the permeation and "inconsumability" of television in rural lives.

Let me elaborate on this point with one last example from the film. In emphasizing the disjointed connection in relation to Ermo as a consumer, the film exploits another moment in the story to enhance the effect of such "connection." It takes place in the scene in which Ermo and Xiazi find themselves in a cheap hotel room. The man comes with a jar of cream as a gift to Ermo. Not knowing what it is for exactly and how to use it, he asks Ermo to take off her clothes, ready to put it on her body. Ermo takes off her top except the bra, which she shows off to him as something new and attractive, asking him whether it makes her look like a city woman. What the viewer sees is a padded bra crudely put together and with too many colors. "City" people, the viewer is aware, would chuckle at her unself-conscious showing off, finding it rather childish or even embarrassing. The man in the film, however, discovers something else: her much bruised arms due to repeated blood drawing. He grabs her arms and demands an explanation. He is upset upon hearing how she got the bruises and tells her that she is ignorant for trying to "cheat" by drinking large bowls of water before having blood drawn each time. At the same time that he scolds her for being ignorant, he himself scoops lotion (presumably for enlarging breasts) out of the jar with several fingers and splashes it onto her body.

The message here is simultaneously condescending and critical. While the two of them are seriously engaged in having an affair and trying to enhance their attractiveness or trying to help the other become more sophisticated based on what they have seen and understood, the film represents all of this as signs of ignorance on the part of these characters who are misinformed beginner consumers. The film does it in a way that betrays a degree of condescension on the part of the filmmaker, regardless of whether or not he intended it. Meanwhile, one cannot but make a connection between these two characters' expressions of desire and that which is being beamed into their lives by television and by the culture that is increasingly informed and shaped by commercially oriented messages. At the same time, however, the representation of Ermo also shows her strong side, regardless of how ambivalently that strength is judged in the film. She is strong-willed, driven, prone to competition, and does not hesitate to stand her ground when, for example, she chooses to make money to buy a television set (as opposed to extending the house as her husband wants), she chooses to end the relationship with Xiazi, or when she chooses to continue to sell noodles back in the township, knowing that what is out there in the larger world can be alluring. Even if unwittingly given, there is agency on the part of Ermo, an agency that is not entirely and readily consumed by the invasive spread of seemingly desirable imagery of the "modern" world.[6]

In this discussion it is neither whether she is condescendingly represented nor whether she is actually a strong woman that is at issue; at issue is how all of these things combined point to the conflicted nature of the sociocultural changes in China and how the contradictions within them motivate, shape, and (mis)inform. It is the implications of the totality of social, economic, and cultural changes represented in these contradictory or conflicting ways that enable the television motif in this film to signify layered questions, some of which I have explored here. Television, therefore, is shown not just as a (bad) thing in and of itself (as most critics tend to assume) but as an embodiment of tensions and contradictions in the changing social and economic relations, in this case, in the parts of rural China where Ermo and her fellow peasants reside.

In this sense, television as a motif has the potential to be evoked in other ways that can help lead to additional understanding of both the cultural phenomenon itself and the social context in which it is produced and received. In the next two films, we will see television employed in different ways as a motif.

### *Unknown Pleasures:* Television as Background and Its Layered Implications

*Unknown Pleasures* (*Ren xiaoyao*) is the third film of Jia Zhangke's so-called trilogy (the first two are *Xiao Wu* of 1997 and *Platform,* or *Zhantai,* of 2000).[7] Set in Datong, Shanxi province, *Unknown Pleasures* is about two young men, Bing Bing and Xiao Ji, who are unemployed, roaming parts of the city (which used to house state-owned factories and their workers and which are now being torn down), restless and directionless. Unlike *Ermo* but like all of Jia's films, *Unknown Pleasures* does not have a clear plot line and is structured, in a pseudo-documentary manner, by the camera that follows the two young men, sometimes together and sometimes separately, in moments of their everyday lives when they find themselves either at home (Bing Bing with a mother who practices Falun Gong and Xiao Ji with an uncle who appears to work at odd jobs), or at a night club, or at a show that advertises a brand of liquor, or at one of the many places where scores of young men hang around (one such place is a former factory turned into a crude entertainment place where young men play pool). While Bing Bing has a girlfriend who is a high school senior getting ready for college entrance exams, Xiao Ji chases after a dancer with a jealous "boyfriend," a former physical education teacher of hers, who prevents him from approaching her. After Bing Bing is laid off from work, he tries to enlist in the army, only to discover that he has hepatitis. Xiao Ji, meanwhile, insists on pursuing the woman who is "taken," only to be beaten up at a nightclub by a group of thugs working for her boyfriend. The "boyfriend," shortly after, is struck by a truck and dies. The seemingly random happenings culminate when, at the end of the film, the two young men try to rob a bank with a fake bomb. The debacle ends with Bing Bing being arrested and Xiao Ji on the run on his motorbike, which dies on him on the newly built highway. He then hitchhikes and is picked up by a vehicle that disappears from the screen leaving behind the open-ended question of what will happen to him. Open-ended question number two is what will happen to Bing Bing. At the police station after his arrest, Bing Bing is ordered by a policeman to sing a song. Startled and uncertain at first, Bing Bing sings a popular song titled "Unknown Pleasures." As he comes to the end of the song, the screen abruptly goes blank and the film ends.

While the film's representation of these aimless youths is reminiscent of the French New Wave cinema (1950s–1960s) or Italian Neorealism (1943–1950), Jia's early-twenty-first-century Chinese version captures a postrevolution ennui embodied by jobless young men, women working in beauty parlors (many as underground prostitutes), unemployed workers of an older generation, and various people who try to eke out a living in one way or another. Stylistically, the film structures seemingly random and mundane happenings among these different groups of people mostly by following the two young men wherever they find themselves. Spatiotemporally, it does so against the backdrop of a city in the middle of physical transformation. With the coal hills looming in the near distance, many long shots, shot on location, capture the city of Datong both in ruins or dilapidation and in the process of being (or waiting to be) rebuilt. Ordinary people are caught in the middle of this transition and do not seem to know where they belong, either at the present or in the future. Their uncertainty lingers, made visible and palpable with the help of a camera, constituting a particular filmic sentiment that captures the sociocultural milieu with uncertainty lingering in the air. Critics have celebrated Jia's concerted efforts in letting his camera show and tell by unrelentingly focusing, through long shots (both in the temporal and the spatial sense, i.e., long in duration and distance of shot), on individuals whose lives are captured in a reversed gaze that both invites and defies interpretation.

The film further complicates the already layered spatial and temporal relationships by consistently noting the presence of television in relation to its protagonists' mundane activities. Indeed, television is employed to allude to less tangible but nevertheless real spatial and temporal dimensions connecting this filmed locale's (uncertain) social and economic transition with the national spread of globalization that helps further define the nature of the transition in question. On the surface, the television motif in this film functions also to show people's lack of interest in what is broadcast on television. While owning a television set no longer has the same meaning it held for Ermo, watching television appears to be of even less interest for many people. The film shows most people ignoring what is being shown and does so by either positioning characters and extras with their sides or backs turned away from the "box" or by not directly showing the television screen. Either way demonstrates another kind of disconnect. Three scenes are particularly poignant.

First is a scene in the little apartment that Bing Bing shares with his unemployed mother, who used to work in the same textile plant that Bing Bing worked at before, as he claims, he "fired his boss." Incidentally, anyone familiar with the history of the People's Republic of China would infer that the apartment must have been assigned by the factory to his mother: it is located in an old residential compound that bears the marks of an earlier era. The buildings, like the characters old and young in the film, though for now still left standing, nevertheless look run down and depressingly grey in the midst of a dilapidated landscape that is in yet another moment of transition. Unlike that bygone Maoist era, however, the remaining living spaces built during that era, though visibly run-down, continue to stand, bearing with them overlapping temporalities in the present. The overlapping temporalities include the socialist era still within living memory and embodied in these not-yet demolished residential buildings, which is juxtaposed with the postsocialist era in which numerous state-owned factories have gone bankrupt, creating a large number of unemployed workers, the youths who have been set loose and try to find their way in the midst of the changes, unfulfilled and with a lack of promise.

In this scene, Bing Bing and his mother are in their little apartment. The camera is largely stationary, and its position captures several small but separate areas within the apartment: the little dining room in the middle with doors that lead to a tiny kitchen, his mother's bedroom, and perhaps another bedroom and bathroom. Bing Bing is having breakfast. His mother, a lackluster woman, walks in and out of the kitchen, the dining room, and her own room. While the two of them are talking without actually looking at each other, we can see that the television in the mother's room is turned on. A news program is running showing, among other things, Colin Powell. He is speaking about the 2001 spy plane incident. For an uninitiated viewer, the showing of Colin Powell may just be another one of those things going on in remote places, but this piece of news is clearly employed in the film to mark the year—2001—in which the film is set. On a symbolic level, the film uses this real historical event, presumably being shown in real time as the event is unfolding, to mark the disconnect between "international" time, "national" time, and "local" time—and, I might add, the individual's time. By way of this disconnect, social problems in the present are critically represented.

Bing Bing's mother, for example, remarks that she has been "bought off" (*mai duan*) by the factory with 40,000 RMB, pointing out this is the final compensation for her decades of work at the factory. Bing Bing does not appear to take much notice of this piece of news—he does not seem to understand the meaning of her being laid off. Nor does he appear to connect with "international," "national," or "local" time. Indeed, his unemployment, his rejection by the army due to hepatitis, and his girlfriend's upcoming departure for school all symbolize his lack of opportunity to "connect" even locally. The presence of television in this scene further demonstrates both his and his mother's generational disconnect with one another as well as with the "international" and "national" times represented on television.

The second scene is in a room in a karaoke complex that Bing Bing and his girlfriend often frequent when they date. The room has at least one couch and a set of karaoke equipment. There they sing karaoke, and the song they sing is, not so coincidentally, the same one that Bing Bing sings at the end of the film at the police station. Besides singing, they also try to have a conversation. As they talk, the camera, at times, cuts to the television set opposite them, showing that they are watching a cartoon show about Sun Wukong, the Monkey King, from the novel *Journey to the West.* It might seem strange at first for the two young grownups to be watching a cartoon show clearly made for children. The film also indicates, however, that the two of them are not really watching it; television, once again, exists in the background and serves largely as background noise. Given that this cartoon was an early one made after the founding of the People's Republic, however, I wonder whether this particular reverse shot, between the two young people and the cartoon show, indicates yet another temporal dimension involving the changed meaning of the Monkey King in relation to youths like this couple. That is, even though the Monkey King was not specifically associated with being young, in modern times, especially during the Mao era, the production of cartoon versions of this cultural icon made the Monkey King a mischievous rebel more suitable for consumption and entertainment by young people. What complicates this seemingly simple change of meaning, however, is that Mao was interested in this character and is reportedly to have half jokingly identified himself with Sun Wukong in his celebration of the need to rebel.[8] But when the cartoon is shown in the karaoke room, Sun Wukong is devoid of this historically specific meaning and is simply a mischievous trickster. While the scene shows a remarkably awkward young couple who are having a conversation facing the television set, as opposed to facing each other, the presence of television effects yet another overlapping temporality that complicates this rather awkward and seemingly uninteresting scene.

In the last of the three scenes, Bing Bing and Xiao Ji are idly standing outside in a neighborhood where a group of old men and young children are watching television. Quickly the viewer realizes that this is supposed to be the moment when the international Olympic games committee is about to announce which city has been chosen to host the 2008 Olympics. The scene is shot from a medium distance with the two young men somewhat centered in the shot. The television screen, however, faces sideways, away from the film's viewer, with only sound indicating what is being shown. The crowd goes quiet, with the two young men being the only ones looking on without emotion, when the former chair of the committee starts announcing the decision. Everyone, again except the two young men, cheers upon hearing "Beijing," and small fireworks go off in the background. With the positioning of the young men and with their nonchalance, the scene once again accentuates the disconnect between them and the overlapping meanings of the time and space they are in, namely, the overlapping of the "international" and "national" temporalities conveyed to them via television. By showing the main characters' eyes turned away from the television set and their disinterested body language, the film manages to convey yet another disconnect between television and its viewers.

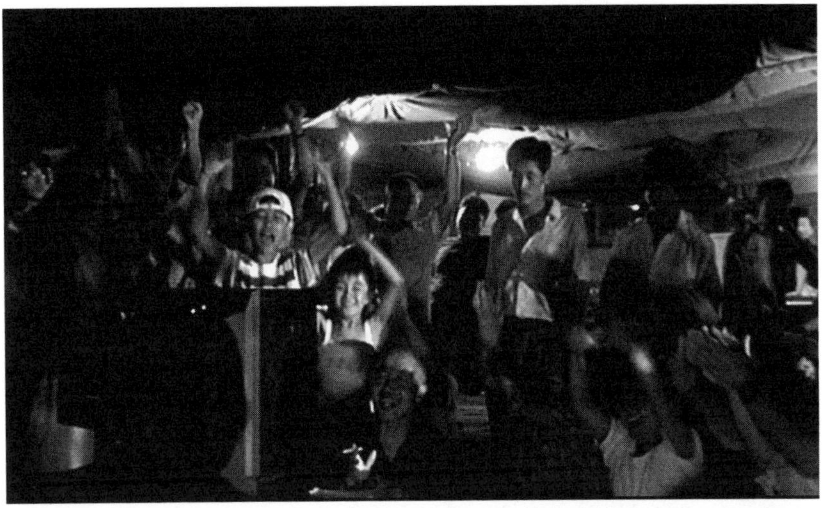

**Figure 1.1.** Bing Bing and Xiao Ji in front of a television set. In this scene the others are excited at the announcement of Beijing being selected as the site for the 2008 Olympic Games. *Unknown Pleasures* (Ren xiaoyao)

Unlike the disconnect seen in *Ermo,* the disconnect in *Unknown Pleasures* indicates that the television set has lost its lure as a meaningful material possession and has become ubiquitous, mundane, and quotidian, with people either paying no attention to it or "performing" disengaged acts of watching. If we recall the point made earlier regarding the filmic form of experimental cinema as cultural critic, *Unknown Pleasures* performs the role of cultural critic, with its visual interpretation and commentary on the disconnect, or the disjointed connect, between youths like Bing Bing and Xiao Ji and the "modernization" temporalities transmitted via televised news. The visualized disconnect manifests a critique of the ideology, practices, and consequences of China's rapid economic reforms aimed at "joining the intentional tracks" (*yu guoji jiegui*) and "moving with the times" (*yu shi ju jin*).[9] By depicting television as an official mouthpiece and simultaneously showing disconnected and tuned-out youth in relation to it, the film's political message cannot be mistaken.

The film, in this sense, dismisses television on the same grounds that most popular culture critics do, that it is too mainstream. The problematics of this film become explicit in the ways in which the youths are shown to have tuned out. Similar motifs—rebellious youths turned off by mainstream culture, which could be rich parents and their lifestyle or radio or television—are employed in films from different countries made at different times including *Rebel without a Cause* (dir. Nicholas Ray, 1955), *The Four Hundred Blows* (dir. Francois Truffaut, 1959), *A Time to Live and a Time to Die* (dir. Hou Hsiao-Hsien, 1985), to name just a few. At the same time, it is conceptually problematic to lump these films together without also realizing the temporal differences and historical particularities that are differently signified.

*Unknown Pleasures*' use of television leaves the relationship between television and everyday life as an open issue for further commentary and interpretation. In subtle ways, the film's representation of the youths' disconnect with television is contrasted with and complemented by its desire-generating and fantasy-forming influence on them. Their imitative acts of night-club hopping, *Pulp Fiction*–like spontaneous robbery, and the Zhao Tao character's Mia Wallace–like hairpiece and crude celebrity status in the local area all demonstrate a disjointed connection between these youths and television, namely, that the latter is also a major source of their daily fantasies and desires. Whether or not intentionally rendered, these details reveal a crucial blind spot in the cynicism of these youths (and, by extension, in many critics' understanding of their cynicism): what informs and shapes their fantasies is not so dissimilar from that which informs the official slogan to join the international track and move along with the times. The same globalizing capitalist ideology, dressed up as personal desires with the right to pursue them, is mediated via the simplistic "join the international track" official ideology and the unmediated flood of consumer-culture-oriented global popular culture on television.

The simultaneous disconnect and connect manifested in this film is realized in a subtle but meaningful (filmic-televisual) intertextual manner, making it clear that the seemingly disembodied stories, be they news, commercials, or imported films, on television have become part of the stories of everyday life. The political and ideological implications, by extension, indicate that the seemingly depoliticized Chinese cultural landscape is far from being so.

### ***Haoren yisheng ping'an* and *Still Life***

*Haoren yisheng ping'an* means "bless good-hearted people," or, literally, "good people, entire life, peace and safety." *Sanxia haoren,* the Chinese title of the film *Still Life,* which literally means "good people of/at/from the Three Gorges area," evokes, more than its English title, implicitly complex contextual and intertextual references and issues televisually. *Sanxia haoren* echoes the title of one of the two theme songs composed for the television drama *Yearnings,* which is one of the most famous and well-remembered Chinese television dramas and is seen as a cultural text that marked the turning point in the era of economic reform from the 1980s to the 1990s. The connection between the title of the film and *Yearnings* is further symbolized by the ring tone on the cell phone used by one of the main protagonists, Han Sanming's character. The film's double reference to *Yearnings* is subtle but nevertheless echoes the pathos conveyed via the latter's melodramatic representations of the life experiences of the main protagonist, Liu Huifang, and via the song that expresses the wish that a "good" person like her will have a good life.

In his usual fashion, Jia Zhangke places his characters in yet another dilapidated locale, this time along the Yangtze River near where the Three Gorges Dam is being built and where extensive (and permanent) demolition is taking place to make way for the reservoir's ongoing construction. This about-to-be-submerged locale is in between visible demolition and its own eventual disappearance, which is constantly indicated in the film when the camera captures, in a few repeated shots, workers writing on buildings where the eventual water level will be. It is also a place that embodies the not so "still life" lived by small communities of natives, migrant workers, and individuals like Han Sanming's character and Zhao Tao's character, Shen Hong, who are there each in search of their "spouses" but in essence are also in a moment of transition. The two characters coexist (although in the film their paths are not to cross), historically, in a shared time and space mixed with both a shared and different past, and an unknown future.

Han's character is a middle-aged man from Shanxi who comes to Fengjie, a county much of which will be under water once the dam is built, in search of his "wife," who is originally from this area. He purchased her about two decades earlier, but she decided to leave him when the local police found out about this transaction. She took their daughter with her, and the man, inexplicably, comes to the region to search for her years later, insisting that he has the right to see his daughter. As it turns out, his "wife" now lives with a much older man who works and lives on a transport boat. Because at first the woman's family—her brothers—refuse to let him know where she and their daughter are, he decides to stick around until he sees her again. In order to make a living while waiting, he takes a job with a demolition team tearing down old and uninhabited apartment buildings from which former residents have presumably departed and relocated to other parts of the province or country. The migrant workers are friendly to him, and he shares lodging with them in a small hostel, which, as it turns out, also will be demolished soon.

About halfway into this character's story, the film switches to the female character, Shen Hong, played by Zhao Tao. Since this character's story does not have much reference to television, I will just briefly point out that the juxtaposition of her story with that of Han Sanming's character adds an additional gendered dimension to Jia Zhangke's exploration of lives in transition and individuals' agency in trying to capture the meaning of their transience as best they can.

Critics have heaped praise on this film, recognizing layered meanings in seemingly simple stories laden with visual cues.[10] Indeed, Jia's camera focuses on the lives of displaced and dislocated individuals whose journeys across various parts of the country, often on the edges of development, tell sobering stories that symbolize social problems, tensions, and contradictions related to the rapid economic changes and their aftermath. Even though on the surface television is not as pronounced a motif as in the previous two films, this film's use of television indicates a subtle and effective take on this prevailing cultural form. In addition to the title of the film, which echoes the strong pathos of the drama *Yearnings,* the television motif is evoked through a seemingly minor character and through his chance, short-lived friendship with the main character played by Han Sanming. Represented as a single thread that is nevertheless a significant component of the main character's experience in the Three Gorges area, this part of the story, like the rest of the film, appears to be random and without a clear and systematic explanation. However the television motif not only adds emotional layers to the film but, more important, helps signify the aforementioned disconnect with overlapping but also conflicting temporalities and their social implications.

The Han Sanming character and the young man come across each other accidentally because they live in the same run-down hostel. The young man is significantly younger than the other men and yet takes a fancy to an old Hong Kong television drama called *Shanghai tan* (Old Shanghai, 1980), which was a great success when it first aired on the mainland in the early 1980s, when the young man would not have been born.[11] He becomes a fan of Chow Yun-fat, who played the main character in the drama, whom he likes to imitate. He likes the drama so much that he sets its theme song as the ring tone on his cell phone. Han Sanming's character sets his cell phone ring tone to the music of one of the theme songs of *Yearnings,* called "Haoren yisheng ping'an." In one scene in the film, the two of them are having a meal in a small restaurant. When he hears Han's character's ring tone, the young man does not recognize its origin. When told that the title is "Bless Good-Hearted People" ("Haoren yisheng ping'an"), he laughs, saying there are no such people anymore. He jokingly calls Han a nostalgic type, to which the latter replies that one should always have something good to remember. The young man then asks Han to ring his mobile, whose ring tone Han does not recognize either. Imitating a signature gesture of Chow Yun-fat in the drama *Old Shanghai,* he points at Han as if with a gun, wondering aloud how it can be that Han has never heard of "Fa Ge" (Brother Fa, Chow's nickname). The film does not stop here with its references to television drama but pushes the multiple temporal references implied in this little exchange much further.

After the exchange in the restaurant and after telling Shen Hong's story, the film again picks up the thread regarding the young man. In a quiet and seem-

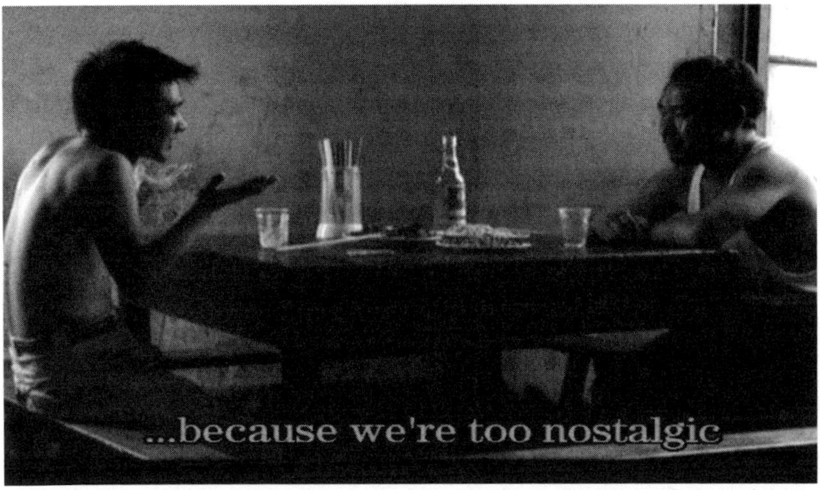


**Figure 1.2.** Han Sanming and Xiao Ma Ge having dinner. *Still Life* (Xihe Xinghui)

ingly random way, the film cuts to a moment when Han Sanming's character runs into the young man on the street. The latter is in a hurry but cheerfully tells the former that he is going to do something and that he will be paid 50 RMB for it. He asks Han to wait for him that evening in the same restaurant. Without further explanation, the young man gets into a pickup truck and quickly disappears from the scene as the truck takes a left turn and speeds off. That evening the young man fails to show up. The next day at his worksite in the midst of piles of demolished bricks, Han Sanming tries to call him. After he dials the number, he hears the theme song of *Old Shanghai* coming from somewhere nearby. He turns around and notices the sound coming out of a pile of bricks.[12] He pushes the button on his phone to hang up, and the music stops. He calls out, pointing at the pile of bricks, while other workers rush to surround it. In the next scene Han is sitting in a partially demolished space in which the young man's body lies underneath a quilt beneath a makeshift shrine. Han sits next to the covered body. As the camera zooms in, we see next to Han a picture of the nameless young man (who has told Han that everyone calls him "Xiao Ma Ge," a nickname taken from Chow Yun-fat's character) posing in a Chow Yun-fat–like gesture. Subtly and not so subtly, the film pushes the television motif further: despite his fantasy that he is Chow Yun-fat's character in a popular televisual story of old Shanghai gangsters, in real life, this Xiao Ma Ge's participation in what appears to be a gang fight brings his life to a premature end.

This entire thread about the young man and his accidental, short-lived friendship with the protagonist are represented with little exploitation of emotion. However, by using camera angles, lingering shots, moments of verbal

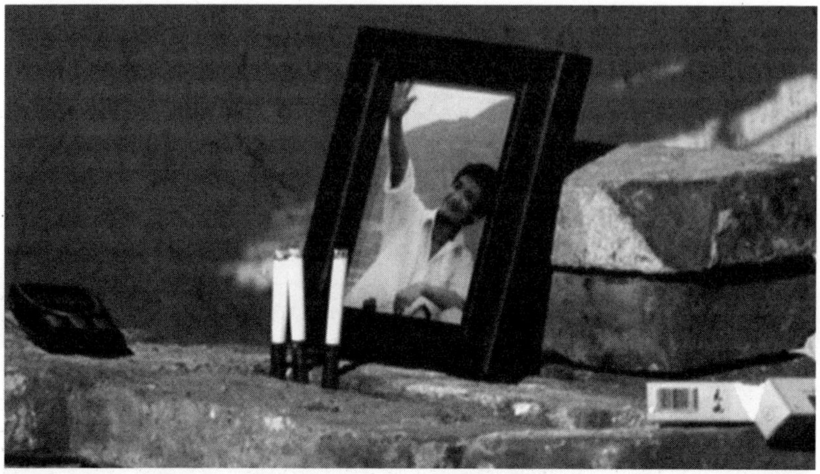

**Figure 1.3.** The makeshift shrine Han Sanming makes for Xiao Ma Ge. The photo shows the latter imitating Chow Yun-fat in *Old Shanghai. Still Life* (Xihe Xinghui)

exchange, and seemingly naturalistic acting, the film manages to tell a heart-wrenching story about a young man whose life is lost in a senseless way. From visual clues one can infer how he meets his end—he is recruited (seemingly by Shen Hong's estranged husband, Guo Bin), with 50 RMB as his payment, to take part in a gang fight. He must have been killed during the fight and is subsequently buried under the pile of bricks where Han Sanming's character finds him. Seemingly quietly—with the violence symbolized by the pile of bricks in the midst of a demolished and about-to-disappear "past"—and almost without a trace, the young man with a fancy for the television drama *Old Shanghai* and its main character has come and gone. He is young, but his short life seems to have included a mixture of hardships, innocence, small hopes, fanciful moments, and eventual destruction. What do his youth and his life stand for when associated with a place in ruins, about to disappear, and yet nevertheless layered with history? To complicate this question further, let me return to Han Sanming's character, his ring tone, along with other snippets shown in the film about his past, his present, and his uncertain future.

In addition to *Old Shanghai,* the television drama *Yearnings* is quietly but strongly referenced in this film. Each drama in its own way refers to moments—in the early 1980s and early 1990s—when the slogan *gaige kaifang,* or reform and open door, signified an optimistically imagined future for China that is both economically developed and socioculturally enhanced. When these relatively old dramas turn up again in this film, however, the time and space they occupy has become further layered with demolished space and individuals in transition with uncertain futures. On one narrative level, the television dramas each tells a story set in a different historical moment in the twentieth century: *Old Shanghai* in the 1920s and 1930s, and *Yearnings* in the 1960s to the early 1980s. The former was made in 1980 and became widely popular both in Hong Kong and on the mainland throughout the subsequent decade. The latter, shown in 1990, was also an instant success but within a different historical moment and with references to different historical issues. Each in its own way is about a not-so-distant past, and each tells a rather linear story with—especially in *Yearnings*—by now rather familiar political implications in relation to the time when it was released: it is time to move away from politics. In *Still Life*, when these dramas turn up again and are symbolized by the ring tones, the lives of the characters in the film signify the sociocultural and economic changes that have taken place during the years since the airing of these dramas and since the hopes, the imagination, and the struggles manifested in these dramas have been crushed, transformed, and rewritten, or are waiting to be rewritten and reimagined. Quietly, but surely, the film manages to revisit those earlier historical moments and question the dominant "modernization" imaginaries by placing them in a time and space where their meanings have to be reexamined.

As old television dramas, their "reappearance" is realized, in this film, via cellphone ring tones and via the short-lived connection between two characters of different generations. Of different social status than the characters in these television dramas—rich old Shanghai families (of the 1920s and 1930s) and urban Beijing intellectuals (of the 1960s, 1970s, and early 1980s)—the young man and the middle-aged man in the film identify with the dramas in relation to their own sense of where they are and what they hope to hold onto. In addition to showing the downside of the "economic miracle" in China, *Still Life*'s use of the television motif recognizes and provides indirect commentary on the impact of television on storytelling via seemingly insignificant individuals' lives.

The notion of *haoren*, or good-hearted person, in *Yearnings*' theme song takes on new meaning in a socially different setting in *Still Life*. *Haoren* today conjures up all kinds of meanings except, perhaps, for someone like Liu Huifang, who is the "good-hearted" character in *Yearnings*. Today, a "good-hearted person" is someone who is poor, so poor that years ago he had to resort to buying a woman to be his wife but who quietly goes about his life in the face of ruins and an uncertain future. Ideologically, then, such a "good person" can provoke controversy. What does "good" mean in today's Chinese context? What does Han Sanming's character mean exactly? What is his agency and what motivates him? If *haoren* here also extends to the young man who cheerfully identifies himself with Chow Yun-fat's character in *Old Shanghai*, what is his "good-heartedness"? With these questions, we realize that *haoren* is not a moral term here but one that hinges upon these individuals' "will to live," their willingness to leave home to make a living selling their labor while continuing to have hopes for themselves. Politically, however, is this not a rather depoliticized sense of being "good," one not oriented toward questioning and challenging social inequality and injustice? The film *Still Life* answers these questions in subtle and often conflicting ways.

While the unclear definition of *haoren* is indicative of cultural, ideological, and discursive changes and uncertainties in postrevolutionary Chinese mainstream culture—indeed symptomatic of its particular kind of depoliticized politics, its unspecific meaning can nevertheless become specific contingent upon historical specificities of social context. The visual particularities employed in this film manifest the interactive dynamics between different individuals and their appropriations of the cultural narratives that are available to them.

The evocation of the two television dramas helps bring to the foreground the fact that, as a dominant form of storytelling, not all television dramas are equal. Some may indeed be ephemeral, while others, at least in China, can be invoked in different historical contexts and can continue to exert an impact, often in different ways due to changing sococultural conditions.[13] It is interesting, therefore, that while Han Sanming's character gravitates toward the sentiment expressed in the theme song of *Yearnings,* the much younger man prefers a drama that was made one decade earlier than *Yearnings* and is about an earlier historical period. The two characters' relationships to the two television dramas as symbolized in *Still Life,* in other words, essentially reorient our sense of the original dramas and help us recognize the complex temporalities that inform the film's representations of these characters. The film not only sheds light on the cultural impact of television drama on individuals, but also, and more importantly, complicates such a cultural relationship via stories about individuals who find themselves in specific social and economic conditions and whose interactions with these cultural texts offer sometimes heart-wrenching glimpses into the layered social and historical temporalities in contemporary China. In short, the multilayered implications and overlapping temporalities, manifested in filmic-televisual intertextuality indicate the extent to which television culture and television drama have participated in constant ideological renegotiations specific to China in the postrevolutionary and market economic reform era.

CHAPTER TWO

# Re-collecting "History" on Television

## "Emperor Dramas," National Identity, and the Question of Historical Consciousness

❏ ❏ ❏ ❏ ❏

Emperors are back, on television. In the last two decades, television dramas about China's dynastic emperors have periodically received widespread popular and critical attention. Although a relatively recent addition, "emperor drama" has become an important subcategory of "history drama" on television. Why emperors? In the West, scholarly attention to this phenomenon has just begun. Ying Zhu's studies on *The Yongzheng Court* (*Yongzheng wangchao*, 1998) (her translation *Yongzheng Dynasty*), for example, situates the making of the drama within the context of contemporary China, recognizing it as "political discourse" in relation to the role of intellectuals.[1] In China, most critics have dismissed the phenomenon as problematic, pointing out what they perceive as inaccurate representations of history or as reducing history to entertainment. Their dismissal, questioning the comeback of emperors, does not entail a clear understanding of the implications of the phenomenon. If "all history is contemporary," the issue is not so much "history" per se as "historical consciousness," a perennial Chinese modernity issue that not only continues to inspire intellectual discourse but also permeates popular culture's representations of history and debates about them.[2] The dynamics between the two seemingly different—intellectual and popular—tracks in the consideration of "history" are characteristic of contemporary Chinese mainstream culture. The "triumphant return" of emperors in popular culture manifests the tensions, the changing dynamics, and the problematics within mainstream culture as China undergoes its latest round of social transformation.

### The Rise of Emperor Dramas on Television and of History as Spectacle

The term "emperor drama" comes from two alternately used terms in Chinese, *diwang ju* or *huangdi ju.* It refers to a phenomenon that began to appear on television in the early 1990s as part of the growing "history drama" subgenre. In the tradition of different forms of drama in Chinese theater, however, "history drama," *lishi ju* in Chinese, is one of the most difficult genres to define.[3] As a "modern" phenomenon,[4] "history drama" existed long before television, mostly as cultural texts theatrically staged, sometimes filmically represented, and alternately identified under the even more all-encompassing genre *guzhuang ju/xi,* or costume drama. On television these dramas range from adaptations of classical novels and tales to adaptations of the modern writings of historical and legendary figures, and they can be either "comedies" or (serious) "dramas." The distinction between history drama and costume drama may be tenuous, but in a narrow sense one can say that the former mainly pertains to narratives that not only have the appearance of China's "premodern" past, but also the appearance of focusing on actual historical and legendary figures. When it comes to representing China's emperors, additionally, the past three decades have seen transregional—including Hong Kong, Taiwan, mainland China, and Korea—exchanges and influences that have contributed to the development of such dramas.[5] Whether or not critics are willing to acknowledge anything "serious" in popular culture's representations of "history," the widespread presence and periodic success of history drama inevitably raise issues about historical imagination, historical consciousness, and historical uncertainty or amnesia.

Televisual representations of "Chinese history" started shortly after the Cultural Revolution (1966–1976), most notably with dramas imported from Hong Kong in the early 1980s. The Hong Kong martial arts dramas *Huo Yuanjia* (1983) and *Chen Zhen* (1984) are two memorable examples. When the former aired, people congregated night after night in places where there were television sets to watch this twenty-episode drama.[6] *Chen Zhen* was aired on the heels of *Huo Yuanjia*'s success and was also popularly received.[7] Their success was an early signal of change in postrevolution cultural production on the popular front that anticipated the return of China's past, fictional or otherwise, as a rich source of narrative materials for televisual display.

With the popular reception of these imported dramas, television drama producers on the mainland turned to classical novels and well-known historical figures for dramatic material. *Honglou meng* (Dream of the red chamber), for example, was made into a thirty-six-episode television serial in 1987, followed by *Xiyou ji* (Journey to the west) also in 1987, with an alleged 81 percent viewing rate (both dramas continued to enjoy reruns as late as 2006).[8] The cultural status of the novel *Dream of the Red Chamber* compelled the director and producers to treat the adaptation with such seriousness that, after they chose actors to play the major characters, they met in a secluded place where the cast read the original novel and discussed it with some of the best-known scholars of the novel at the time.[9] This artistic care manifested an elite's desire to own the interpretation of the classics. As time went on, such artistic care was less practiced, signaling a diversification of the forces that participate in the production of popular representations of the classics. With *Sanguo yanyi* (Romance of the three kingdoms), which came late in 1994 and was followed by *Shuihu zhuan* (Outlaws of the marsh) in 1996, television adaptations not only helped popularize traditional classics, but they also demonstrated the power and potential of television as a medium to represent the past in ways no other cultural form or medium had been capable of before.

It was not until 1991, when Taiwan and the mainland coproduced *Xishuo Qianlong* (Playfully told tales of Emperor Qianlong) was shown and popularly received on the mainland, that past emperors become a special category on television. *Playfully Told Tales of Qianlong*, much to the chagrin of scholars and critics, ushered in a new variety of "history drama" that was later identified as the "emperor drama."[10] The emperor drama did not quite solidify as a noted cultural phenomenon until the appearance of a series of dramas about emperors from the Han, Tang, Ming, and Qing dynasties, all made by mainland producers.[11] Since then, Chinese viewers have periodically been given doses of an emperor drama, either in the *zheng shuo* style (seriously told, or serious style) or the *xi shuo* (playfully told, or playful style).[12]

Representations of emperors, like no other history drama, involve acts of "(re-)collecting," as defined by Susan Pearce, a range of historical and fictionalized figures and fake historical material objects to create a make-believe (but authentic-appearing to many viewers) diagetic world within which "history" is projected "as if it really happened that way."[13] The popularity of these dramas indicates, in the words of one Chinese critic, "an enthrallment" with past emperors.[14] Emperor drama evolved on television throughout the 1990s and beyond, becoming more and more spectacular.

Although this phenomenon has remained on the periphery of China studies in the West, within China numerous short essays have been written in response either to a single drama or to the phenomenon as a whole. They reflect a range of positions and, combined, manifest differences and contentions that exist within the community of critics. There is a journalistic immediacy to many of these critical responses, and they tend to emphasize errors in terms of historical accuracy, a lack of "seriousness" in the playful style, or some drama's "unconventional" or unorthodox interpretations of an emperor.[15] Many criticisms are expressed in familiar oppositional terms such as truth versus fiction, high culture versus low culture, avant-garde versus mainstream, elite culture versus popular culture, or historical memory versus historical amnesia. These dichotomies manifest a familiar tension in modern China on the issue of how to understand and explain "tradition"—specifically China's "premodern" history—within the "modern" context. They also indicate, I would argue, that "popular culture" is at the same time deeply entangled with the modern Chinese elite's and intellectuals' sense of uncertainty and crisis, and with a modern Chinese "historical consciousness" that is characterized by this sentiment of uncertainty and crisis (I will return to this point in the last section of the chapter).

In the next two sections, I examine "playfully told" and "seriously told" emperor dramas. The former variety reflects the influence of Hong Kong and Taiwan popular culture on mainland Chinese mainstream culture. Using two dramas, *Kangxi weifu sifang ji* (Emperor Kangxi traveling undercover) and *Huanzhu gege* (Princess Huanzhu) as examples, I speculate about how such influence helped produce a "cool" type of emperor within the larger context of the postrevolution era. In examining the "seriously told" category, I focus on two of the most celebrated and critically acclaimed emperor dramas, *Yongzheng wangchao* (The Yongzheng court, 1998) and *Han wu da di* (Emperor Wu of the Han dynasty, 2004). Both dramas are directed by a woman director, Hu Mei. Although I do not delve into the gender aspects of the genre here, the fact that these two dramas are directed by a woman is worth exploring, both in the context of gender politics in general and in the context of the changing and changed role of women in cultural production in particular, in post-Mao and the post–women's liberation contemporary China.[16] Focusing on the narrative structure of these Hu Mei–directed emperor dramas, I examine the extent to which the representations of emperors as (tragic) "national heroes" are symptomatic of changing dynamics within mainstream culture in which "history" is reimagined through the reconstruction of (new) national myths. The melodramatic mode of heroism manifests what Ying Zhu identifies as a "totalitarian nostalgia," to be sure, but, as I argue in this study, its "melodramatic politics" is informed by the inherent tensions in modern Chinese historical consciousness itself, an issue with far wider implications.

## Who Is Afraid of Emperors, Whether Kangxi or Qianlong?

The first television drama about an emperor to be widely circulated and popularly received on the mainland was *Playfully Told Tales of Qianlong*, aired in 1991. The timing is worth noting. Similar to the importation of dramas like *Huo Yuanjia* and *Chen Zhen* from Hong Kong in the early 1980s, the making of *Playfully Told Tales of Qianlong* and *Yearnings* in the early 1990s signaled another moment of change, in this case from the Enlightenment-oriented *jingying wenhua*, or elite culture, of the 1980s to a culture dominated by popular cultural products, including those from Hong Kong and Taiwan.[17] This shift corresponded with underlying structural and ideological changes in the quick-paced economic reforms of the 1990s whose cultural manifestations and their implications have been the subject of heated intellectual debates in China.[18] Indeed, a powerful cultural flow from these regions into the mainland, including Deng Lijun's music (Deng Lijun was the most popular Taiwan/Hong Kong singer in mainland China in the 1980s), Jin Yong's martial-arts novels, and Qiong Yao's romantic fiction, heralded a "postmodern" taste for global, cosmopolitan entertainment with a preference for the cool and playful.

Television culture in the 1980s was still preoccupied with what might be identified as "serious" cultural issues largely defined by intellectuals.[19] Dramas like *Huo Yuanjia* and *Chen Zhen* were well received for more than their entertaining martial arts intrigues. Their central themes—patriotism, righteousness, and (manly) heroism—were familiar ones to the mainland viewers, while their melodramatic codes were made afresh with stories that would not have been allowed to be told publicly during the Cultural Revolution. These popular dramas ran parallel with what Chinese writers, poets, filmmakers, and scholars were trying to do in the 1980s, namely, flooding China's cultural scene not only with "new" ideas and artistic experimentations, but also with new entertainment products. These imported dramas helped bring back legendary historical figures who would not have fit the model of "revolutionary hero" during the Cultural Revolution but would be readily identified and celebrated as "national heroes" in the post-Mao era. The central themes of these imported popular dramas, in other words, corresponded well with the elite culture of the 1980s, which was itself filled with a (male) desire for "authentic" cultural roots, for "manly men," and for a different type of hero.[20]

The appearance of *Playfully Told Tales of Qianlong* shortly after the 1989 social upheaval and political and military crackdown, in contrast, coincided with the arrival of (1) an all-out economic development phase in the post-Mao reform era and (2) a change in the cultural scene that would decentralize intellectuals' position in mainstream culture. It is not an exaggeration to suggest that the success of *Playfully Told Tales of Qianlong* helped usher in an additional influx of Hong Kong and Taiwanese (as well as Japanese and Korean) popular cultural products in music, literature, film, and television.[21] The influx of these products would play a role in the formation and production of a glamorized popular visual culture in China, adding yet another layer of difference and ambivalence to its mainstream culture. Signifying these changes, the image of a smiling (and even goofy) Qianlong corresponded with what can be identified as a depoliticization process in the contemporary mainstream culture. I use the notion of depoliticization here advisedly in the sense that Wang Hui discusses in his article "Depoliticized Politics: From East to West," in which the seeming depoliticization of the popular culture is in fact full of political implications.[22] In the context of China's economic reforms of the last thirty years, the political implications of "depoliticization" reside in the coexistence of a collective retreat from the legacies of the twentieth-century Chinese revolution and a gravitation toward the "modernization imaginary" of the late-twentieth-century version, an imaginary that is largely contained within the logic of globalized commercial capitalism. The "transregional" flow of cultural products from Hong Kong and Taiwan to the mainland, to reiterate, took place within this larger cultural and political development.[23] In many of these cultural products, certain melodramatic narrative codes—such as a strong pathos or overwrought emotions—are toned down and replaced with "postmodern" ones, including random use of dehistoricized time and space, a corresponding request for suspension of disbelief, and excessive play in turning "heroes" into "antiheroes," all of which is geared toward an ahistorical playfulness. The return of emperors in playfully told tales was premised on related logic.

The notion of *xishuo* in Chinese implies not only comedy, but also "poetic license," in this case license to render emperor stories without much historical basis. The poetic license employed in the playful tales does not lead to the creation of a trickster like Sun Wukong (the Monkey King) in *Journey to the West* through which the "sacred," the powerful, and authority are all made fun of. Instead, the playful dramas, as it were, turn the emperor himself loose. In many cases, they freely deploy the emperor outside the court in disguise and turn him temporarily into someone else—a beggar, a shopkeeper, a passer-by, a father, or a son—to witness the "real" world and to set what is wrong out there right. In other cases, they create comical situations in which the emperor appears foolish, stubborn, loving, and therefore human all at the same time. Emperors are "re-collected" as a type of "cool" hero who is human and therefore prone to foolishness. Let me offer two textual examples.

*Emperor Kangxi Traveling Undercover* can be said to be the first major mainland Chinese version of the playful style of emperor drama. It consisted of five *bu,* or series, the first of which appeared in 1999 with a splash. It had thirty episodes within which there are four separate stories, each ranging from seven to nine episodes in length. This structural model was repeated in the following four series of *Emperor Kangxi Traveling Undercover.* Combined, the five series tell about twenty stories in which Emperor Kangxi disguises himself as someone else and travels to a particular place to investigate one thing or another. Within each of these smaller stories, the emperor almost always travels with his most trusted eunuch and favored concubine, and there is always an episode of romance (a comparison to James Bond comes to mind). Given that the emperor's decision to travel in disguise is often prompted by news about corrupt local officials,

Kangxi in these serials is essentially turned into a detective of sorts. At the same time, because he is the one with ultimate power, his detective work, although full of twists and turns due to inevitable occurrences of misunderstanding, is always unequivocally triumphant. As a James Bond–like romance magnet, the emperor is also always placed in the position of the "knowing subject"—that is, he is never going to commit to the women who express interest in him and to whose interest the emperor does not hesitate to respond—a power position that answers to no one except, presumably, his own conscience.

Building the narrative structure of these serials around the idea of *weifu sifang* (meaning to pay a visit, to explore a situation, or to investigate undercover) by an emperor is reminiscent of a rather traditional ideal about an official's willingness to *ticha minqing,* or experience the situation on the ground firsthand. Whether or not this ideal was practiced by any emperor in history, it is believed to have been practiced by some officials or legendary figures who are mythologized for their uprightness, sense of justice, and ability to solve crimes. Assigning Kangxi to about twenty undercover investigations (in a total of five series) is in essence the latest expansion of this cultural ideal.

From one story to the next, Kangxi travels at will from the south—Suzhou, Yixing, and Anqing—to the north—Shandong, Shanxi, and within Beijing itself—accompanied by only a handful who know who he is. The disguised emperor is put in a certain degree of danger—hence drama—such as being pursued by local thugs or their dogs, having to fight with local soldiers who take him for a criminal, becoming a coolie in a mine, where he is punished for wanting to help a "fellow coolie," becoming a low-ranking local official having to deal with the local gangsters, or being put in jail by corrupt local officials (who do not know who he really is). As a melodrama would have it, he is always able to escape unscathed and, more important, triumphant, with "bad" people duly punished and "good" people duly rewarded. As such, Emperor Kangxi in these playfully told tales is not unlike modern Hollywood superheroes such as Superman, Batman, Spiderman, and 007. Most of them have "superhuman" powers that make them undefeatable. At the same time, they also have a "human" side with which they live a seemingly ordinary life. More often than not, there is romance on the side, even though most of the romances do not come to a good end. The popularity of such heroes, as critics have argued, manifests the modern-day human condition, which is marked, by a profound sense of uncertainty. As a type of Chinese modern-day *chuanqi,* or strange tale, playful Kangxi dramas echo the same sense of uncertainty and a similar desire for superhuman heroes, who, through some struggle, can always set things right. Issues of historical accuracy, as a result, do not apply. I will return to this comparison after I offer additional examples from the *Huanzhu gege* (Princess Huanzhu) serials.

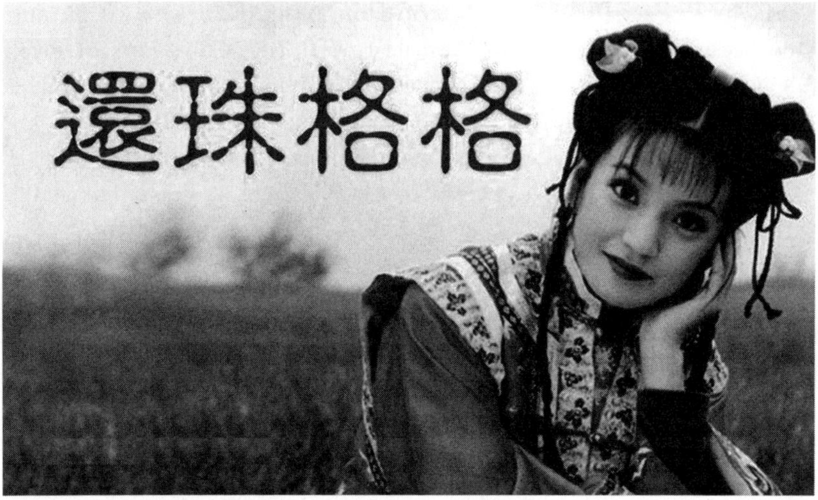


**Figure 2.1.** Xiao Yanzi. *Princess Huazhu* (http://image.baidu.com)

Scripted by Qiong Yao, the best-known contemporary Taiwanese romance novelist, the first twenty-four-episode *Huanzhu gege* serial, a coproduction by Taiwan and the mainland, was aired on the mainland in 1998. By then Qiong Yao had long been a household name on the mainland. Throughout the 1980s, television dramas based on her novels, such as *Zai shui yi fang* (On one side of water), attracted widespread popular attention as soon as they were shown there. Ever since then, Qiong Yao's novels and their film and television adaptations—always about romantic love and its impossibility and always represented in a unabashedly sentimental way—have exerted substantial influence on the mainland. Not directly about an emperor, *Huanzhu gege* belongs to the playfully told tales of emperors in that the protagonist, Xiao Yanzi (literally, Little Swallow), is placed in the Qianglong court, and her relationship with Qianlong constitutes the key component of the drama.

In the story, she is mistakenly taken to be Emperor Qianlong's long lost (out of wedlock) daughter Xia Ziwei. Much of the rest of the story takes place inside the court with the emperor playing a major role in the dramatic evolution and resolution of this case of mistaken identity. What makes this serial (and the following two additional productions) "playful" is the character Xiao Yanzi, who is armed with funny lines in her conversations with the emperor and others, making her a favorite character among devoted viewers.[24] Narratively, her loveliness—she is lively, cute, and articulate—is what makes her succeed in persuading the emperor that, despite the fact that she has deceived him by pretending to be his daughter, she deserves his understanding because she did not intend the mistaken identity to happen. Together with the next two serials of the same title, the theme of this drama hinges on how this unlikely heroine, Little Swallow, ultimately manages to "cleanse" the darkest human souls and to soften the most powerful human being, the emperor. Placing a number of additional good-hearted young individuals (who are unlikely characters to appear there) in an imperial court, Qiong Yao continues her style of modern-day sentimental "strange tales" and essentially creates Qianlong in the image of Kangxi in *Kangxi weifu sifang ji:* a humanized individual who nevertheless possesses larger-than-life power. Through Xiao Yanzi, additionally, Qianlong is represented as an emperor with feelings.

Qianlong, a grandson of Kangxi who became the fourth Qing dynasty emperor in history, returns again and again on television as the favorite emperor in playfully told dramas of emperors. Historically, as the Qing emperor with the longest reign (which lasted sixty years, after which he ceded the throne to his son in 1795 before he died in 1799), Qianlong presided over one of the most prosperous periods of the dynasty. But he is also known for his propensity to extravagance and for many controversial decisions, ranging from conducting a literary inquisition (*wenzi yu*) to promoting and protecting He Shen, a known corrupt official, to refusing Western demands for trade. In the playfully told dramas, however, his stature is significantly softened, and he becomes a loving father, a lustful man with power over any woman he wants, and a sometimes confused emperor who does not know how to distinguish between bad and good. Like many temporarily misguided father figures in typical Hollywood productions, Qianlong the emperor is able to learn lessons along the way and to acknowledge that he was wrong and to express willingness to mend his ways. At the same time, the

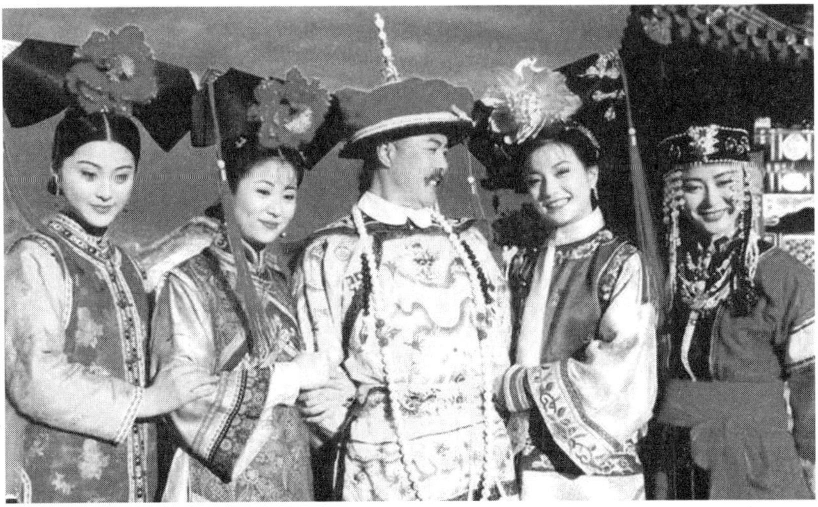

**Figure 2.2.** Xiao Yanzi with Qianlong and others. *Princess Huanzhu* (http://image.baidu.com)

emperor is always the one who not only ultimately rights the wrongs, but also grants "happiness" to the "good" people who deserve it. As a result, it goes without saying, these playfully told tales unfailingly end happily ever after.

Recall the point made earlier regarding the comparison between playful representations of emperors and characters such as Superman, Batman, Spiderman, and 007. The linkage between the two seemingly very different types of representations and characters is that, as heroes, they possess both superhuman and human qualities, and as a result they are always capable of saving the world from troubles or destruction, and doing so in a "cool" way.[25] What is "cool" in playful dramas, specifically, is that they play with the "throne" by making it appear funny and quotidian, with desires, flaws, and faults not too different from those that most ordinary moderns are prone to. The emperor together with his idiosyncrasies is thus wrapped up under a cover that says "cool." History does not quite apply. Making emperors in the image of contemporary "cool" culture not only succeeds in turning "history" into an infinite source of entertainment material but also succeeds in flattening history out into the latest version of a game show. As in a game show, history becomes a virtual world made up in any way the game players fancy. What kind of historical consciousness, if any, does all of this reflect?

The answer lies in the question of what informs such "playfulness." Scholarly attention to Hong Kong and Taiwanese cultural influences (mostly in film) on the mainland tends to hail the transregional exchanges for injecting into Chinese mainstream culture large doses of "cultural difference." Looking beyond a postmodern proclivity to celebrate difference merely for difference's sake, one can infer from this celebration another one that celebrates "different" historical choices and experiences from regions or countries where revolution has always been a negative concept and where modernization is presumed to have been achieved without revolution. It is still fresh in our memory, for example, that throughout the 1980s and 1990s (until the "Asian meltdown" in 1997) the economic successes of the so-called four little dragons—Hong Kong, Taiwan, Singapore, and Korea—were hailed as proof of the success of the "Confucian work ethic." Underlying those celebrations was a devaluation of modern Chinese revolutionary historical choices and experiences, with a seemingly logical conclusion that the "backward" mainland Chinese ought to emulate those regions and countries not only economically but also culturally. This simplistic "better economy equals better culture" logic is buttressed by the flow of global capital and corresponds to the mainland Chinese desire to modernize and a willingness to downgrade their own historical choices and experiences. This ideological readiness deconstructs the modern Chinese trauma-oriented sense of history, while at the same time serving up another version of history in a different pot labeled with the word "play." To be willing to play in today's world order and being "playful" according to its logic is "cool."

Since being "cool" has become a major component of the postmodern logic in the latest round of globalizing capitalism, the global spread of the culture of the "cool" becomes a powerful informing force that, with a nod toward a depoliticizing (and dehistoricizing) "playful" irony, is license to deconstruct that which is "serious" or "traumatic." In this context the "transregionally correct" playful representations of China's past implicitly function to deconstruct the "trauma-oriented" mainstream Chinese intellectual and revolutionary traditions. The key action in this deconstruction game is to turn a negative historical symbol—the emperor—into a modern-day superhero. Ironically, however, the opposition of playful and serious styles that results helps reveal additional ideological tensions within contemporary Chinese mainstream culture in which the struggle between what is considered traditional and what is modern continues to remain a serious national preoccupation.

## Re-collecting Emperors as National Heroes, Melodramatically and Ambivalently

In the *zhengshuo,* or serious, style, the creative impulses stem from the "old-fashioned" grand narrative from a "modern" perspective, treating emperors not as postmodern "cool" heroes but as modern national ones. Generally speaking, the serious style of emperor drama derives from the familiar narrative style found in adaptations of classical novels such as *Romance of the Three Kingdoms* and other kinds of so-called *xinbian lishi ju* (new history drama). Their creation may well have been inspired by the success of *Romance of the Three Kingdoms,* which was shown on television in 1994. Based on the classical novel of the same title, the eighty-four-episode drama was shot on a scale unseen in any previous television drama regardless of genre. Though the drama is characterized by a crudely designed mise-en-scène, the feel of the large scale comes from the large collection of characters and the various battle scenes in the novel. Among the so-called four best-known classics (*si da mingzhu*), *Romance of the Three Kingdoms* is perhaps most closely related to events in history, specifically the historical period around the Three Kingdoms, the state of Wei (AD 220–265), the state of Shu (AD 221–263), and the state of Wu (AD 222–280). Although the period lasted less than one hundred years, it has left Chinese culture with numerous legendary historical figures, and their stories have continued (and will continue) to capture people's imagination. As such, this eighty-four-episode television drama can be seen as a (melodramatic) prototype of the serious-style emperor drama in which themes such as heroism, power struggles, good versus evil, and loyalty versus disloyalty loom large. In emperor dramas, dynastic emperors have become cultural icons and are represented in ways that are reminiscent and characteristic of the legendary figures in *Romance of the Three Kingdoms,* often as tragic heroes. What has followed in the making of serious-style emperor dramas, in other words, has not diverged far from the prototype. This continuity ensured additional melodramatic possibilities, in terms of both structure and content.

Narratively, almost all the serious-style emperor dramas begin in the later years of an old emperor in decline and tell of his passing along with the struggle that ensues in the consolidation of power by the young emperor. This narrative structure allows for considerable poetic license—for melodrama—in the focalization of characters and stories, arrangements of plots, and, above all, the imagined dialogues. In many of the melodramatic moments with regard to these characters there is a thinly disguised fascination with the power struggles waged within the logic of the political structure of the dynastic system. The narrative structure helps focus on the fate of the individuals who either actively or passively participate in such struggles. The relationship between the narrative structure and representations of characters is a key element in our understanding of the historical imagination manifested in these dramas. At the same time, the representations of the emperors as (male) individuals within a political power structure carry with them a projection of modern and contemporary ambivalence and desire that needs to be examined and understood.

Compared with such seriously told emperor dramas as *The Kangxi Court* (Kangxi wangchao) and *The Qianlong Court* (Qianlong wangchao), Hu Mei's *The Yongzheng Court* (1998) generated heated debate, in part because this drama portrays Yongzheng as a sympathetic figure, which is different from the customary interpretation. Based on Eryuehe's literary representation of Yongzheng in his novel *Yongzheng huangdi* (Emperor Yongzheng), the televisual representation of the emperor pushes the envelope in placing Yongzheng in a more sympathetic light.[26] Instead of portraying him as a ruthless and brutal ruler suspected of gaining his position by altering his father Emperor Kangxi's will, Hu Mei's televisual version, following the original novel, portrays him as just the opposite: he is an upright individual who not only is favored by his father Emperor Kangxi and legitimately inherits the throne, but is also a hardworking emperor. Throughout the drama, additionally, Yongzheng is framed within a narrative structure that sets him up against the conspiracies of a number of his brothers, who constantly conspire to overthrow him. Above all, Yongzheng is represented as a tragic hero.

For example, as this forty-four-episode drama begins against the background of the last years of Kangxi's reign, and power struggles are already taking place

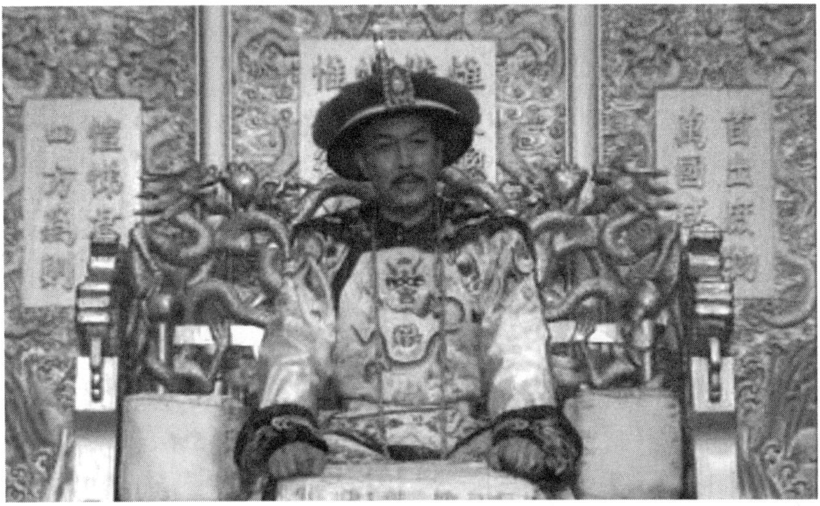

**Figure 2.3.** Yongzheng takes the throne. *The Yongzheng Court* (Zhongguo Guoji Dianshi Zonggongsi)

oriented around the choice of the next emperor, the first episode shows Yongzheng as *si ah ge,* or the fourth son, of Emperor Kangxi, together with the thirteenth (younger) brother, on a mission ordered by the emperor to collect taxes in a province. Instead of placing them in an official mansion or governmental quarters, the drama shows them walking in the street, witnessing the cruel treatment of ordinary people by local officials. When they interfere, because no one knows who they are, they are rudely challenged and disregarded. With this scene setting the tone from the opening, the drama places Yongzheng in a positive light in direct contradiction to the customary belief that Yongzheng was a ruthless ruler. Indeed, how can a hardworking and sympathetic prince who tries to honestly carry out his duties not ultimately manage to win his father's trust and subsequently his throne? Duty and honor are already written into the representation of the young prince.

It is along these lines that *The Yongzheng Court* differs from *The Kangxi Court.* While the latter focuses on many details on Kangxi's relationships with his mother and some of his concubines, *The Yongzheng Court* offers little narrative space for significant female characters or for Yongzheng's personal life. Instead, it stresses his "manly" stoicism by showing how he struggles against difficult odds, especially when shunned and isolated by most of his brothers, and by emphasizing that he lives a simple life without interest in material gain and that he is kind to individuals who work for him regardless of their family background. In the midst of all of this, however, he is also shown as a participant in a power struggle capable of acting decisively and ruthlessly when need be.

The narrative focus on the transition of power from Kangxi to Yongzheng and the subsequent positive portrayal of the latter as emperor thus reveals an ambivalent awareness on the part of the producers of the drama. On the one hand, through all the major characters, whether sympathetically portrayed or not, the drama demonstrates how they are part of a political system within which they are constructed and conditioned and in which they carry out their beliefs and ideas. The system is shown to be cold and ruthless, a familiar perspective shared by most modern Chinese, who view the dynastic past critically. Yongzheng's ascendance to the throne and his efforts to establish and maintain his legitimacy become the overall narrative focus of the serial that, along with the various plots and subplots focusing on the roles of different individuals in various power struggles, help foreground the workings of a system in which the motif of conspiracy looms large and in which power struggles are the major driving force that informs the behavior of individuals including the emperor.

On the other hand, the drama focuses on Yongzheng, offering a sympathetic representation of an emperor who has traditionally been portrayed as someone shrouded in suspicion. By placing him in the forefront of real sociopolitical issues that were reportedly plaguing the Kangxi court, the drama shows the "fourth son" to be someone who is willing to uphold principles regardless of whom he might offend. In this way, the drama sets up its value orientation when it comes to this controversial Qing emperor, suggesting that it is possible that history's unkindness toward Yongzheng may have come about because he offended many in the power system. He is portrayed as a lonely monarch, an "individual," who, faces the risk of being overthrown by his grudging brothers. The drama also sets him (and his thirteenth younger brother) apart from their gangster like siblings led by *ba ah ge*, Kangxi's eighth son. By placing Yongzheng's struggle with his brothers within the context of a real power struggle in which the former represents what is important for the empire at large and the latter are shown to be power hungry, the drama reverses traditional accusations against Yongzheng for, among other things, being cruel to his brothers and for driving some of them to an untimely death. The collection of individuals surrounding the emperor and the system within which the logic of their behavior is understood are represented in ways that support Yongzheng in what he has to do. The drama does not aim to show him as a kind-hearted emperor but, rather, as a tragic hero and individual who is subject to the limitations of the system in which he operates but who can nevertheless be understood through a different—more sympathetic—historical lens. The same melodramatic model of representation will be repeated in another one of Hu Mei's emperor dramas, *Emperor Wu of the Han Dynasty.*

While the majority of emperor dramas have taken place in the Qing court, *Emperor Wu of the Han Dynasty* takes the viewers to a much early historical period (156–87 BCE). Structurally speaking, early parts of *Emperor Wu* also consist of stories of transition of power, from Emperor Jing of the Han (Han Jing Di) to his son Liu Che, who became Emperor Wu (Han Wu Di). There are numerous power struggles involving Emperor Jing's mother, his brothers, his sister, his wives, and circles of individuals associated with these relatives of Emperor Jing. When Liu Che comes to power as the heir, he is too young to carry out his duties and much of the power to make decisions falls into the hands of his grandmother. In this drama, unlike in *The Yongzheng Court,* Hu Mei has added major narrative lines that involve female relatives of both emperors. The grandmother of Emperor Wu is particularly powerful, but female power is also represented as somewhat irrational. Everybody is involved in power struggles and risks punishment if not careful (and almost everybody, in effect, is punished). Once again, power struggles are fully employed narratively for melodrama and for us to explore their meanings further.

Using biographical clues from the *Historical Records* (*Shi ji*) and the *Book of Han* (*Han shu*), two of the most influential history books of all time, the producers of the drama focus the "great feats" of Emperor Wu mainly on his long-term efforts to defeat the Xiongnu (a nomadic tribe in the north and northwest who were a formidable force threatening the Han court), enhancing the heroic warrior image of the emperor. Against the historical background of war with the nomadic Xiongnu, this drama examines other historical figures and the significance of their roles. By dramatizing the difficulties Emperor Wu initially encounters because of philosophical differences with his grandmother on how to govern, the drama further weaves in the controversy for which the emperor is remembered, namely, his role in elevating Confucianism to the state ideology at the expense of other schools of thought. The matriarch is a faithful follower of Daoism and believes that the best way to govern is *wu wei er zhi*—governing through inaction. The young emperor, however, breaks away from the control of his grandmother and her ideas, and embarks on years of fighting with the Xiongnu and eventually succeeds in pushing them farther west. In the process, however, the young emperor grows into an angry old man alienated from just about everyone around him. He continues to dodge "bullets" from various directions, but as time goes on, he becomes the victim of his own power and its uncertainty, growing more isolated and lonely. Narratively framed in this way, this emperor is represented in the same vein as Yongzheng, namely, as a tragic figure both despite and because of his "great feats." In both cases their "great feats" are accompanied by deadly power struggles and great sacrifices in terms of their humanity.

The drama's unique beginning and ending further complicate the implications of the representations of Emperor Wu. The drama is bracketed with a repeated scene of a dialogue between the aged Emperor Wu and Sima Qian, a contemporary of the emperor and the author to whom the *Historical Records* is attributed.[27] In the drama, the meeting takes place after Sima Qian has finished writing the *Historical Records*. Emperor Wu has read the text and is enraged by it. The repetition of the dialogue is intriguing.

The scene begins with an overview shot of the grand palace in which a tiny figure is seen walking with a cane toward a huge hall—someone has been summoned by the emperor. As he walks in, he kneels down in front of the emperor, reporting that "the guilty servant Sima Qian" has arrived. Thus begins the dialogue between the two, which I will quote in its entirety:

> EMPEROR WU: After reading your book, I fell ill. This experience has taken at least one year out of my earthly life. Aren't you satisfied? You want me to have you killed, so that future generations can praise your loyalty and righteousness and curse me for being a tyrant. But I am most definitely not going to satisfy you in this way.
>
> SIMA QIAN: Your Highness, your heart is as grand and deep as the oceans and cannot be fully understood by someone like me.
>
> EMPEROR: You can have the books back, but there is no need for you to start another one. I have been advised to have the books burned, but I have rejected the idea. As far as I am concerned, even though they cannot be viewed as official historical records, they can be left behind as representing the views of one historian.
>
> SIMA QIAN: Your Highness, you always take a long view and keep in mind the needs of generations to come. Your humaneness is not easily understood by ordinary souls; perhaps I simply do not have any right to comment on Your Highness.
>
> EMPEROR: Do you think you truly understand me? Many things only heaven ultimately knows. Whatever has happened and whatever has not happened, I have no opportunity to change them nor can they be changed.[28]

This exchange can hardly be construed as a dialogue. The emperor's wrath is aimed at what the historian has written, and yet the historian is shown to be somewhat apologetic for having written something that enraged the emperor. Sima Qian is made repeatedly to raise the possibility that he may have failed to truly understand the emperor.

Given that Sima Qian's *Historical Records* has indeed become the "history" based on which various early historical figures have been remembered and understood (or not), this imagined dialogue between the emperor and his biographer seems to give the emperor an opportunity to have his say, or, more

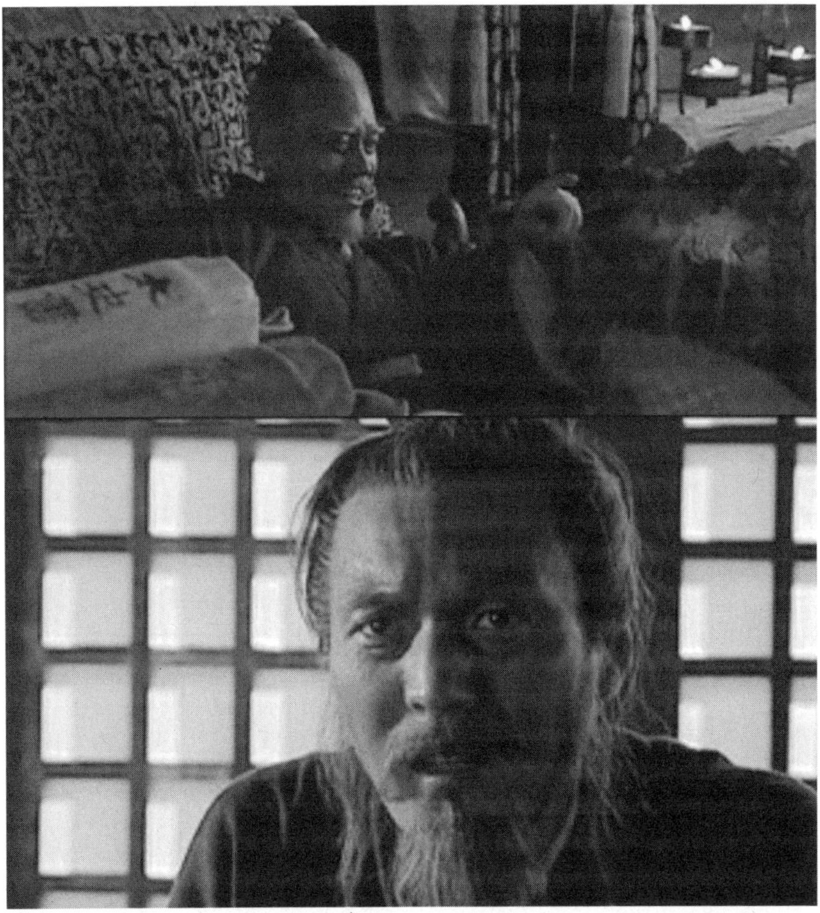

**Figure 2.4.** A shot reverse shot of Emperor Wu and Sima Qian during the meeting that opens and concludes the drama. *Emperor Wu of the Han Dynasty* (Zhongguo Dianying Jituan Gongsi)

accurately, gives the producers of the drama a chance to offer their views on historical judgments in relation to a figure like this emperor. With its emphasis on the question of whether or not history—as written by historians like Sima Qian—has truly understood someone like Emperor Wu (and, by extension, anyone like him), the drama appears to add a (postmodern) twist to such issues as history, historical writing, and historical recording. The wrath displayed by Emperor Wu toward Sima Qian brings to the fore issues regarding the role of historical recording and the act of reading (and, by extension, collecting and re-collecting) in response to "history."

The uncertainty that Sima Qian expresses is also expressed in *The Yongzheng Court* in the song that accompanies the opening credits. Sung by the well-known contemporary pop singer Liu Huan, the song expresses uncertainty (about historical judgments) with a defiant sentiment: "When it comes to commenting on the accomplishments and failures of heroes of the past, who really has the final say? Good or bad, let others judge; even though you work hard for the country, you cannot prevent bad names from being thrown at you after you are gone." Even though no direct identification is made here, these lyrics put a philosophical spin on the drama's representations of Emperor Yongzheng.

What does such articulated uncertainty mean? In the case of *Emperor Wu,* although the drama claims to be based on Sima Qian's *Historical Records* and Ban Gu's *Book of Han,* when it opens and ends with a dialogue between the emperor and the historian, the drama does not appear to identify with the historians' representations but proceeds, instead, to represent the emperor in a more positive, if not also ambivalent and ambiguous, manner. On the one hand, by claiming that the drama is based on two well-known history books, the producers claim a degree of historical authenticity. On the other hand, by creating the dialogue between the emperor and Sima Qian, they seem to want to make the drama more than what the history books offer by adding their own interpretations of the relationship between historians and the historical figures they record.

Anyone familiar with Chinese history knows that *Historical Records* is considered to be the first Chinese history book written in a biographical style (*ji zhuan ti*), with many more to follow in later dynasties. History books from fairly early on, in other words, came to be mixed with historians' decisions of what and whom to record and how to present history. In a sense, we can say that emperor dramas on television are modern popular culture's parodies of such esteemed history books as *Historical Records,* with their own (re)interpretations and opinions written into narrative representations. Those familiar with Chinese history also know that Emperor Wu had Sima Qian castrated after the latter allegedly defended a general by the name of Li Ling, grandson of Li Guang, upon his arrest. Li Ling, who surrendered to the Xiongnu, was one of the best-known generals in Emperor Wu's military. So, at the time of the dramatized meeting, Sima Qian would have lived through the consequences of his disagreement with the emperor; indeed, he is remembered as having decided to live on, despite the humiliation of his punishment, solely for the purpose of finishing what Sima Tan, his father, had started, namely, the book *Historical Records.* Throughout dynastic and modern Chinese history, *Historical Records* has enjoyed an esteem that few other history books have ever enjoyed. In this television drama, however, the usual esteem for the historian is questioned with the repetition of the scene in which the historian is made to appear uncertain about his own judgments.

By creating and repeating such a meeting and dialogue between the emperor and the historian, the drama, made in the early twenty-first century, puts the historian in an ambivalent light while at the same time implicitly shedding a different light on history. It does so by evoking a familiar modern ambivalence toward China's dynastic past but is unusual in the degree of sympathy directed toward Emperor Wu, showing him as a tragic hero who nevertheless was able to accomplish "great feats." Throughout the drama, this theme is repeated both visually and verbally at the beginning of each episode, where superimposed on the image of Emperor Wu are the words "he established unprecedented honor for a country; he gave a people long-lasting self-confidence; his dynasty became the permanent name of a nationality."[29] The images situate the man as the center of focus for the "moderns" to see, a lonely old man, the product of his own times, and yet living on through history. Right there on the screen, with words, image, and music, another emperor "hero" is added to the collection.

Implicit in this latest induction of emperors into the modern (myth-making) hall of fame of (tragic) heroes is an indication of the nature of depoliticized politics in the context of postrevolution China, where many modern (and revolutionary) "heroic" figures, real or fictional, have lost their appeal. Widespread ambivalence toward the People's Republic of China's official ideology (which still represents itself as "communist" and as a force to struggle for socialism) and its authority leaves today's China's "hall of fame" for heroes increasingly occupied by those who are neither "modern" nor "Chinese" along with such ancient emperors as Emperor Wu of the Han dynasty and Emperor Yongzheng of the Qing dynasty as its latest occupants. Even though it has become a cliché to state that "all history is contemporary," when it comes to emperor dramas on television, the ambivalence identified here signifies that what is represented in these dramas indeed pertains more to the historical consciousness in contemporary China than to specific emperors. The ambivalence is the product of modern Chinese history, where experiences and the "modern" lens have fostered ambivalence toward so-called premodern (dynastic) history, revealing modern Chinese intellectuals' anxiety over China's national and cultural identities.

## A New Collective Imagination? Contending "Historical Consciousness" in Contemporary China

The two different styles of emperor drama manifest changing dynamics in Chinese mainstream culture in relation to representations of history and, by extension, in relation to the issue of modern Chinese historical consciousness.[30] The playful style lightens up the historical imagination by turning emperors into cool superhuman heroes capable of human feelings and of being good rulers. Its playfulness downplays the "burden of history" (*lishi de fudan*) and deconstructs the trauma-oriented Chinese historical consciousness by playing up the postmodern sense of irony that renders that sense of history "uncool." The serious style, in contrast, revisits "history" by focusing and shining a spotlight on a group of formerly "deposed" historical figures in an ambivalent (but far less negative) manner. These two types of emperor drama, each in its own way, have generated discussions and sparked debates on how to understand such "new" representations of "traditional" Chinese history and culture, and what it means when past emperors are "excavated" as main characters in contemporary popular televisual tales of "history." Most of the popular and critical responses to these dramas in China, to echo an earlier point, further demonstrate entangled tensions and ideological struggles within mainstream culture, especially with regard to the question of historical consciousness, an issue to which I now turn.

Even though her discussion of the drama *The Yongzheng Court* does not focus on the drama itself, Ying Zhu's discussion of the context in which the drama was made is on target. Her discussion points to the changing political and intellectual dynamics in post-1989 China as a way to understand this drama. I would like to expand the discussion by noting that the "triumphant" comeback that dynastic emperors have enjoyed in cultural representations is essentially a return to familiar tensions in modern Chinese historical consciousness vis-à-vis the enormously complex modern Chinese experience.[31] The question of how to deal with "tradition" and "history" has continued to be an intrinsic part of being "modern" as a Chinese and also, as a result, has remained a recurrent issue for those who study modern China. In the past several decades, a Foucauldian-genealogy-informed historiography in the China field in the West has arisen to question the historical resources that informed "modern Chinese historical discourse," treating that consciousness as no less than the mimicry of a West-originated Enlightenment-oriented grand narrative of history.[32] Perceived from this perspective, history and emperor dramas of the serious style—especially given the ambivalence they exhibit—can appear problematic precisely because they continue to echo the trauma-oriented modern Chinese historical discourse. In response to the prevailing genealogy-informed historiography, Wang Ban argues for the need to distinguish "historical sense" and "sense of history." Quoting Michael Roth, he states, "The historical sense aims at a relentless genealogical dismantling of the discourse-power nexus and takes sadistic delight in parading its contingent mechanisms and arbitrary violence. The sense of history, on the other hand, is 'animated by a desire to give meaning and direction to the present by finding its development in the past.'"[33] "A sense of history," he further argues, "has to be based on an articulated unity, continuity, and solidarity of purpose—rearticulated in the genealogical ruins of dismantled History. Thus the retreat from the political-ethical horizon is also a withdrawal from historical discourse. If all history lies in ruins, how are historical agents supposed to write alternative histories and act alternatively to change the repressive History?"[34] If "the notion of history is bound up with modernity,"[35] how do we understand the televisual representations of emperors within the context of contemporary China's ongoing quest for modernity and, more important, in relation to the ongoing debates about "modern Chinese historical consciousness"?

With these questions in mind, let me now turn to one particular critic's response to the phenomenon of the emperor drama, which I will treat as yet another cultural representation of the issue of historical consciousness. Let me preface the following discussion by pointing out that, while there has been criticism of emperor dramas in China, most critics tend to express their displeasure or criticism in short essays without fully analyzing the manifested sense of history in these dramas.[36] The same is true of this critic except that his essay is a celebration of such dramas. And this critic's celebration of the emperor drama exists alongside his recent dismissal of the importance of Lu Xun in contemporary China. Given that Lu Xun is arguably the most influential modern Chinese intellectual and that his sense of history remains an important point of reference in any discussion of "new (Chinese) historical consciousness," and given also that debates about Lu Xun function as an important gauge for understanding changes, tensions, and problems within mainstream culture, the coexistence of the two critiques may not be coincidental.

In his comments on the 2004 hit *Emperor Wu of the Han Dynasty,* Zhang Yiwu, a Beijing-based scholar-critic hailed the series as symbolizing the beginning of a new Chinese historical consciousness.[37] He is quoted as saying that "*Emperor Wu of the Han Dynasty* shows that the imagination of emperors, which prevails in recent years, has not dried up. It is still an important part of the contemporary culture that cannot be parried."[38] After comparing the series with *The Yongzheng Court* by the same director (Hu Mei), Zhang states that *Emperor Wu of the Han Dynasty* "speaks highly of his great feats... in a big way. This is very rare in China where individualism and heroism were absent for thousands of years."[39] This has come about, according to Zhang, as a "result of the fact that China is thriving and powerful." Zhang continues: "People's enthrallment with Emperor Wu is actually their desire for a brand new century. The new development of Chinese history requires new collective imagination. This is the key issue that the television drama has highlighted."[40] Whether the critic is accurate in stating that "individualism and heroism were absent for thousands of years [in China]," he is presenting a contrast with his call for a "new collective imagination," a new (Chinese) historical consciousness, which he declares that the television drama *Emperor Wu of the Han Dynasty* helps place in the foreground.

Rather than ambivalence, Zhang sees in this (and other similar) dramas something different and presumably new. According to the enthusiastic comments quoted above, what is new is what he identifies as a "new historical consciousness" or "new collective imagination." Using a collection of words and phrases from Zhang's comments—"individualism and heroism," that China is "thriving and powerful," and the Chinese people's desire for a "brand new century"—this presumed new historical consciousness seems to be one that bursts with pride and confidence in the "feats," "power," and "grandeur" all symbolized by this emperor. For those who are familiar with modern Chinese history, however, none of this is particularly new. The hailed "new collective imagination" can be easily traced to the power-and-wealth-oriented "modernization" imaginary that has been promoted by generations of Chinese elites since the mid-nineteenth century. Comparatively speaking, what is new is the fact that today's China is experiencing rapid economic growth, and the desire and imaginary of the earlier generations of Chinese elites for China to become strong and wealthy is becoming a more tangible reality. Historically speaking, therefore, in his celebration of this "new" reality, the critic is in fact echoing an "old" modern Chinese dream. Given that in Chinese intellectual and public discourses what is identified as new and what is old often carries a value implication, a more important question to ask is what is "old" in relation to what he celebrates as "new?" Not surprisingly, the critic is ready with an answer.

In arguing that current historical conditions in China require the Chinese to acquire a "new" historical consciousness, Zhang recommends a collective, or national, retreat from what he identifies as the trauma-oriented glorification of "tragic heroes" of the past. In citing a study by the Japanese China scholar Ozaki Fumiaki, he enthusiastically hails the supposed fact that, finally, young Chinese today are showing less interest in such pivotal modern intellectual figures as Lu Xun.[41] Zhang celebrates this development as signifying that "Chinese modern consciousness" has turned a final corner at the turn of the new century. If Chinese (youth) are finally able to transcend Lu Xun and his legacy, he echoes, this would truly signal the beginning of a "new" Chinese historical consciousness. Without questioning whether the decreased interest in Lu Xun is based on an informed understanding of his legacy and whether it entails a collective transcendence beyond Lu Xun or, for that matter, whether a (supposed) lack of interest in Lu Xun among the Chinese young actually amounts to a kind of historical amnesia that indicates a decreased historical consciousness, Zhang enthusiastically embraces this "discovery." He follows up by claiming that it is time that Lu Xun, instead of being recognized as a living critical force that directly or indirectly informs modern Chinese historical consciousness, be rendered innocuous like such historical figures as Qu Yuan, Li Bai, and Du Fu.

The connection between the critic's unqualified celebration of emperor dramas and the (supposed) marginalization of Lu Xun among the young suggests a contrast between "new" and "old"—emperor dramas represent what is new, whereas Lu Xun represents what is old. However, if we juxtapose the critic's call for Lu Xun to be relegated to the ranks of such historical figures as Qu Yuan, Li Bai, and Du Fu with his celebration of the televisual representations of *Emperor Wu of the Han Dynasty* for manifesting a "new collective imagination," we realize that, rather than anything actually new, Zhang's call for a "new collective imagination" mainly pertains to a negative judgment of the "critical historical consciousness" represented by Lu Xun.[42] What has "flared up" (to borrow the familiar term from Walter Benjamin) in this double celebration is, in effect, a reappearance of some of the issues of (Chinese) modernity that continue to dog contemporary Chinese intellectuals.[43] What may indeed be new here is a blatant celebration of emperors and of *daguo yishi* (literally, "consciousness of a big nation"), or an empire mentality. But then again, if we recall what Yan Fu did at the end of his life—as someone who had translated major Western books on political theory at the turn of the twentieth century and had envisioned being modern in the image of the powerful and wealthy West—in turning to support Yuan Shikai's failed attempt to become emperor shortly after the Republican revolution in 1916, we are actually confronted with a modern desire for power and wealth, which is at least more than one hundred years old. In this sense, the new/old dichotomy that the critic suggests does not quite apply; the real issue lies elsewhere.

As my previous discussion demonstrates, the seriously told emperor dramas so celebrated by Zhang Yiwu are actually still governed and informed in part by a sense of crisis and uncertainty. As my reading of the relationship between the political system and the emperor also indicates, there is a clear thread of ambivalence dominating the representations in these dramas. In celebrating the emperors' accomplishments, the dramas struggle with details of the process through which these emperors are supposed to have achieved them. Those narrative details manifest a modern awareness that, either consciously or subconsciously, questions the structural reasons for the various plots and schemes staged by different groups of individuals and for the fate of those individuals, who are products of the system and whose fate, as a result, is inevitably tragic. As such, one can suggest that in these emperor dramas there continues to be something allegorical in their melodramatic representations: in essence their stories keep returning to issues related to what is "traditional" and what is "modern." As allegories, they simultaneously reveal the "dirty secrets" of the political system and function as an agency that at once questions and sustains a cultural/national identity via such revelation. They also manifest, in the words of Michael Herzfeld, a Chinese version of "cultural intimacy" resulting from China's more than a century long struggle in coming to terms with modernity, a struggle that has been expressed mainly in an ambivalent manner. This ambivalence has continued to inform the tensions within Chinese mainstream culture between the power and wealth based modernization imaginary and the critical modern historical consciousness represented by Lu Xun, as seen in the case of emperor dramas.

Despite efforts from certain corners inside and outside the mainstream culture to retire Lu Xun and his legacy, Lu Xun's sense of history continues to remain highly relevant. Indeed, given the structural problems of global capitalism becoming increasingly manifested in the social, economic, environmental, cultural, and ideological domains in China one decade into the twenty-first century, Lu Xun's sense of history actually becomes more relevant and essential in China's ongoing struggle to make sense of its modern experiences. Lu Xun's critiques were relevant when China was subject to the abuses of colonial powers and continue to remain so when China is becoming stronger. For Lu Xun, the desired modern Chinese historical consciousness is not oriented around "power" but is self-aware and self-critical, capable of maintaining vigilance against the unquestioned acceptance of any seemingly new and fashionable slogans. That is why, while Zhang is in a hurry to retire Lu Xun, others insist on the importance and relevance of Lu Xun and on the need to revisit his "critical historical consciousness" in the hopes of better articulating issues and problems of the present.[44]

It is in this sense that serious-style emperor dramas' ambivalent representations of emperors in effect help continue to demonstrate the tensions and contradictions in modern Chinese historical consciousness and mainstream culture, especially when perceived in gendered, ideological, and social terms. The ambivalence may also be a sign of uncertainty about, or a blind spot in the understanding of, the significance of one's own historical experiences and the nature of one's own historical agency. Let me conclude by enumerating a few general observations about the problematics of the emperor drama phenomenon and its melodramatic politics (manifested by way of representing emperors as tragic but national heroes). First, these dramas tend to manifest a blatant masculinist subject position, in which male heroism is still "naturally" related to concerns of history and of the survival of the nation. Indeed, when the emperors are collected, framed, and represented as tragic heroes (here we cannot but be reminded of Zhang Yimou's *Hero* and the controversies surrounding the film), the historical consciousness manifested is nothing particularly new.[45] What is new, if anything, is that it signifies a change in the mainstream culture from the besieged male mentality of the 1980s into a culture whose psychodynamic orientation is no longer dominated by a perceived "lack" (of male potency). Emperors represented as heroes have emerged to replace abject male characters, thereby masking the "lack" with powerful individuals. Thus, even though representations of emperors are highly ambivalent, the collection of emperors on television constitutes a cultural phenomenon that could not have been possible throughout much of the twentieth century (until the era of economic reform).

Second, in cultural terms, this ascending power-oriented vision and logic compel Zhang Yiwu, the critic in question, to dismiss Lu Xun's critical historical consciousness and to conclude that Lu Xun's critical spirit is outdated. This reevaluation of the re-collected historical figures, emperors on one side and Lu Xun on the other points to a number of underlying issues in the mainstream culture of postrevolution and market-reform China, including how to reevaluate such historical legacies as the May Fourth New Culture Movement and its leading intellectual representatives, the (Chinese Communist Party–led) revolution, and so-called traditional culture. In the history museum envisioned by the critic, emperors are re-collected and elevated to the major exhibition hall while intellectuals such as Lu Xun are packed in boxes to be stored in the basement. If this is what he envisions and celebrates as the "new historical consciousness" and "new collective imagination," as I have just argued, there is nothing particularly new. This vision not only continues to manifest the tension within modern Chinese historical consciousness, in which the two dimensions, power and enlightenment, of the modernity imaginary are deeply intertwined. It is also indicative of the ideological repositioning among contemporary Chinese intellectuals in relation to their views of China's modern historical choices, experiences, and legacies.

We now come to the third point: much is in flux but also at stake with regard to Chinese historical consciousness in the age of postrevolution market reform. The widespread cultural interest in emperor dramas is accompanied by a shadow process of re-collecting or "remembering" what are deemed to be important historical experiences. Closely examined, however, we find in Zhang's celebration of the televisual "collection" of emperors not so much a new collective imagination as such but an ideological position toward which some elites have gravitated. In this sense, if we look again, we may come to realize that emperor dramas are actually the shadow images of a changing (changed?) historical consciousness informed by a depoliticized ideological position.

In the end, emperor dramas and critical responses to them are symptomatic of the changing and contradictory nature of contemporary Chinese mainstream culture, especially of its uncertainty about how to reaffirm China's own historical agency, fully acknowledge its own historical choices, and examine their successes and failures without subscribing to either a postmodern nihilistic cynicism or a simple-minded nationalism. At the same time, emperor dramas, their popular reception, the debates about them, one representative critic's contradictory responses, and various other related intellectual concerns continue to constitute the complexity of and agency within mainstream culture. In this sense, we can say that the emperor dramas, like the other subgenres I study in this book, function as "open-ended" texts that invite both cultural and historical readings not only into the texts themselves, but also out into the social, economic, cultural, and political realities of market-reform-era China.

CHAPTER THREE

# In Whose Name?

## "Anticorruption Dramas" and Their Ideological Implications

❑ ❑ ❑ ❑ ❑

Since *Heavens Above* (*Cangtian zaishang*) was aired in 1995, anticorruption drama has been one of the most popularly received television subgenres in China.[1] Between 1995 and 2005, anticorruption drama became a mainstay in programming on television channels at all levels, thereby periodically making corruption a publicly aired social problem on television.[2] Since corruption has plagued the reform era in China and is generally believed to have gone from bad to worse, especially since the early 1990s, the popularity of such dramas is easy to understand. Jeffrey Kinkley's recent study of the anticorruption or, in his words, "political novel" in "late socialist China," offers a timely exploration of what "corruption" means in contemporary China, especially with regard to popular political novels and their implications.[3] He insightfully observes that "the novels' formal realism is debatable, but they were arguably the works of their day that 'spoke truth to power.' They gave the Chinese people *stories* about where their social and political problems came from, and these narratives resonated with familiar takes from Chinese history and literature. As a sanctimonious charge, these novels also made the decadent lifestyle of the rich and infamous fascinating. Corruption itself and the power struggles it causes were enshrined *as* popular culture" (italics original).[4] Kinkley points out that this kind of political novel helps broaden the idea of corruption, which "is more a matter of linguistic usage and freedom of expression catching up with very old ideas of corruption as general social decay,"[5] and that "'anti-corruption fiction' and its mass media adaptations" as a genre have been "a Chinese way of addressing a variety of fundamental popular complaints and protest and riots organized to express them."[6]

This chapter focuses on the anticorruption televisual subgenre, which enjoys a much wider viewership than its counterpart in the form of the novel. As Kinkley points out, many of the anticorruption novels by such writers as Lu

Tianming, Zhang Ping, and Zhou Meisen have been adapted into television drama. In some cases, such as that of Lu Tianming, what became a novel was originally conceived as a television drama script.[7] Other works, such as those by Zhou Meisen, tended to be snatched up for adaptation right away, and the author assumed an active role in the adaptations.[8] This speedy genre crossing in popular representations of corruption was partially driven by the market and partially, as Kinkley notes, attributable to the fact that popular culture's representations of anticorruption themes essentially functioned as popular expressions of discontent. Indeed, it would take the state's censorship—in the form of new regulations issued in 2004—for the much more widely viewed and influential anticorruption television drama to disappear from prime-time broadcasting (from 6:00 p.m. to 10:00 p.m.).[9] But the blatant official censorship is indicative of the power (and related problematics) of this televisual subgenre. To expand on Kinkley's findings, this chapter takes up what he dismisses as the "formulaic" narrative style of the anticorruption novel and "its mass culture adaptations" by, first, fully acknowledging its melodramatic characteristics and, then, examining the melodramatic codes and the politics (and their historicity) within. More specifically, I explore the extent to which televisual representations of corruption and anticorruption activities pertain to some frequently evoked notions such as *fa* (law), *fazhi* (rule by law), *fazhi* (rule of law), *quanli* (power), and *quanli* (rights), and various structural, ideological, and sociocultural issues related to them. By focusing on the dramas' "melodramatic politics" in relation to these issues, we may be able to shed more light on what is underneath the "formulaic" narrative style of the anticorruption drama.

### (Re)contextualizing the Phenomenon

To be sure, as a mainstream cultural phenomenon, anticorruption dramas—which have been simultaneously encouraged and censored by governmental authorities—have functioned vicariously as a way for the public to vent its discontent toward the rampant existence of corruption. At the same time, this function is also complicated by a changed and changing mainstream ideology and unstable "meaning negotiations" within that ideology. The potentially subversive nature of anticorruption dramas can, in turn, explain the uncertain fate of this subgenre on television. Such uncertainty is symptomatic of the tensions in cultural production in China when real social issues are tackled and mediated by such a medium as television. Ironically, therefore, on the one hand, televisual representations of corruption and dramatized struggles against it help foster and reinforce a public perception that the "state" (*guojia*) or the government (*zhengfu*) is on the side of ordinary people in wanting to tackle the problem. On the other hand, the constant censoring, especially the regulations issued in 2004 that resulted in the removal of anticorruption dramas from prime time and in drastic cuts in granting licenses (issued to production companies that intended to make anticorruption dramas), are indications of a discomfort on the part of the state authorities toward the presence of such dramas. Anticorruption dramas inevitably serve as a constant reminder of the darker side of society or, worse (to the ambivalent state authorities), a major venue for expressing social discontent and criticism disguised as entertainment.

Cynical critics may not feel particularly surprised to see the official "pushback" on this cultural phenomenon, because those critics tended to doubt the social and political effect of the phenomenon to begin with. This "cool" reception echoes Lu Xun's critical assessment of "exposé literature" of the late nineteenth century. He pointed out that such "exposé" literature often lacked a real understanding of underlying social and structural problems.[10] Exposing the dark side of society, in other words, does not in itself entail a clearer understanding of the underpinning structural issues. The difference between the exposé literature commented on by Lu Xun and contemporary anticorruption dramas, however, is that, while some of the dramas do suffer from a similar problem of mindless melodramatic dramatization of violence and criminal activities, others nevertheless try to connect the abuse of power and uncertain definitions of such notions as power, rights, and rule of law to the problems of the existing power structure, and to represent them in ways that are not welcomed by those in power. The periodic success of such dramas and their impact is precisely why the making of anticorruption drama in China has never been free from the watchful eye of the state. As melodramas that inevitably aim at maximizing their entertainment value, they nevertheless push the boundaries in negotiating with different existing cultural and ideological legacies. A meaningful study of this cultural phenomenon, to echo Kinkley, must recognize that governmental control and censoring of anticorruption dramas, the popular reception of such dramas, and the critical suspicion and dismissal of their significance on the grounds they lack real political challenge, all constitute part of the tension and contradictions in the production and reception of the anticorruption subgenre on television in China.

If anticorruption as a subject matter for storytelling is "socially correct"—in that it emerged in response to rampant corruption viewed as a negative by-product of the economic reform—its popularity as a shared social reaction is by no means represented, criticized, and judged in a uniform and monolithic manner. Recognizing the contradictions within televisual representations of anticorruption themes, I am interested, to echo a point made in my introduction, in the coexisting but different discourses, the "polyphony" or dialogism and their ideological implications, in different anticorruption dramas. In whose name is anticorruption activity carried out, and who is said to benefit? How is corruption defined and represented? How do we recognize and understand the ideological tensions and implications within different televisual representations of anticorruption themes? To what extent are these representations informed by and do they inform the rise of a normative understanding of "law" and "rights," and a particular kind of legalist language? In what ways, if any, do such popular cultural texts echo contemporary intellectual debates in China regarding China's path to modernization and quest for modernity and the tensions within such debates? With these questions, I hope to explore the extent to which different cultural, historical, and ideological ideas, traditions, and legacies are evoked and struggle and negotiate with one another in the anticorruption drama's textual representations. It is also my intention to speculate on both the ideological possibilities and the limitations of the different discursive appropriations of notions of "law" (*fa*), "rule by/of law" (*fazhi/fazhi*), "power" (*quanli*), and "rights" (*quanli*) in relation to some of the dramas' critical representations of the abuse of power (*quanli*). Finally, I am also interested in the extent to which the complexities within such a "mainstream" popular cultural phenomenon tell us about the relationship between culture and social transformation in contemporary China. But before addressing these questions in the context of a few specific anticorruption dramas, I will offer a brief description of the development of this televisual subgenre between 1995 and 2005.

As mentioned, *Heavens Above* was the first anticorruption drama seen on television in which relatively high-level corruption—the abuse of power for self-interest and personal gain—was dramatized. In addition to representing high-level corruption, the drama also set a critical tone as coded in the name of the drama, *cangtian zai shang,* or "heavens above." As the drama's scriptwriter Lu Tianmin recounts, it took quite some time before his script was approved and the drama was produced. This fact alone makes one realize that such a "mainstream" cultural phenomenon did not emerge without rejection and censorship and that behind-the-scene tensions would set the tone for the production and the representations contained within anticorruption dramas. To put the drama in context, as China's "market reform" was pushed further into high gear after Deng Xiaoping's 1992 tour of the south, what had become a major source of discontent among ordinary people in the late 1980s was becoming even more of a blatant social problem in the 1990s and a (potential) political liability to the Communist Party–led Chinese state.[11] Officially waged campaigns against corruption—openly acknowledging and indignantly calling for a struggle against it—were an indication that corruption in officialdom was implicitly becoming part of the legitimacy issue facing the ruling party. At the same time, "anticorruption" also appeared to be a socially correct banner that the ruling party could uphold without necessarily having to confront its underlying structural problems or reformulate its "marketist" (*shichang zhuyi*) ideology.[12]

The success of *Heavens Above* marked the rise of anticorruption drama as a new televisual subgenre and helped set the "tone" (as in "main melody," or *zhuxuanlü*) to promote a morally correct way of being an official, signaling that the state was interested in combating the increasingly rampant spread of corruption by way of *yu jiao yu le* (teaching through entertainment). This institutional propagandistic instinct and orientation reached a new high when, a few years after *Heavens Above* was aired, the film *Shengsi jueze* (A life and death choice, 2000) was promoted by the governmental machinery in an all-out campaign through organized screenings, viewings, and discussions.[13] What has happened since then, however—corruption has continued unabated—reveals the lackluster nature of officially organized propaganda campaigns, especially with regard to corruption. Indeed, the officially organized public promotion of the film (a kind of organized public campaign that by the time *A Life and Death Choice* was aired had become rather rare) indicated the presence of underlying worries about the linkage between the government's legitimacy and the rampant (and out-of-control) nature of corruption at all governmental levels and to the ineffectiveness of previous officially promoted moral lessons. Along with melodramatized "moral" appeals such dramas also always end with (the threat of) punitive consequences. The reality of the last two decades, however, has demonstrated that neither appealing to moral conscience nor the threat of punishment has accomplished much in terms of stamping out corruption. Corruption has remained as rampant as ever, if not more widespread, as power and economic interests and opportunities have become increasingly intertwined with one another. The only change, ironically, may well be a growing sense of cynicism that has permeated the populace. Today, official calls for stopping corruption sound hollow and beget more cynicism.[14]

At the same time, anticorruption television dramas are not produced in a uniform fashion without potential for critical engagement.[15] Some of the well-received ones have not only functioned to keep the issue of corruption in the public view, but also and more importantly, they have taken time to probe and raise questions about the various social and structural aspects of the problem. Regardless of official censorship, of increasing market-oriented pressure that affects ways in which anticorruption stories are told, and of scorn on the part of critics, there are always dramas whose "serious" nature indicates a desire and effort to penetrate the surface of corruption-related crimes and violence and to examine the inner workings of officialdom and, either consciously or unconsciously, question the nature of its power structure, underlying logic, and its changed and changing value system.[16]

Two main types of anticorruption dramas have evolved, one, represented by dramas adapted from (or scripted by) writers like Zhou Meisen, Zhang Ping, Zhang Chenggong, and Lu Tianming who tend not to orient their stories around the crimes related to corruption, and another that tends to be more crime-related and constitutes the main body of the subgenre. Of the first type the most notable dramas are those adapted from Zhou Meisen's novels or scripted by him.[17] Zhou Meisen dramas, as I call them, do not focus on actual acts of corruption and deal instead with the inner workings of officialdom. Because of this focus, Zhou has reportedly objected to the *fanfu* (anticorruption) label put on his novels and dramas, identifying them instead as *zhengzhi xiaoshuo* (political novels) or *zhengzhi ju* (political dramas). I will return to this point when discussing one of his dramas, but suffice it to say that Zhou Meisen dramas have indeed been one of a kind on television, with the result that the writer himself has become one of the best-known writers in contemporary China.[18]

The second type of anticorruption drama is crime-oriented, but within it one can make a distinction between more violent and less violent examples. The former sometimes spill over into a related subgenre—cop dramas, or *jingfei ju/pian*—and have exhibited a tendency to become increasingly violent. As a result, many such dramas tend not to be picked up by television stations and instead end up in video stores (or stalls of pirated copies sold by small-time vendors). The less violent ones are noted for their entertaining stories and interesting characters. Indeed, television drama has a generous amount of narrative time (and space) to tell a story, which encourages complicated plots and melodramatic stories. They also tend to be dialogue-oriented and character-driven.

In the last ten years, a large number of anticorruption dramas have been created.[19] By my own account, at least forty of them can be identified.[20] It is not an exaggeration to suggest that the combination of viewers' interest and market forces made the decade between 1995 and 2005 a golden age for anticorruption dramas. But the recent official censorship has made the entire subgenre all but disappear from the public's attention in the last two years.[21] Such censorship indicates, as I have pointed out, that anticorruption dramas ought not to be readily dismissed as cultural texts merely manipulated by the state and the market.

With corruption and anticorruption activities as their central topic, dramas in this subgenre may choose to focus on different types of corruption and their related issues, with larger thematic issues such as "power," "rights," and "social justice" as part of the anticorruption discourse and its melodramatic renditions. Given contemporary China's historical context, these renditions are informed by a mixture of different historically and ideologically motivated social and discursive positions—and, by extension, different voices—that coexist in post-revolution and market-reform-era China, which are manifested, in this case, in the mainstream culture's tackling of the corruption problem. In the anti-corruption subgenre, such sociocultural particularity is in part manifested in the evocation of such familiar iconic terms as *guojia* (nation), *renmin* (people), *laobaixing* (ordinary folks), *quanli* (rights), and *fazhi*. But the question is from what perspective and with what clarity and what conviction are these terms evoked?

The dramas I discuss below are some of the most popularly received ones, including *Guojia gongsu* (Sued by the state), *Hongse kangnaixin* (Red carnations), *Gongan juzhang* (The police chief), and *Hei dong* (Black hole). I am not able to offer a comprehensive reading of each drama but will mainly focus on their shared melodramatic, but nevertheless different, renderings of the relationship between morality, law, and power. I will examine the ways in which each drama assumes its "moral" authority in its critique of power abuse. Exploring their implications, I will connect them to some of the most heatedly debated social and political issues in today's China.

## In the Name of the "People"? *Sued by the State*

*Sued by the State* (2003) is one of the Zhou Meisen dramas. It focuses on the uncovering of a network of corrupt officials, both at the city and the provincial level, all the way to a vice governor. The drama begins in a fictional city, Changshan, where a devastating fire destroys a well-known nightclub and kills more than 150 people. As the investigation proceeds, the case becomes increasingly complicated by attempts from certain corners of officialdom to cover up, interfere, or sabotage the investigation. Led by the district attorney Ye Zijing, the investigation persists under dangerous circumstances—indeed, the investigators themselves are some kind of "underground workers" (*dixia gongzuozhe*)—until their efforts succeed in uncovering (legally obtained and permissible) evidence that links attempts at sabotage all the way to Wang Changgong, the vice governor. Apparently, Wang has received bribes from people whom he helped to obtain major contracts, but, in order to prevent the bribes from being discovered, he goes all out trying to cover them up. The drama shows him going so far as to order a key witness to be killed by the city police chief. He tries to convince his lover, Zhou Meili, not to admit to their illicit relationship or provide information about the whereabouts of the money, but Zhou Meili eventually relents. With the information she provides, the investigators are able to obtain written documents directly linking money they have confiscated to Wang. Predictably,

Wang is arrested. Instead of ending at that point (as most anticorruption dramas do), however, the drama goes on with his trial. The trial ends the narrative but not without a long speech by Ye Zijing summarizing the case.

The skeletal plot line summarized here is a familiar one, identical to that in other (especially Zhou Meisen) dramas such as *Zhigao liyi* (In the name of the highest principle), and *Juedui quanli* (Absolute power). In their efforts to demonstrate how easily power is abused, these televisual serials raise and dramatize a major question regarding the relationship between power and responsibility, on the one hand, and power and self-interest, on the other. What is there in the existing power structure that can ensure the promotion of the former and limit the latter? While subtextually *Sued by the State* is unaware of the fundamentals of such a question in relation to its own story, textually, however, it does try to tackle the question of how to explain corruption and how to stop it. In addition to the overall melodramatically structured (mini)stories that indicate the struggle between "good" and "evil," these textual attempts culminate with the very speech—narratively shown as a closing argument in court—made by Ye Zijing.

Indeed, as in the good old melodramatic tradition, the drama sets Ye Zijing up as the hero, the "good guy." Dramatizing the extent to which she refuses to be frightened and succeeds in bringing Wang to court, the drama situates its moral center around this character, a female district attorney with moral courage and integrity. Like the "good" officials in similar dramas, Ye Zijing is represented in a way reminiscent of the "model cadres" (*mofan ganbu*) that the Chinese Communist Party used to promote and, as such, would strike anyone who is familiar with today's Chinese society as too good to be true.[22] But the familiarity of such a character and especially the idealism that comes with her representation in a rapidly changing but morally uncertain society can still evoke a response powerful enough to help suspend disbelief.

Framed as a closing argument, Ye's speech in many ways sounds more like an extended editorial, anticlimatic in that the speech is no longer part of the story but a means to transmit an official pronouncement. It is interesting, however, to note the moral tone of this speech and the coexistence of ideological conviction and uncertainties within it. For this reason, I will quote a major portion of the speech:

> This case is both Wang Changong's personal tragedy and that of the people of [the city of] Changshan.... [And yet] Wang still wants to appeal to our conscience and consider his contributions to the city of Changshan. But where was his conscience when, while tens of thousands of mine workers in the South Mine [Nanbu Meikuang] were facing the possibility of being plunged into extreme poverty [*jidu pingkun*], he

> received a bribe of as much as 4.8 million yuan, when he was willing to let wrongly accused workers be executed for a lesser crime, when he interfered with the investigation and went so far as to order the city's police chief to murder an important witness? As a party official, do you have the conscience to face the ruling party [*zhizheng dang*] that you once were part of, the People's Republic [*renmin gongheguo*] that gave birth to you and brought you up, and the five million kind-hearted ordinary people [*wubaiwan pusu shanliang de baixing*] in this city? I am afraid the truth of the matter is that you have never truly believed in the Party, the People's Republic, and ordinary people.
>
> Today [in court], the conscience of the People's Republic has achieved a victory [albeit one] soaked in tears and blood. But what about the rest of us? Officials at all levels in the city must shoulder different responsibilities, including legal, leadership, and humanitarian responsibilities, for the deaths of 156 people in that fire. The state apparatus of Changshan has been running under weakened conditions.... As part of this gigantic operating machine [*pangda he longlong yunzhuan de jiqi*], have any of us asked ourselves whether or not we have contributed to its weakening and whether given [enough] power, we will also end up being corrupt?... [Despite success in prosecuting this case,] in the face of these questions, I remain heavy hearted.

As the speech is given, it is accompanied by grand orchestra music and images that cut between the Communist Party flag, the People's Republic of China national emblem, the somber-looking courtroom, the judges and audience within it, and the solemn-looking Ye Zijing standing tall while making the speech. The visual cues are indeed formulaic, reminiscent of a party congress meeting rather than a wrapping-up session by a prosecutor in a courtroom.

Formally this speech is not unlike the ending of many traditional Chinese vernacular stories and novels in which the narrator inserts a moral warning after the end of a dramatic story, except this time the "warning" is rendered in a modern political discourse both visually and verbally. At the same time, however, given its context and larger implications in today's China, packed within the seemingly familiar and old-fashioned political speech are not-so-subtle changes in official ideology and the uncertainties found within them. First, the speech, like most of the anticorruption dramas, makes a connection between corruption and the abuse of power, but it does so by evoking *liangxin*, or conscience. If *liangxin* implies a question of value, or *jiazhiguan*, the contour of the speech fails to lead to that end, an indication of both an assumption and an uncertainty about what values and ideals are worth upholding and for what reasons. Second, as a result, the speech makes a quick jump between *liangxin* and *guojia, renmin, baixing* (ordinary folks), and *zhizheng dang* (ruling party), thereby finding a moral high ground without indicating the need to explore

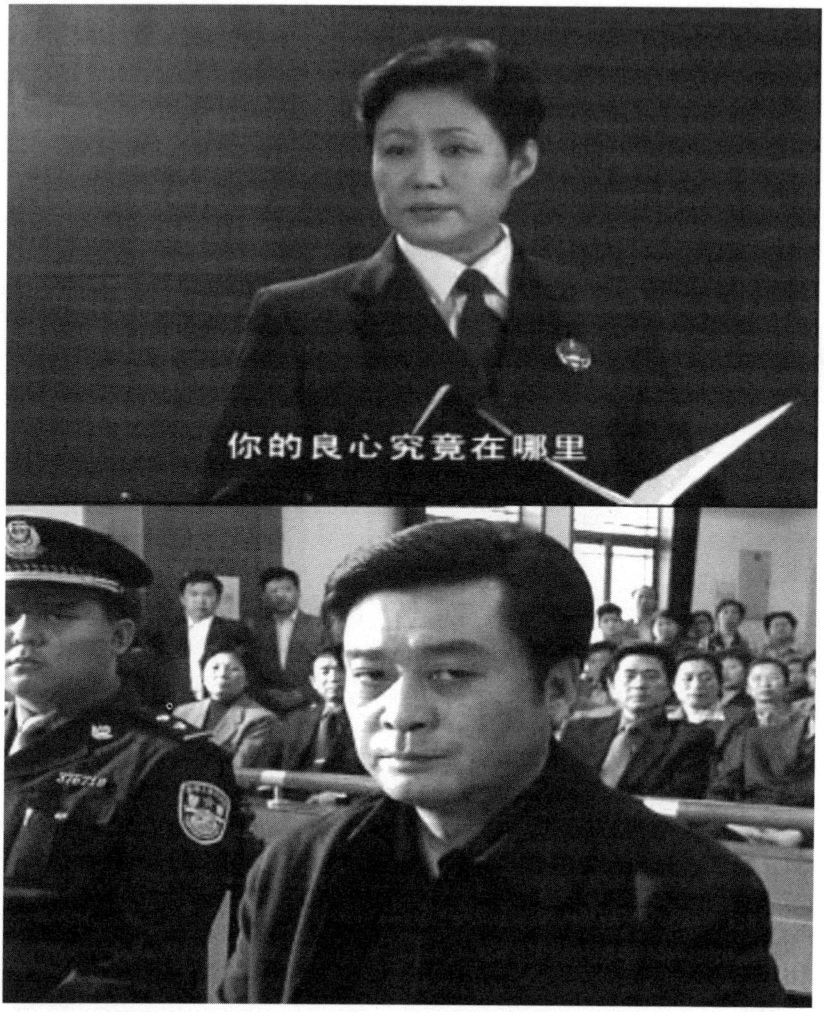


**Figure 3.1.** A shot reverse shot of Ye Zijing making a speech in court with Wang Changgong as the defendant. *Sued by the State* (Qilu Yingxiang Chubanshe)

why these categories remain significant and in what ways the existing power structure and its marketist ideology have significantly weakened the social and political importance of these categories within a (no-longer-so-naive) free-market-oriented modernization discourse.

The juxtaposition of the four categories in the speech is therefore indicative of an ideological uncertainty, if not complete confusion, within the mainstream culture. On the one hand, the linkage is a familiar one with an unquestioned conviction that the four categories belong to one single entity that is China. In the Chinese Communist Party's revolutionary and socialist discourses, *guojia* is closely identified with *renmin* or *laobaixing:* the founding of the People's Republic was in many ways a major historical moment for the symbolic appropriation of the category *renmin,* by the winning party, to connect the newly founded nation-state with the Chinese "people." Even though the term *laobaixing* did not become a more populist-sounding term than *renmin* until after the start of the reforms, both *renmin* and *laobaixing* were used to refer to major social and political forces in the revolution led by the Chinese Communist Party and subsequently comprised a positive political category in the party's revolutionary discourse. Despite the capitalist turn in the post-1992 market reforms, these terms continue to be evoked in official discourse in today's China, but in the context of that turn, which has profoundly changed social relations in China, the social and political content and therefore the meanings of these terms have also changed. Ye Zijing's speech, however, does not demonstrate recognition of such changes and continues to assume that the state apparatuses and the people are one and the same. In this sense, one can say there are two levels of irony manifested in Ye Zijing's speech.

On the first level, the irony lies in the question raised by the speech itself when Ye wonders aloud whether officials like Wang Changgong have ever believed in the words that stipulate the responsibilities of a Communist Party cadre to the ruling party, the People's Republic, and ordinary people. Although the speech continues to mention these categories together, Ye's references to these high-sounding terms fail to indicate that the connection between them has in actuality fallen increasingly apart in both the social and the political sense. They sound like mere moral embellishment not unlike *shuojiao* (preaching) words found at the end of traditional fiction, that is, they tend to sound clichéd. On the second level, the irony is that the speech, by way of attacking corruption and the lack of belief in the Communist Party's (seemingly outdated) idealism, reveals the truth about one aspect of the social and political reality in China: many cadres and officials have joined the party not so much for its (stated) ideals or the responsibilities that come with power. Power is alluring because of its close proximity to self-interest.

At the same time, history amply demonstrates the possible rupture in meaning reconstruction; what is seemingly old and outdated can be made anew. Part of the reason that such a speech may still resonate with ordinary people (as evidenced by the popularity of all of the Zhou Meisen dramas) is that these terms can still conjure up the positive values promoted by revolutionary and socialist ideals and practices. What needs to be questioned in Ye's speech, in this sense, is not so much the mere—clichéd—use of these terms but the lack of attention to such questions as Who are the *laobaixing* and the *renmin?* In what sense are they part of the *guojia?* Do they really have rights and a say in deciding what *guojia liyi* (interests of the state) and *renmin liyi* (interests of the people) are? What is the relationship between the interests of the *guojia* and those of the *laobaixing* when the former are in fact becoming increasingly divided among and controlled by interest groups? How does one really speak of the difference between the *quanli* (power) of the state and the *quanli* (power) of the people within that context?

We may entertain the possibility that, even though these questions remain dormant in Ye's speech, they are nevertheless indicative of the presence and memory of a value system and ideals (albeit many of which were unfulfilled and are presently marginalized or rendered illegitimate) that can be made anew, melodramatically, as a critical force in today's China. One recognizes such possibility in the dramas themselves. When, for example, it comes to the rights of the workers—the tens of thousands of miners mentioned in Ye's speech—*Sued by the State* raises the issue by contrasting Wang Changgong's corruption with the dilapidated conditions of state-owned mines, with the lives of the workers who are now laid off and facing economic hardships, and also with one particular character, Huang Guoxiu, who happens to be Ye Zijing's husband. Huang is the party secretary of the city's bankrupt state-owned mine and is now nicknamed *yaofan shuji,* literally, "the party secretary who begs for food (on behalf of the miners)." Although much of this is in the background of the drama, Huang's role in the story—by repeatedly bringing up the conditions of the workers and begging for funding—keeps as part of the narrative the fate of ordinary workers, the question of fairness, and the workers' rights to enjoy the fruits of their labor and, by extension, their contributions to society. Indeed, why do miners in a state-owned mine have to lose their jobs, and why are they pushed to a level of poverty so quickly and without debate?

Ironically, however, limited by the melodramatic mode of expression, instead of realizing the potential to focus on such questions, the drama falls back on promoting "good/clean officials," or *qingguan,* who are shown to be the ones concerned with the interests of the ordinary people, especially social groups like laid-off workers, migrant workers, and peasants. Similar textual practices can also be found in other anticorruption dramas. One ready example is a Huang Guoxiu type of character in *Zhongcheng* (Loyalty, 2001), also a Zhou Meisen drama. The character, Tian Liye, is represented (even more movingly as a character than Huang) as a good/clean official. Tian takes his responsibilities as an official seriously and disregards his own self-interest (for example, he forbids his sister to take a job offered on account of his position). In the drama, he ends up sacrificing his own life in order to prevent a possible ecological disaster from happening to both workers of a joint-venture chemical factory and people downstream of a river. The problem lies in the fact that, even though representations of such "good" officials function to link the rights of workers, migrant workers, and peasants, their narrative function in the dramas tends to be more of a suture than critically deconstructive. Given the lack of real attention to the rights issues of those ordinary people, these morally upright officials are no more than "feel-good" elements that mainly function to suture the rupture caused by the unequal relationship between those in power and those without it, and to bridge the deepened and widened gap between the interest groups in the state and ordinary people in contemporary China. While the state continues to rely on the term "people" to claim its legitimacy and moral authority and while "people" can in turn demand the state to "serve the people," the relationship between the two, both in Ye's speech and in much official discourse, remains relevant but also unclear, abstract, and manipulatable.

#### In the Name of Rule of/by Law? *Red Carnations*

Like *quanli* (power) and *quanli* (rights) in Chinese, *fazhi* (rule of law) and *fazhi* (rule by law) are also homonyms. Scholars have criticized the legal system in contemporary China for putting emphasis on writing laws but little emphasis on establishing a genuinely independent legal system, and they identify this situation in China as "rule by law," not a "rule of law." In China, however, despite attempts by critics to clarify the two terms, they are often used interchangeably: hence my use of "rule of/by law" to refer to the notion of the two Chinese homonyms.

In most anticorruption dramas, *fa,* or law, is assumed to be a weapon against corruption, and legal professionals (lawyers, district attorneys, and policemen) are part of the anticorruption forces. With courts (as part of the setting) and lawyers (as major characters) becoming major components in many of the stories, anticorruption dramas appear to take on a normative legalist way of representing issues related to "law," or, to echo Xingzhong Yu, they assume a "legal-fetishism" without fully recognizing why and in what ways law is the ultimate weapon for fighting corruption and, for that matter, the means for ordinary people to find protection for their own interests.[23] Indeed, anticorruption dramas function as an advocate normalizing "law" and "rule by/of law" as a magic bullet to solve the problem of official abuse of power. Such a law-fetishism behaves not unlike the high moral stance claimed for the aura of the "state." In this mind-set, the notion of *fa* is assumed to be part of the market economy and as such it remains not only blind to marketist ideology, but also functions to help normalize it. Meanwhile, "law" enters popular culture via dramas like this, adding meaning to the drama's own melodramatic rendering of the notion of law.

*Red Carnations* (2000) was popularly received when it was shown on television, hailed as a different kind of anticorruption drama. The drama tells its story through intriguing characters including Lan Sihong, the CEO of a large state-owned company, or SOE (state-owned enterprise), named Da Hua, and Zhou Ruobing, a lawyer. Both are women. The latter works for a law firm representing the company but later ends up working with the police to investigate what turns out to be a scheme to sell a major state-owned enterprise to a nonexistent German company (which means the sale is essentially a secret way of selling the enterprise to Lan Sihong and her cohorts, who are state officials appointed to run the enterprise). The exposed corruption in this case focuses on the real problem of the sale of state-owned enterprises by or to those who run them, a shockingly serious but underreported corruption-related problem since the 1990s. What is interesting about this drama is its focus on two levels of corruption of which the more immediate level—the acceptance of bribes by officials—exists only as the cover for the more serious and dangerous corruption, namely, the eroding or selling out, of state-owned capital (known in Chinese as *guoyou zichan liushi*),[24] which is carried out via a complicated and carefully planned scheme. In this particular drama, the scheme is limited to Lan Sihong and her associates' sale of the state-owned assets to a nonexistent foreign company set up by a relative who is in actuality a Chinese restaurant owner in Germany. As serious as the corruption and crime exposed here is, the narrative detail is nevertheless indicative of either censorship or ignorance on the part of the producers and fails to penetrate the real issue at hand, namely, that the real sell-out in China does not only take place at a low level. Nor does the sell-out, as the drama suggests, mean that those who carry out the corrupt transactions will benefit only through direct monetary gains. The real sell-out of state-owned capital in China has in fact comprised turning state-owned enterprises into rent-seeking activities by the powerful without much public knowledge, scrutiny, and understanding of what that means. The melodramatic use of a (female) lawyer as hero, therefore, reveals the limitation of such a narrative mode, especially when it tends to direct the public attention toward individual crimes and the seeming usefulness of the court (as opposed to revealing the structural and systemic problems that still await much-needed public debate). What is more, when the drama ends with a speech, further questions arise regarding exactly in whose name the anticorruption battle is waged.

The speech is given by Zong Ming, head of the anticorruption office, who is sent to investigate the Da Hua case, and is a good example of mainstream thinking about how to stop this kind of corruption. At a meeting (instead of a court) in the last episode, Zong, head of the team that has investigated this case, discusses the "lessons" of officials like Lan Sihong who are placed in the position of managing SOEs. He begins by pointing out the change in Lan Sihong from a "good" person (who has spent years taking care of her bedridden husband, adopted a little girl she found on the street, and managed to turn a steel plant established in the 1950s into the Da Hua conglomerate trading company that has gone international [*yu guoji jiegui*]) to someone who unscrupulously schemed to steal tens of millions in state-owned capital. What, Zong asks, caused such a change in a good person? He goes on to argue that this has little to do with the failure of the party's "thought work" (*sixiang gongzuo*) but everything to do with the issue of a problematic "mechanism" (*jizhi*) (which essentially means system). After quoting Deng Xiaoping, who allegedly stated that a good system can turn a bad person into a good one and a bad system can make a good person bad, Zong argues that Lan Sihong is a typical good person turned bad under an unreasonably established system (*bu wanshan de jizhi*). What needs to be improved, therefore, is the system. Zong concludes by offering three specific suggestions to amend the system:

> First, the reward mechanism needs to be improved. SOE managers are still considered cadres and are compensated as state officials would be. No matter how well the enterprise performs, their compensations are not matched accordingly. This can affect these people psychologically. On top of that, when they are compensated the same way as officials whose enterprises are poorly run and lose money, there is essentially the problem of inequality, which can generate resentment and corruption.
>
> Second, the retirement system is not well established. As a result, there is the "age fifty-nine phenomenon" in which a cadre close to that age [and even younger these days] would want to do something before he or she steps down to secure his or her years in retirement.
>
> Third, and also most important, the supervising mechanism remains weak. When the factory-manager-responsibility system [*changzhang zhi*] was established, it was done for the purpose of improving management. When such a position is not properly checked, however, the system can be easily turned into one in which power is concentrated in one person [*yizhang zhi*]. Everything is decided by that person, one signature can sell out a huge amount of state-owned capital, and one word can decide the fate of thousands of workers. Sometimes, such a concentration of power in one person can become concentration of power in one family and even a mafialike organization. Power without supervision, or checks and balances, can be like an out-of-control wild horse, dangerously terrifying. Fortunately, this time, owing to two good lawyers and someone willing to sacrifice her own feelings for justice, we were able to solve this case. What we need, I argue, is a good management system for SOEs so that this ancient country of ours will one day stand up among the world powers.

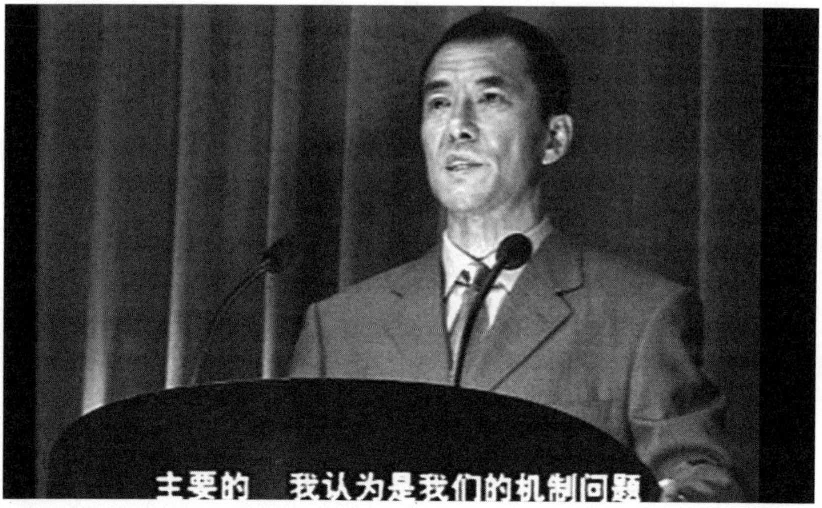


**Figure 3.2.** Zong Ming gives a lecture after the trial that convicted Lan Sihong. *Red Carnations* (Beijing Dianshi Yishu Zhongxin Yingxiang Chubanshe)

This speech is filled with contradictions. On the one hand, it appears to argue for the need to check power by establishing "proper" mechanisms. When it comes to the third point, especially, Zong is making a liberal argument appealing for power to be checked via a well-established system. He does not, of course, go on to explore how to establish such a system. On the other hand, the speech is littered with appeals to treat officials that manage SOEs like highly paid CEOs of private companies (owned by international corporations), using logic that represents a typical mainstream self-interest-driven argument for the "rights" of those in power. Within this logic, the problem with Lan Sihong is not so much her greedy desire to be compensated as the unfortunate fact that she does not go about it in a "correct" way. The "correct" way, according to Zong, is to systematically, and therefore legally, establish a reward system that compensates people in accordance with how much profit they help generate. The underlying logic is that such individuals ought to enjoy more "rights" for compensation. This is in fact a manifestation of the established logic in today's China, where monetary rewards are viewed as the most meaningful forms of reward and acknowledgment. In many ways, this speech is a blatant advocation of the mainstream marketist ideology in today's China, which has accepted, without question, the management-worker hierarchy based on the capitalist private corporate management model. The role of the workers and the issue of labor are rendered invisible within this logic and hence never mentioned in Zong's speech.

Zong's speech is particularly telling in light of the latest worldwide economic crisis, which originated in the United States and has been identified as the worst since the Great Depression in the late 1920s and early 1930s. The speech is indicative of the increasingly dominant ideological position within the Chinese Communist Party and the Chinese government promoting the need to emulate the logic of the market economy, especially the kind in the United States that supports and rewards the power of capital (at the expense of labor). It is against this larger global capitalist context, in relation to the social and economic changes in China and the ideological tensions with regard to those changes, that we can better understand the difference between Zong's speech and the earlier speech by Ye Zijing. Compared with the central argument in Ye Zijing's speech, Zong's skews the issue of moral authority away from iconic symbols such as *guojia, renmin*, or *laobaixing* into the abstract notion of *jizhi*, or mechanism, further blurring, diluting, or making invisible the social—class—content within these notions and the distinction between the relationship of power and self-interest and that of power and responsibility. While this drama—along with using a lawyer as the central protagonist and hero—ends with a call to establish a "fair" mechanism or system and therefore appears to be more legally oriented and practical, its notion of *fa* and its assumption of moral authority smack of law-fetishism based on a received marketist ideology. The concerns demonstrated here are aligned with the "rights" of those already in power. When it comes to *Red Carnations*, then, the difference between a "bad" lawyer and a "good" one is no more than that the former serves those in power stealthily, while the latter argues for a way to do it openly and "legally."

## Idealism as Specter? "Fallen Angels" in *Black Hole, The Police Chief,* and Other Anticorruption Dramas

Related to the layered implications of what is "good" discussed above, the "bad" or "evil" is also frequently represented in a less-than-clear-cut fashion. Indeed, the anticorruption discourse and its melodramatic manifestations are complicated by the ambivalent representations of what I call "fallen angels," the major villains in many anticorruption dramas, and by the complex role played by "value," or *jiazhi guan*, in relation to issues of corruption.

Examples of "fallen angels" include Zhou Mi in *Daxue wuhen* (Snow-covered traces),[25] Nie Mingyu in *Heidong* (Black hole), and Zhong Liuyi in *Gongan juzhang* (The police chief) (and to a large extent, I might add, Lan Sihong in *Red Carnations*). All of these characters are middle-aged individuals who have become "successful" (or, to echo a trendy term in Chinese, *chenggong renshi*) but who have for different reasons turned into "villains." The reason that I refer to them as "fallen angels" has to do with the fact that, both textually and subtextually, the dramas mix their past lives with their present ones, thereby offering a collection of ambivalently represented villains. In so doing, the narratives raise questions regarding the relationship between specific changes in the postrevolution economic reforms and the quality-altering changes in these individuals: what has changed them? Can the crimes they have committed be explained away simply in legal terms by the lack of a systematic prevention mechanism that limits the relationship between power and personal gain and by the lack of a well-thought-out compensation mechanism? The representations of these "fallen angels" appear to answer both yes and not entirely.

*Black Hole* (2001) is a more violent story than the other dramas discussed above.[26] Chen Daoming, one of the best-known actors in contemporary China, plays the major villain, Nie Mingyu, son of the mayor of the fictional city Tiandu and CEO of the city's best-known business enterprise. The drama focuses on the power of "princelings"—the children of high-ranking officials—and their associates. The violence in this drama takes anticorruption dramas' representations of corruption one step further by probing into the link between corrupt officials and mafialike groups, some of which are led by well-connected princelings. It dramatizes the extent to which such a linkage can lead to senseless crimes, while probing the implications of the loss of ideals and the rise of cynicism in postrevolution China on the part of those who grew up during the Mao era. Nie Mingyu is an "insider" whose cold-blooded cruelty and cynicism is said to have developed upon seeing how easily those in power can be corrupted. His cruelty, in other words, is blatantly linked to the death of an ideal. The residue of this ideal is symbolized in a peculiar manner by Nie's playing the accordion with a group of men of his age—they play revolutionary music from the Mao era. It is also symbolized by the secret room built within the walls of his hypermodern office. This hidden room, in which Nie is periodically shown to sit, is supposedly a replica of the office of his army company leader, and it is in this room in which Nie ultimately commits suicide (I will return to this point shortly).

The drama goes so far as to show how Nie's father, the mayor, though prevented from learning much about how his son has achieved his business "success," eventually chooses to protect his son once he is confronted with the truth that the latter is in danger of being exposed. The "morally upright" individual in this drama is Nie's adopted brother, Liu Zhenhan, who happens to be a police officer and who also happens to be assigned to investigate Nie's case. The "coincidence," needless to say, ensures the many melodramatic moments in the drama but also sets up a "good" versus "evil" dichotomy with subtextually significant turns and twists. Coming from a humble background and deeply indebted to Nie's father, who adopted him as a child, and to Nie Mingyu himself for having once saved his life while they both served in the army, Liu

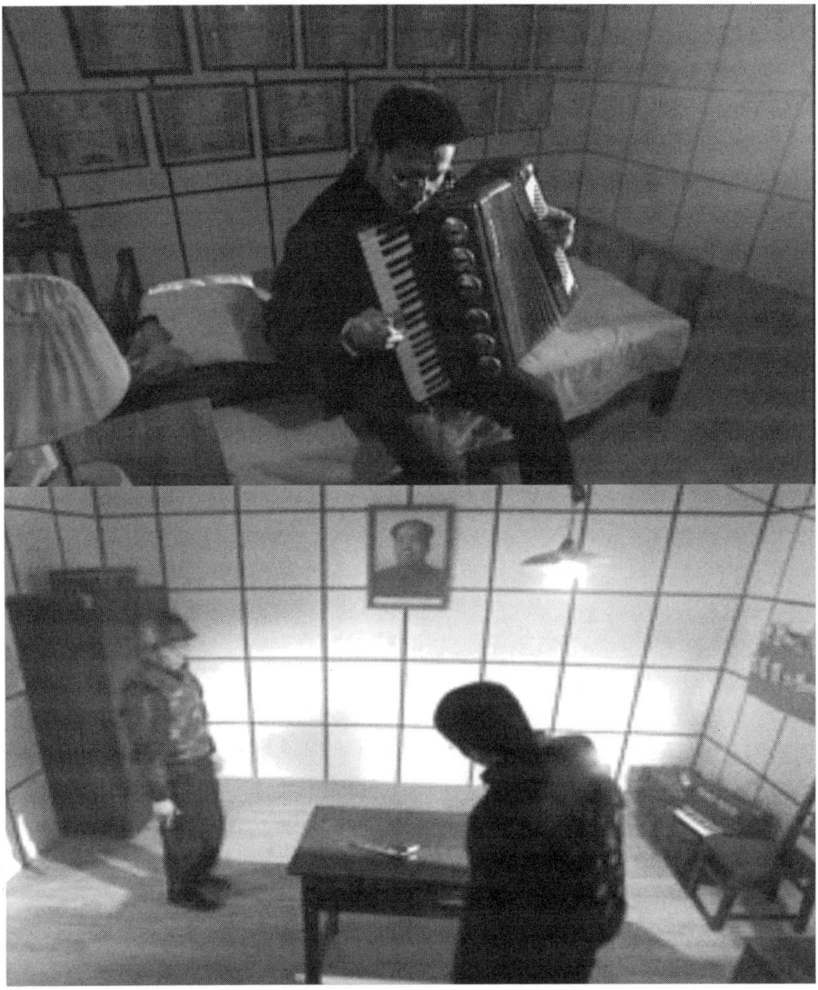

**Figure 3.3.** Nie Mingyu playing the accordion in the secret room. And Nie Mingyu and Liu Zhenhan in the same room before the former commits suicide. *Black Hole* (Xizang Yingxiang Chubanshe)

is a man struggling with himself. When chosen to investigate Nie Mingyu and his company for alleged smuggling, for running underground gambling parlors, and for murder, he has to struggle between his sense of responsibility and justice, on the one hand, and his sense of indebtedness toward Nie's family, on the other.

Similar shades of ambivalence are echoed in other anticorruption dramas. Among them is *The Police Chief*, which addresses princeling-related corruption but does so in an indirect way—focusing on one of its victims-turned-victimizer. The drama tells the story of Zhong Liuyi, owner and CEO of a private company who is shown as someone on a mission of vengeance: he schemes to corrupt as

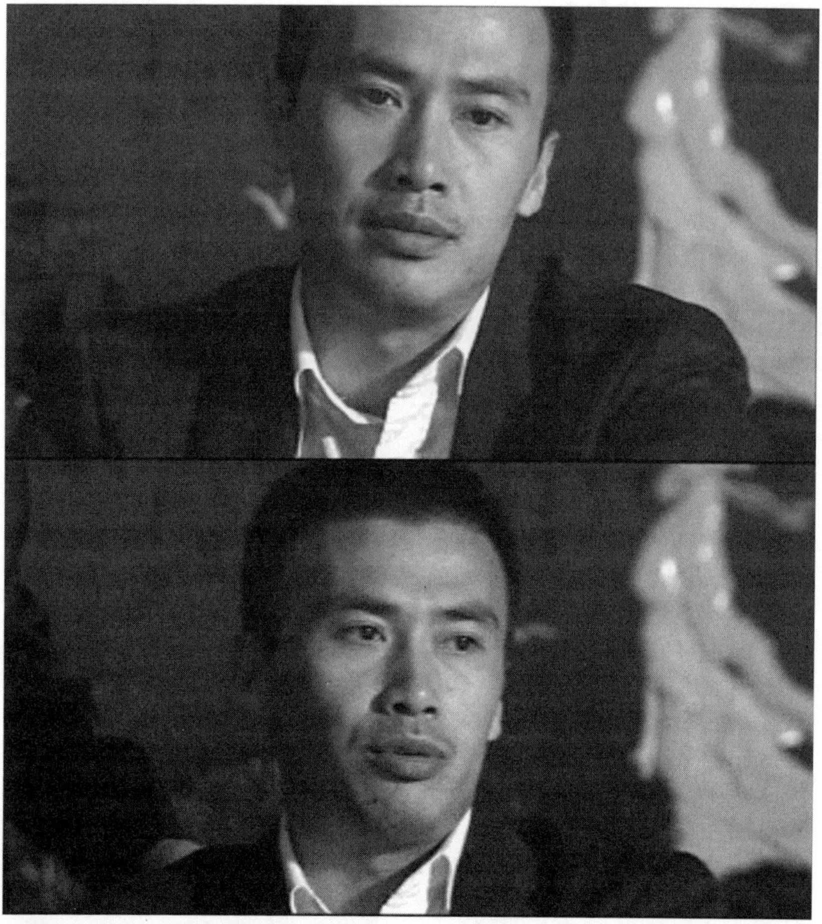

**Figure 3.4.** Zhong Liuyi talking to an official with contempt. *The Police Chief* (Qilu Yingxiang Chubanshe)

many officials as he can. Zhong makes reference to *Jidushan bojue* (Le Comte de Monte-Cristo) in this drama of vengeance, which has its origin in the fact that Zhong Liuyi, coming from a humble family, was once used and misused by a group of princelings who essentially sacrificed him when their illegal business activities were exposed.[27] Zhong Liuyi had to go to jail in their place and, in return, he is given a short prison sentence and provided with seed money to start his own business after his release. Upon his release, however, he finds out that his mother worked herself to death trying to accumulate enough money for her son by collecting garbage, while disregarding her own health. This is not an unfamiliar narrative device employed to intensify the protagonist's sense of injustice and to justify his sense of vengeance. Indeed, both his imprisonment and his mother's death are "good" versus "evil" melodramatic elements with strong subtextual implications that function as the prequel to this drama of vengeance in which unequal social relations between those in and not in power are accentuated and linked to the onset of economic and market reforms. Even though the drama sets up the police chief as the main hero who eventually succeeds in "defeating" Zhong, much of the narrative is about Zhong and is dramatized in a highly ambivalent manner. Closely identified with a major type of corruption, Zhong is represented as both victim and victimizer in the context of the economic reforms.

Nie Mingyu and Zhong Liuyi occupy opposite ends of the social spectrum in relation to power, but the dramas involving these characters hint that inequality became intensified and radicalized with the onset of market reform and by the enormous consequences of the direct link between power and the "rent-seeking" behavior of those in power. Their stories address the question of how to understand the changes in these individuals from Mao era youth with ideals to criminals intent to destroy. While the dominant view provides a ready conclusion—that these youth were cheated by the Chinese revolutionary ideals and the death of their ideals can only lead them to cynicism and nihilism—the way these dramas represent the characters' connection with their idealist past does not answer the question in such a simplistic manner.

As mentioned above, Nie Mingyu in *Black Hole* and Zhong Liuyi in *The Police Chief* are both villainous characters and "successful" businessmen. At the same time, they are from opposite social backgrounds, and their criminal activities have seemingly different motivations. In Zhong Liuyi's case, especially, his success is motivated by a desire for revenge, and his way of going about it is to corrupt as many officials as he can. There is a vigilante impulse in his schemes to take revenge against the powerful on behalf of the socially powerless like he and his mother were. Nie Mingyu is also intent on revenge of a sort. The drama repeatedly shows his seeming contempt for officials and his alienation from his high-ranking official family even though he actually benefited from it as long as his father remained in power (as the mayor of the city). Represented as a cold-blooded person who heads a mafialike company that runs underground gambling parlors and smuggles high-end automobiles, among other things, Nie also plays the accordion, sometimes with a band but most of the time in the secret room tucked away in his hypermodern office. The three narrative details—the accordion (which was a key music instrument during the Mao era), the music he plays, and the secret room—are all reminiscent of the socialist era, and they curiously connect him more closely to Zhong Liuyi. In Zhong's story, Mao era references are made by evoking nineteenth-century European literature—especially that in the critical realism tradition—and a sense of class difference sharpened via his own experiences in postrevolution and reform-era China. Like Zhou Mi in *Snow-Covered Traces* and Lan Sihong in *Red Carnations,* representations of these characters' former lives share references to a less corrupt and more idealistic past. What is the "moral" in such references in relation to these "villains"? Nostalgia or something more complex than that?

Anybody who has watched *Black Hole* cannot but be struck by the cold-blooded nature of Nie Mingyu and his associates nor can they forget the contrast between his past and present symbolized by the secret room in Nie's office, which is a peculiar replica of a typical Mao era military officer's room. The contrast and juxtaposition is peculiarly jarring within the context of what Nie's company represents and the network of corrupt officials—the "black hole"—he has managed to establish throughout the provincial and city power structure. Tucked away in Nie's hyperpostmodern-looking office, what does this replica symbolize? In many ways, it does not seem to symbolize anything other than a space occupied by the newly rich Nie Mingyu. But can Nie embody both eras in the way the drama shows him to—that there is a part of him that continues to harbor a desire for a more innocent time? Or does the drama subtextually indicate that while individuals in Nie's position may find a way to reconcile the difference between the two eras, in actuality the two are not really reconcilable, and hence the replica is not a reminder of values, ideals, and passion from the past but rather suggests their death (along with the death of the army company commander and Nie's suicide)? Indeed, every time this room is opened and occupied by Nie Mingyu, the space feels cold and lonely. Does the periodic focus on this space, with Nie in it, signify mourning of the past, or is it a cynical way of playing with the symbols of that past? The truth may lie somewhere in between, thereby revealing the uncertainty on the part of the producers as well as their censors and viewers about how to gauge that immediate past that is in many ways still part of those who grew up during the Mao era.

Nie Mingyu's adoptive brother Liu Zhenhan, in contrast, though without an external space to attach to, may well symbolize the residues of the idealistic spirit of that era. The irony is that without occupying a physical space that juxtaposes and symbolizes two very different social and political imaginaries, Liu Zhenhan and his associates in the police force are represented as the "bodies" whose comings and goings around the city and its adjacent areas connect the rapidly changing society and the uneven meanings found in that change. Their pursuit of Nie and his cohorts function to show a setting in which all kinds of social elements coexist, some in search of survival and some seeking to comprehend the rapid changes taking place around and inside them. With a mix of characters, both "fallen angels" and "heroic" legal professionals, we find the specter of idealism still lurking, with tremendous uncertainty, in the fast-changing social landscape of China. Within the same rapidly changing system, what historical, sociocultural, and political legacies, traditions, and ideals can continue to be evoked as more than a specter from the past?

## Back to the Question: In Whose Name?

After watching *Black Hole,* a friend of mine remarked, dismissively, that he did not believe there could be policemen like Liu Zhenhan and others in his team in today's China. They are too good to be true, he claimed, emphatically. Whether his claim is accurate is not the issue here. His assumption—that such shows are not realistic and therefore propagandistic—is echoed by many more sophisticated viewers and critics. To me, however, the seemingly unrealistic and melodramatic downside is an interesting narrative inroad into locating ambivalence and criticism of the "social reality" of contemporary China. Ambivalence and criticism are found in the different voices identified and discussed above. On the one hand, the stories in these dramas are about corruption in officialdom.[28] On the other hand, they also demonstrate an array of perspectives and ideological positions that inform their specific representations. When seen together, these dramas touch upon a range of areas in which corruption is becoming rampant: officials whose power is essential to the formation of an extended network of power and corruption, officials of state-owned enterprises in relation to the loss of state-owned capital and bankruptcy, the rise of mafialike organizations and their deepening connection with officials, and more. At the same time, they also rely on the belief that there are always some idealists in both officialdom and the legal profession who will rise to the occasion and expose the corruption and thereby correct the wrong, rehabilitate the wronged, and restore order. Indeed, given the narrative structure of television dramas that requires a positive ending—that the "bad" are duly punished—it is not difficult to guess who in these dramas wins at the end. This is the basis of the shared theme in such dramas that anticorruption activities are made possible and fought for mainly by morally upright individuals—be that a district attorney, a lawyer, or a policeman. Like the use of *qingguan,* or good/clean officials, resting one's hopes on *fazhi,* or rule by law, via "morally upright" legal professionals is another feature that helps these dramas to "suture" the rupture in their narratives: in the end anticorruption forces always prevail. This "good"-ultimately-triumphs-over-the-"bad" logic, in other words, tends to smooth over the ideological uncertainty displayed within them.

At the same time, the polyphonic nature of these representations indicates rapidly changing cultural logic as well as internal tensions. As such, contemporary anticorruption dramas do more than simply expose corruption (as Lu Xun once observed). Anticorruption dramas offer up a range of complex issues that call for debate and discussion. Representations of corruption and anticorruption activities are related to some of the seminal issues facing China's quest for modernity throughout its modern history and in this latest round of that quest in particular. These issues include questions regarding the nature of the "state," the definition of "people," who has the right and power to decide how wealth is distributed, the concept of "law" in relation to "traditional values" of morality and rights, and the relationship between social and personal interests.

It is in relation to these implications that I want to conclude by pointing out one glaring limitation of the anticorruption televisual subgenre as a whole. The subgenre displays a glaring absence of dramas that address the widespread struggles between ordinary people—peasants and migrant workers, especially—and corrupt officials. The absence of representations of this particular social reality further reflects the limitations of mainstream culture. Focusing on the struggles mainly between "good" and "bad" officials, these dramas continue to operate within the existing power structure without fully recognizing that the rights of ordinary people are the source of legitimacy that provides the right for the existing power structure to continue to exist.

CHAPTER FOUR

# Beyond Romance

## "Youth Drama," Social Change, and the Postrevolution Search for Idealism

❑ ❑ ❑ ❑ ❑

Across the heavily advertised landscape of contemporary China, many of the billboards highlight "youth" (and femininity), demonstrating globalizing consumer capitalism's conquest of yet another new frontier. In this new frontier, the desire economy has significantly changed what it means to be young in China. But questions about the relation of these changes in the youth culture to the larger context of modern Chinese history and the latest social transformation in China remain underexplored. "Youth" is a key social, cultural and political marker in modern Chinese history. Youth-oriented "visuality" at once manifests desire and ambition, but also anxiety, uncertainty, disappointment, despair, as well as resistance, all of which cut across a much wider, deeper, rapidly changing and palpably troubled social landscape. Youth drama as a subgenre on television offers yet another interesting example of mainstream culture's representations of social contradictions and ideological tensions.

### Changing Meanings of Being Young and the Rise of Chinese-Made Youth Dramas: A Few Historical Pointers

Throughout much of the twentieth century in China, "youth" has been prominently associated with various forms of radicalism and revolutionary idealism and with social, cultural, and political changes brought about by reforms and revolutions.[1] To better understand youth-related issues in contemporary China, manifested via youth drama on television, it is necessary to recognize their historical specificities. Given the limited scope of this chapter, I would like to briefly mention a few points of contention in relation to the major historical periods of the twentieth century.

Beginning with Liang Qichao, who coined the term *shaonian Zhongguo,* or young China, around the turn of the twentieth century, *shaonian* and *qingnian*—both refer to being young or young people—emerged as a "new" and "modern" cultural and political imaginary for nation building.[2] As such, "youth" was poised to become a particularly meaningful modern symbol, as well as a powerful social and political force, throughout twentieth-century Chinese history.[3] The first and most well-known historical event directly associated with youth was the May Fourth New Culture Movement (1915–1927). On May 4, 1919, three thousand university students in Beijing demonstrated at Tiananmen, or the Gate of Heavenly Peace, against the Western powers' decision, negotiated at Versailles, to hand over a German concession in China to Japan.[4] This demonstration ignited a nationwide nationalist movement and gave the New Culture Movement its identity as being prominently associated with the radicalization of modern Chinese youth.

At the same time, May Fourth–related youth identity coexisted with other "modern youth" imaginaries and identities informed by socioeconomic and ideological forces, making issues of youth symptomatic of the larger ideological tensions and political struggles throughout the first half of the twentieth century in China. Images of youth in both May Fourth literature and other popular and "modernist" literature and culture represented the variety of identities. Young protagonists in Yu Dafu's "Sinking," Guo Moruo's implicit identification with Werther in translating Goethe's "The Sorrows of Young Werther" into Chinese, Lu Xun's "Regrets for the Past," Ding Ling's "Miss Sophia's Diary," Ba Jin's *Family,* and Xiao Hong's and many other young women writers' stories are some of the well-known "May Fourth" literary representations that directly address the social and cultural conditions that young men and women were confronted with in a society deep in social, political, and national crises. In addition to these literary representations, youth and their issues were also represented in so-called Mandarin Duck and Butterfly and modernist literature, in which the connection between youth and "modern" desire and its anxiety also loomed large. Together with other forms of representation, such as film and popular magazines, these cultural products revealed the complexity of the pre-1949 urban social, cultural, and political scenes in which representations of (urban) "youth" were symptomatic of the social contradictions and political and ideological struggles of the time. Despite the different political forces and ideological persuasions, however, the immediate national crisis China was facing conditioned a strong association between "youth" and the revolutionary spirit for national salvation. Although the May Fourth culture movement has been under critical scrutiny and even under assault in academic circles in the late twentieth century, one of the long-lasting legacies of the movement continues to be its critical and independent spirit.[5]

During the Mao era (1949–1976) after the founding of the People's Republic of China in 1949, the official discourse continued to uphold a "revolutionary spirit" (*geming jingshen*) in the education of youth.[6] As I have discussed elsewhere, young people (*qingnian*) would be molded according to the discourse of *qingchun,* or more precisely *geming qingchun* (revolutionary youth), in which a connection between youth and "revolutionary ideals" was emphasized.[7] Before the Cultural Revolution (1966–1976), young people were educated to see themselves as revolutionary successors, but their education was nevertheless a mixture of modern science, (selected) Western classics in literature and arts, (selected) traditional cultural materials, orthodox Marxist principles, and revolutionary ideals. The Cultural Revolution changed all of this, and its aftermath led to the emergence of a Chinese version of a "lost generation" who found themselves disillusioned by revolutionary ideals. As the Mao era yielded to the post-Mao era of the early 1980s, the decade would witness a collapse of revolutionary ideology and the unraveling of the *qingchun*-related idealism, signifying yet another round of changes in ideological and discursive struggles symbolized by "youth."[8]

In the 1980s, along with the return of "rusticated youth" to the cities, the post-Mao era witnessed an emergence of old and new political and ideological forces whose voices would further contribute to the weakening of the Mao era's revolutionary ideology. Via media and literature, many young writers and intellectuals joined forces in promoting "thought liberation" (*sixiang jiefang*) and in "reevaluating" (*fan si*) what they believed to be China's problems. On the popular front, the much-publicized debates in the early 1980s generated by "Pan Xiao's letter" and Zhang Hua's death, in the then widely read magazine *Youth of China* (*Zhongguo qingnian*), are well-documented examples of the early post-Mao era's public reevaluation of the "value" of being young (*qingchun de jiazhi*).[9] In literature, especially in "educated-youth literature" (*zhiqing wenxue*) and "roots-searching literature" (*xungen wenxue*), which emerged in the mid-1980s, young writers questioned the Chinese Communist Party–led revolution with stories highlighting its violence, destruction, and failures, manifesting the shared disillusionment of the time. Through the fate of their characters, these young writers questioned whether the revolution had succeeded in moving China in the "right" direction.[10] Q*ingchun* would become one of the first cultural categories to be cut adrift from the Mao era's revolutionary discourse and, like gender identities, it would become subject to cultural and ideological reconstruction.

Indeed, appearing on the cultural scene of the 1980s, the aforementioned cultural activities and their products would eventually merge into an "ideological preparedness" for the notion of youth to be delinked from its revolutionary and political orientation and reconstructed by a "modernization"-cum-consumer-capitalist imaginary. The appearance of new phrases that contain *qingchun* within them is symptomatic of the changes in the meaning of "youth." If the word *qingchun* in Chinese emphasizes a temporal dimension or the duration of being young (as opposed to the word *qingnian,* which specifically refers to people who are young), the word *qingchun* in *geming qingchun* (revolutionary youth) and in *qingchun ouxiang* (youth idol) nevertheless denote very different historical and temporal imaginaries. While *qingchun* in "revolutionary youth" is associated with the history of Chinese revolution and emphasizes a teleological connection between the present and an (imagined) better future, *qingchun* in the latter expression orients around a seemingly permanent state of the present that nevertheless emphasizes the ephemeral and fleeting nature of time and the time-sensitive "value" of youth. In the latter case, associating youth with such a temporal value, though relatively new to China, is a time-honored marketing practice deeply entrenched in the desire economy of consumer capitalism. The underlying logic of *qingchun ouxiang* informs the visible changes in the reform-era youth-related discourse and helps explain why today at the end of the first decade of the twenty-first century in China, the word *qingchun* is often associated with such terms as *qingchun fan* (youth as a bowl of rice) or *qingchun buzai* (youth fleeting away), emphasizing the need to make the best use of something that is fleeting in nature.[11] Following this logic, the visually enhanced youth in the postrevolutionary era symbolizes the impact of consumer capitalism in transforming the meaning of youth from its earlier social, political, and historical orientation to a seemingly pastless and futureless temporal one that emphasizes the importance of arresting the present.

At the same time, the social reality in contemporary China is far from a postmodern pastless and futureless recycling of fragmented realities of the present. Indeed, across the tension-filled contemporary social landscape in China, the rapid influx of the youth-embodied desire economy has inevitably had to contend with a mixture of cultural and historical legacies whose presence as part of modern Chinese history continues to inform different responses, including an uncertainty, if not a critical sense, about the value of such an economy. It is with this understanding that I now turn to the phenomenon of Chinese-made youth drama.

I refer to the subgenre as "Chinese-made" for a reason: it emerged against the backdrop of the widespread popularity of non-Chinese-made—principally Japanese and Korean—youth-idol dramas (*qingchun ouxiang ju*). Technically, "youth-idol drama" did not become a major phenomenon on television in China until the 1990s, when a large number of such dramas, first from Japan and later from Korea, flooded Chinese television screens.[12] Varying in length from ten episodes to hundreds, these dramas possess an identical melodramatic narrative formula.[13] They unfailingly focus on love relationships between young individuals, mixed with tales of misidentification, misunderstanding, and familial interference. As a rule, these shows are visually formulaic but nevertheless pleasing to the popular taste—with beautiful young actors and a "tastefully" designed mise-en-scène—and narratively melodramatic and sentimental. They are reminiscent of a Chinese version of modern middle-brow fiction (such as Mandarin Duck and Butterfly literature or fiction by Qiong Yao) focusing mainly on rich and middle-class "family matters" with their complex relationships and individuals' struggles within.[14] To date, while often looked upon with a cool detachment by critics in China, imported youth-idol dramas remain highly popular. Despite recent regulations that have pushed most of these non-Chinese dramas out of prime-time slots and even though many do not get to be screened on television (and as a result become popular buys from the pirate DVD vendors who lurk on various street corners),[15] they have exerted a powerful influence on the development of contemporary Chinese youth culture.[16]

What is interesting about this phenomenon is the fact that, while Japanese and Korean youth dramas have been popularly received in China, most domestic—Chinese—efforts at making a similar type of drama have failed to register viewers' interest.[17] Indeed, as popular, attractive, and entertaining as youth-idol dramas may be if they are from Japan or Korea, if they are set in contemporary China, stories about affairs of young people from urban, white-collar, and wealthy families tend not to meet with the same interest from the viewers, who tend to dismiss them as poor imitations.[18] Chinese youth dramas would have to be different to be "believable." As it turns out, they would have to be more in touch with social reality and social problems. Contemporary China's social reality, in other words, functions to inform the reception and then the production of Chinese-made youth drama.[19]

In what follows, I will focus on three types of well-received Chinese-made youth dramas and their best-known texts. In the first case, I have chosen the dramas by the so-called master of Chinese youth drama, Hai Yan. Focusing on the narrative patterns and the young characters represented in Hai Yan's dramas, I explore what the representations of these young characters share and what social and ideological implications are entailed in the commonality in Hai Yan's dramas. In the second case, I examine the phenomenon of what I term "post-youth" youth drama. By "post-youth" I refer to dramas that focus on the generation of Chinese who were born and grew up during the Mao era but who encountered significant changes in their lives during the post-Mao era. I examine the ambivalence expressed within those dramas in which their main characters live through two sharply different eras. I am interested in exploring the "unseen rhythms" that inform their representations at a time when former "revolutionary youths" are compelled to learn quickly to survive in the new postrevolution reality. I am interested in both the implications and the limitations in the dramas' representations of such tensions. In the third case, I turn to what I call "counteridol" youth drama, examining especially one of its latest representatives, *Shibing tuji* (Soldiers, be ready, 2007). Focusing on its main character, Xu Sanduo, and the popular following this unlikely "hero" has generated, I speculate on why an unconventional "youth idol" has successfully managed to capture the public's imagination.

### Youth, Beauty, and Violence as the "Social" in Hai Yan Dramas

The first wave of popularly received Chinese-made youth dramas would come to be identified with two individuals, Zhao Baogang, a television drama director, and Hai Yan, a writer.[20] Today, both names have become synonymous with Chinese-made youth dramas.[21] The collaboration between the two has produced a few popularly received dramas, including *Yong bu mingmu* (Eyes forever open, 1999) and *Na shenme zhengjiu ni, wo de airen* (With what to save you, my loved one, 2002).[22] Adopting one element that made Japanese and Korean youth-idol dramas popular, their dramas are also about impossible love between beautiful and young couples. As such, both Zhao Baogang and Hai Yan are nicknamed *yanqing dashi,* or masters of love stories.[23] At the same time, there exists an important difference between the two men.

Most of the Zhao Baogang–directed dramas are known for the director's skill in visually enhancing mise-en-scène and creating a sentimental mood, projecting a strong sense of melancholy when a passionate love ends tragically or simply goes nowhere. Regardless of whether a story is set in the early twentieth century or in contemporary transnational environments, most of Zhao's dramas, offering viewers little sense of history, function mainly as a cultural vehicle in conveying a sense of longing for a desired private domain.[24] Within the context of contemporary China, such sentiments befit the newly rising, for lack of a better word, "middle class" who orient their attention toward carving out a materially comfortable and emotionally safe "private" haven for themselves. Because of that, Zhao Baogang's dramas are often compared to dramas adapted from Qiong Yao's fiction, carrying with them a strong petit-bourgeois flair reminiscent of early-twentieth-century "middle-brow" fiction popular among city dwellers. Most of Hai Yan dramas differ in that they tend not to focus on the rising middle-class desire for a glamorous lifestyle or, for that matter, on melancholic longing and visual beautification, all of which constitute the signature of Zhao Baogang–directed dramas.[25]

Hai Yan's main protagonists are almost always placed in social settings that are neither private spaces as within a family nor public spaces such as a work place.

More often than not, his main characters are part of the floating population on the move and on the margins, often in transit, from one place to another or from one position to another facing an unknown future, all reflective of major social changes in reform-era China. The desire and the drive that accompany such human migration as represented in the dramas help capture, perhaps despite the writer himself, the complexity of the social context and the cultural milieu in which the (uprooted small-town) youth search for meaning. In this sense, one can see Hai Yan dramas as a mix of nineteenth-century European critical realism with melodrama and Chinese social particularities, manifesting issues much larger than the angst and predicaments of being young and emblematic of a society in search of a moral direction. While the focus on the young in Hai Yan's dramas does not escape a familiar collective and seemingly clichéd desire for *zhen, shan, mei,* or truthfulness, kindness, and beauty, respectively, his narrative renderings of such desire are not deployed in the "beauty for beauty's sake" manner found in Zhao's dramas. Hai Yan's young protagonists tend to find themselves in a time and place where the "reality" is rampant with corruption, unquestioned and unexamined desires, out-of-control greed for material possessions, and a lack of a clear value system. It is the messy complexity of the Hai Yan dramas' representations of youth that merits our further critical attention.

Even though the first television adaptation of one of Hai Yan's stories appeared in 1988 as *Plain-Clothed Cops,* he did not become a household name until his second drama, *Eyes Forever Open* (1999), many years later. Suddenly, viewers began to be drawn to the young characters in Hai Yan's dramas. *With What to Save You, My Loved One* (2002), *Your Life Is So Passionate* (Ni de shengming ruci duoqing, 2001), *Love Is Sweet and Cruel* (Yi chang fenghua xueyue de shi, 2004), *Jade Goddess of Mercy* (Yu Guanyin, 2003), and *Ordinary Life* (Pingdan shenghuo, 2004) generated further enthusiasm from viewers. One after another, the young and beautiful protagonists managed to touch the public in such a way that those who played these characters became stars, giving the actors an aura that comes from the characters they have played and turning the actors themselves into contemporary youth idols.

Because some of the more important implications of Hai Yan's dramas derive from his representations of young and beautiful protagonists, I would like to provide a few examples. The young protagonists from *Eyes Forever Open, Jade Goddess of Mercy, With What to Save You,* and *Ordinary Life* each have different stories, and yet together they demonstrate a shared narrative pattern—indeed with all the necessary melodramatic elements—in which these characters are situated within a harsh and often unforgiving social reality.

Hai Yan's second drama, *Eyes Forever Open,* managed to capture the imagination of its viewers with the creation of a young, flawed, but pure at heart (male) character, Xiao Tong. Its narrative structure—a mixture of love relationships and criminal activities that require not only the presence of the police in the narrative but, more important, a narrative space in which the dark side of the society is dramatized—was also to become the signature narrative structure of Hai Yan dramas. The story centers on two relationships, one between a police woman and Xiao Tong, a college student whose vision was saved by the cornea of the police woman's fiancé when he died in the line of duty, the other between the same young man and a young woman with criminal ties. The former relationship develops in relation to the cornea transplant, after which a superficial kind of "transference" takes place when the young man begins to feel attracted to the police woman even though she is older. As the plot develops and while Ou Qingchun, the police woman, does not know how to respond to a younger man's attraction, an accidental encounter brings him into the life of a rich businessman's daughter, Ouyang Lanlan. She fancies him and starts pursuing him. Xiao Tong in turn is asked by the police to take advantage of the opportunity, and as a result he becomes a temporary undercover agent for the police pretending to be her boyfriend. Because the criminal family is forced to be on the run, Xiao Tong must go along, all the way to a Tibetan region where the family hides from the authorities. In the end, the mission costs him his life, but he is supposed to have remained true to the police woman. This drama is said to be the first in which a relationship between an older woman and a younger man is positively portrayed. But more important, it helps establish Hai Yan's narrative pattern in which a young protagonist can be placed in a harsh environment and yet can still remain "true" and "good." The death of the young protagonist is another indication that Hai Yan's love dramas differ from the dramas with happy endings (*da tuanyuan*) found in traditional Chinese theater and in Hollywood films; Han Yan's dramas tend not to end happily ever after.

*Jade Goddess of Mercy*, though arguably more about its main female character, An Xin, is nevertheless narrated by Yang Rui, whose "growing up" journey begins with his meeting An Xin and proceeds with his eventual loss of the woman and his journey to her home province to both look for her and find out who she is. Early in the drama, Yang Rui has a chance encounter with An Xin, who works as a janitor at the sports club where Yang Rui practices boxing. This encounter turns out to be "fatal" for Yang Rui because he gradually falls for this young woman who is "wrong" for him in every sense of the word: she is a migrant worker doing a menial job, she appears to be somewhat secretive, she already has a child and turns out to be someone who was once married but whose husband was killed because of her own bad judgment, and she has been placed in a witness-protection program because the killer of her husband is still at large. All of these "wrong" factors turn Yang Rui's life upside down. He loses his job (his father also loses his job because of Yang Rui), has trouble finding and keeping another job because of the constant meddling of his vengeful former girlfriend (who goes so far as accusing him of bribery, an accusation that lands him in jail), and eventually loses An Xin, the object of his love (who decides to punish herself for the deaths of her husband and her son by disappearing from Yang Rui's life and by, presumably, returning to her job as an undercover cop). In the end, after going through much hardship and still unable to be with the one he loves, Yang Rui decides to remain loyal to An Xin. This over-the-top love drama managed to become a huge hit when it aired in 2003.

Seemingly centering on Luo Jingjing and her relationships with two young men, the drama *With What to Save You* in many ways is more about the two young men, a handsome young lawyer, Han Ding, and a migrant worker, Long Xiaoyu, who is accused of murder. The young lawyer is so taken by Luo's beauty and so wants to marry her that, at her request, he agrees to be the defense lawyer for Long Xiaoyu, whom Luo Jingjing supposedly is really in love with. Long Xiaoyu is the opposite of the young lawyer; he is from a small town and so poor that after the death of his father he had to drop out of college to become, first, a factory worker in his hometown and, then, a migrant worker in a different city. The poor young man needs a defense lawyer because he is accused of murdering his former girlfriend, a young woman who is portrayed as pretty but with a crude, petty intelligence. Han Ding sacrifices himself (by not studying for the exams to go abroad) and successfully defends Long, only to find out later that Long did indeed deal the last blow to his former girlfriend, effectively killing her. Long then commits suicide in the house of the dead woman, Siping,

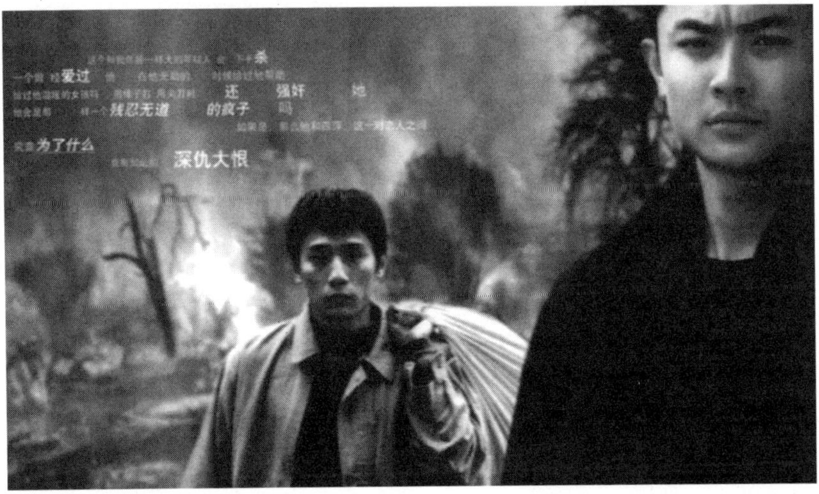


**Figure 4.1.** Han Ding with Long Xiaoyu in the back. *With What to Save You My Loved One* (Beijing Dianshi Yishu Zhongxin Yingxiang Chubanshe)

where Long once spent a long period of time taking care of her sickly mother when Siping was away working in another city. Narrated in part with the voice-over of the young lawyer Han Ding, a large portion of the story, consisting of conversations between Han and Long Xiaoyu in a prison meeting room and lengthy flashbacks, turns out to be about the efforts by Long Xiaoyu, to move beyond the lowly state of a migrant worker, first innocently, then with much apprehension, and finally with violence. Like the two dramas described above, this one is also sympathetic toward the two young (and handsome) male characters who in their own way are shown to be kind and "good," one lucky enough not to be poor and the other not so lucky.

Lastly, in *Ordinary Life,* the protagonist Ding You is a young and innocent woman who, escaping the bullies in her hometown who sexually harass her, travels to the capital city of her province in search of a young man that she has had a long and secret crush on only to find herself incapable of escaping forces that drag her through a rude awakening in the capital city. Much of the story centers on her life in a big city where Ding You's search for her youthful crush leads her farther away from him and to other unexpected events, including being pursued by the only son of a rich businessman, witnessing his parents being robbed and murdered, and feeling obligated to become his fiancée. Eventually, the harsh reality smashes all her dreams and causes her, like An Xin, to disappear into the sea of people never to be heard from again.

By way of these characters, we can see more clearly what Hai Yan's protagonists come to represent: the young, the beautiful, and the innocent in relation to the rapidly changing world around them. The conflicts and violence in a society undergoing rapid transformation take place at the expense of the young, the beautiful, and the innocent. Few of these characters have a complete family and most are on the move, either running away from their hometowns (Ding You and, to an extent, An Xin) or moving from one place to another as migrant workers (Long Xiaoyu and his former girlfriend whom he killed), as an undercover agent for the police (Xiao Tong and An Xin), or in search of a loved one (Yang Rui and Ding You). All of them, additionally, inadvertently find themselves cut adrift from the people that they knew and having to experience "growing pains" in a much harsher environment. These characters collectively define the "Hai Yan formula" in which his young, beautiful, and innocent protagonists are placed in social settings in which they are confronted with rapid social changes, economic uncertainties, and sometimes violent consequences. How are we to understand such a formula?

Hai Yan's youth-oriented melodramas resemble literary and filmic works from different cultures that also use youth as focus to explore social ills. In the context of contemporary China, aspects of these dramas are reminiscent of not only of the tradition of "critical realism" and its melodramatic mode that was welcomed by the left-wing writers and filmmakers of the 1930s, but also of the contemporary "urban generation" films made by such directors as Jia Zhangke.[26] To be sure, compared with the portrayal of the characters in such films as *Xiao Wu*, *Platform*, and *Unknown Pleasures* by Jia Zhangke, Hai Yan's dramas seem so stuffed with events and so filled with melodrama and (sometimes overly charged) emotions that they fail to leave the viewer enough time and space to reflect. Indeed, noted for their antimelodramatic representations of young characters, Jia's films are lauded for employing a style that helps "document" a generation of "lost youth" who are situated, socially and economically as well as symbolically, in the middle of nowhere when the market reforms are rapidly changing the world around them and leaving them behind to bear the brunt of the consequences. The long shots, stationary cameras, and slow cuts all capture youngsters suffering from indirection and ennui and engaged in mundane and unremarkable activities in a life that does not get them anywhere. By showing the lives of the young as a rather empty experience, Jia's films offer a powerful sense of the problem facing certain social groups, especially young people from rural areas and small towns as China continues its path of modernization and development.

At the same time, the busy narrative details and dramatic events in Hai Yan's dramas are emblematic of a society busy with indirection. Without the prospect of living happily ever after, the young protagonists portrayed in Hai Yan's dramas in fact function quite like Jia Zhangke's characters in exposing the problems of a social environment and in doubting the possibility of finding personal salvation or locating ideals in such private space as the home.

In *With What to Save You*, for example, it is the character Long Xiaoyu and his tragic life experience that help make the representations of the other young characters in the drama more meaningful. In the story, Long does not appear until after Han Ding's encounter with Luo and after a sequence of events that leads Luo to agree to live with Han. When Long does appear, he is already on the run, pursued for allegedly murdering his former girlfriend. From the moment that he appears, this young man's story will symbolize the theme typical of Hai Yan's narrative structure—dragging the young and the innocent through the mud of crime, murder, and the dark side of society. Performed by the now-famous young actor Liu Ye, Long Xiaoyu is portrayed sympathetically as a young man whose sincerity and whose life story convince the viewer that he is wrongly accused. This sympathetic perception is enhanced when Han Ding manages to prove that Long was wrongly convicted and saves Long from execution when the latter is already on his way to the execution site. And yet, at the end of the drama, Long is found guilty for having actually dealt the young

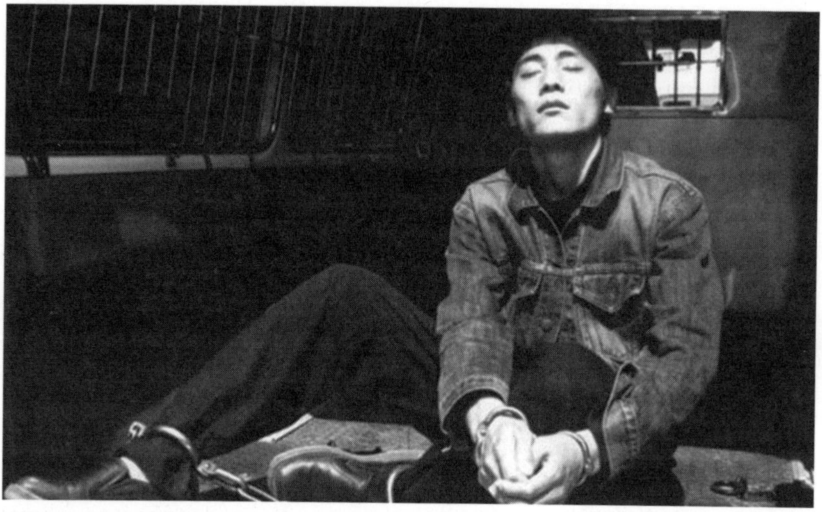

**Figure 4.2.** Long Xiaoyu locked up. *With What to Save You My Loved One* (Beijing Dianshi Yishu Zhongxin Yinxiang Chubanshe)

woman the fatal blow after she was stabbed by a group of thugs. Legally, the "innocent" is not so innocent, after all.

In the drama, much of Long's experience is narrated, via flashbacks, within the confines of an interview room in prison. The prison setting further enhances the harsh reality that Long finds himself in, but what he tells Han Ding, his lawyer, about his life before prison makes it unclear whether this imprisonment is worse than the life he has lived. While one is not sure meetings between client and lawyer like the ones shown in the drama actually happen in prisons in China and whether such meetings last as long in real life, the drama gives Long ample time to tell his own stories, thereby making it possible for the viewer to sympathize with him. The sympathy toward Long is achieved because Long's tragic end is due in essence to his poverty; a perfectly "good" kid is pushed by forces beyond his control into a violent end simply because his desire to move beyond poverty motivates him to resist his "fate." Once again, the drama lays a major part of the blame at the feet of a society in transition that is harsh to the poor and the powerless. Poverty and the struggles against it constitute the underlying theme in the drama that helps make the portrayal of Long Xiaoyu compelling.

The link between poverty and Long, and the sympathy that is meant to be generated in the viewer are echoed in *Ordinary Life* when Ding You's story reveals a similar theme: a perfectly innocent young woman, after going to the city in pursuit of her dreams, is put through a series of harsh and even deadly events only to find her dreams crushed and her life turning from bad to worse.

Like Long Xiaoyu, the death of Ding You's dreams begins with her own and her sister's desire not to be poor, although the social stacks are set against both of them. *Pingdan shenghuo*, the Chinese title of the drama *Ordinary Life*, is meant to demonstrate the irony in Ding You's experience: what is ordinary about life is when one realizes that it always involves the death of dreams in the most violent and yet also the most mundane fashion.

To reiterate, ostensibly about love between the young and the beautiful, Hai Yan's dramas are more about the crushing of love and desire experienced by the young and the innocent because of their poor social status and circumstances and forces beyond their control. His representations of the young protagonists of the twenty-first century echo their nineteenth-century critical realist counterparts, in which youngsters are confronted by forces in a society that both lure them with material gains and also prevent them from achieving such gains. Melodramatic and emotionally manipulative as the Hai Yan formula may be, situating his young protagonists in a harsh reality nevertheless helps unfold the social dynamics and related problems in a postrevolution China undergoing development-oriented market reforms. In this sense, similar to many other subgenres in television dramas, Hai Yan's youth dramas do not shy away from representing the harsh reality in which his young protagonists exist. What is more, by situating the lives of these and other young characters within the context of rapid socoeconomic transformation and within the social settings of the floating population in particular, Hai Yan's stories indicate that, on the one hand, the revolutionary concept of youth from the Mao era has become a distant memory at best, and, on the other hand, the lure of "youth" as a marketable category—as "bowl of youth" for the young—essentially remains just that, a lure. More often than not, his young protagonists find themselves trapped in a rapidly changing and increasingly unfamiliar social environment in which they nevertheless must make sense of their own lives.

As a result, these dramas tend to strike a deeper social note than is apparent. The "fairy-tale" like quality in Hai Yan's representations of youth can be understood as a narrative lure into representations of a harsh reality. The pure, the good-hearted, and the beautiful—*zhen, shan, mei*—quality of his young characters manifests a sentiment—indeed a strong pathos—that can be identified in terms of, to borrow Rey Chow's words, "sentimental fabulation," but that sentiment stems from a tradition that is critical of social injustice and, within the contemporary context of China's market reforms, of the rapid and under-challenged reshuffling of social and economic relations and conditions.[27] The sentimentalism is also symptomatic of the limitations of dramatic representations portraying the increased (and increasing) polarization of the rich and poor in China. Despite the criticism that resorting to melodrama for articulation of criticism tends to lead to no more than momentary sympathy, if it is sympathy without condescension, however, this emotion may well be where social sentiment resides, a first necessary step for social action. I will return to this point in the concluding part of the chapter.

### *Age of True Feelings* and "Postyouth" Youth Dramas

By "postyouth" dramas I refer to a small but visible group of dramas that focus on a generation whose youth straddles the Mao and post-Mao eras—those who grew up during the Mao era and who "came of age" during the post-Mao economic reform era. The most popular series in this subcategory of youth drama are *Xuese langman* (Romantic life in brilliant red, 2004), *Xuese langman II* (also known as *Yu qingchun youguan de rizi,* or Days of being young, 2005), *Zhenqing niandai* (Age of true feelings, 2006), *Xuese qingchun* (Youth in brilliant red, 2005), and *Xingfu xiang hua'r yiyang* (Happiness is like flowers, 2006). We must note at the outset that many of the viewers whose lives during the Mao era are supposed to be represented in these dramas are said to have found the representations largely inaccurate. Some have taken serious offense with what they see as distorted representations, while others dismiss them for their lack of in-depth understanding. The question, still, is what makes such dramas popular, and what their popularity means. Most of these dramas share a similar representational pattern—starting with the main characters' lives during the Cultural Revolution and following them into the reform era, in which they experience drastic changes. I will focus mainly on one drama, *Age of True Feelings,* but would like to do so by way of *Romantic Life in Brilliant Red,* the first such drama to appear in China.

*Romantic Life in Brilliant Red* effected the successful inauguration of the "postyouth" drama. It appeared at the time when China's reform era entered a third phase of economic reform in which society began to face serious human, social, and environmental consequences of the development-oriented economic miracle. At the same time, the title of the drama also suggests that the drama is a "typical" postrevolution production representing Mao-era youths' experience of going through two very different historical periods by reevoking their lives during the Mao era, mainly through a nostalgic and ambivalent lens.

*Romantic Life* stars Liu Ye and Sun Li, two well-known young actors in contemporary China (made famous by, among other things, their roles in some of Hai Yan's dramas). It starts at the beginning of the Cultural Revolution, when the protagonists find themselves freed from both school and familial supervision. As such, the portrayal of the main characters reminds one of Wang Shuo's fictional (and filmic) representations of *da yuan* youth ("big courtyard," referring to the living quarters of various central administrative organs, either civilian or military, commonly found in Beijing during the Mao era).[28] Either consciously or unconsciously following Wang Shuo's portrait of this generation of Mao era youth, Wang's imitators have largely stayed within the same formula: the protagonists are the children of high-ranking officials, and they had the "privilege" of enjoying the chaos brought about by the onset of the Cultural Revolution. While the children of revolutionaries are expected also to be "revolutionary," Wang's stories in essence poke fun at the revolution by representing the refusal of these youngsters to subscribe to revolutionary ideals. Unlike Wang's stories, however, *Romantic Life* (and other similar dramas) is more reflective, although the reflection is filled with contradictions and uncertainties.

The term *xue se* in the drama's title, which literally means "bloody red," can be rendered in English in a number of ways. Given that the story is about a group of Mao era youngsters and their experiences during and after the Cultural Revolution, this "redness" is obviously associated with the revolution led by the Chinese Communist Party. Because the revolution was "communist" in nature, in English the color red referred to within this context would have negative implications, including an implication of violence. In Chinese, however, the connotation is more layered. In the entry on this drama in *Baidu baike*, a Chinese equivalent of Wikipedia, there is a "word definition" (*zici jieshi*) that defines *xuese langman* as (1) cruel but exciting youth, (2) a pure sense of romance emitting from the bottom of one's heart, (3) romance that is adventurous, and (4) a youthful era that is deeply marked by the eras of war and revolution.[29] This mixture of meanings are at once revolutionary and postrevolutionary. On the one hand, revolution is still associated with the country achieving national sovereignty and ridding itself of imperialist aggression, and the color red continues to be associated with the lives of Mao era youth and the spirit that they were brought up with and that they revolted against shortly after the Cultural Revolution. On the other hand, revolutionary ideals that used to be symbolized by the color red have now become a blur overshadowed by a collective farewell to the revolution in the post-Mao era. It is this mixed and contradictory connotation that makes the dramas that portray this specific "postyouth" generation worth discussing further.

In one dialogue, for example, we find a commentary on the generation portrayed in the drama:

> We have wasted too much of our youth. That was a youthful age filled with an overblown sense of our selves, which at the same time was quite ridiculous. There coexisted laughter and tears, youthful spirit and decadence, sweet feelings and silliness, self-confidence and uncertainties. We were sensitive, stubbornly partial, and we

> insisted on being this way, pretending that we were strong. We would easily hurt others but could also easily feel hurt by others. We pursued moments of decadent enjoyment and indulged in moments of lonely beauty. We strongly believed that we were different and that the world would change because of us. When we woke up, we were no longer young, and we realized that our future was no longer infinite. Then again, when had our future been infinite? For a brief moment [after our awakening], we thought we had grown up. Until one day, we finally realized that, besides desires, growing up also includes courage, responsibility, inner strength, and a necessary willingness to sacrifice. In real life, we are in fact still like children, yet to grow up, yet to understand what love is and how to be loved.[30]

The irony is that, despite the Wang Shuo–esque cynical tone generally present in the narrative, this passage contains a sense of idealism that does not exist in Wang Shuo's fictional representations of youth. The idealism—conveyed via the quote above—refers to the ideals of an earlier period of modern Chinese history when being young would indeed mean more than indulging in one's desires and would indeed be characterized by "courage, responsibility, inner strength, and a willingness to sacrifice."[31] As we will see shortly, this idealism is re-evoked within the postrevolution era when being young has become directly linked with the desire for material gain; its re-evocation pertains to today's social reality and exists with an ambivalence toward both this generation's own youth and their loss of idealism. To elaborate on this point, let me now turn to *Age of True Feelings*.

Directed by Gao Xixi, another well-known director of television dramas, *Age of True Feelings* tells the story of a group of educated youth after they return to the city (from the countryside), where they are compelled to live a life unavoidably shaped by the economic reforms. In this sense, this drama functions like a sequel to *Romantic Life*s. The story begins, during the Cultural Revolution, with the three male protagonists trapped in a small mine located in the countryside, where they have been sent as educated youth. This opening sequence lingers on this scene for quite some time, presenting a dialogue taking place among the three young men, who are waiting with some hope but without certainty of being rescued. Feeling that they may not leave the mine alive, they begin to confess to one another their desires and thoughts, among them, feelings toward a fellow female educated youth, He Ying. He Ying, meanwhile, is frantically trying to get help from the local officials to rescue the three young men. Thus introducing its four major characters, the drama quickly ends the opening sequence with the three being successfully rescued. Shortly after, Hao Jiefang, who is from a high-ranking military officer's family and who is also He Ying's "official" boyfriend, leaves to join the army. He "entrusts" He Ying to the care of Zhao Penghui

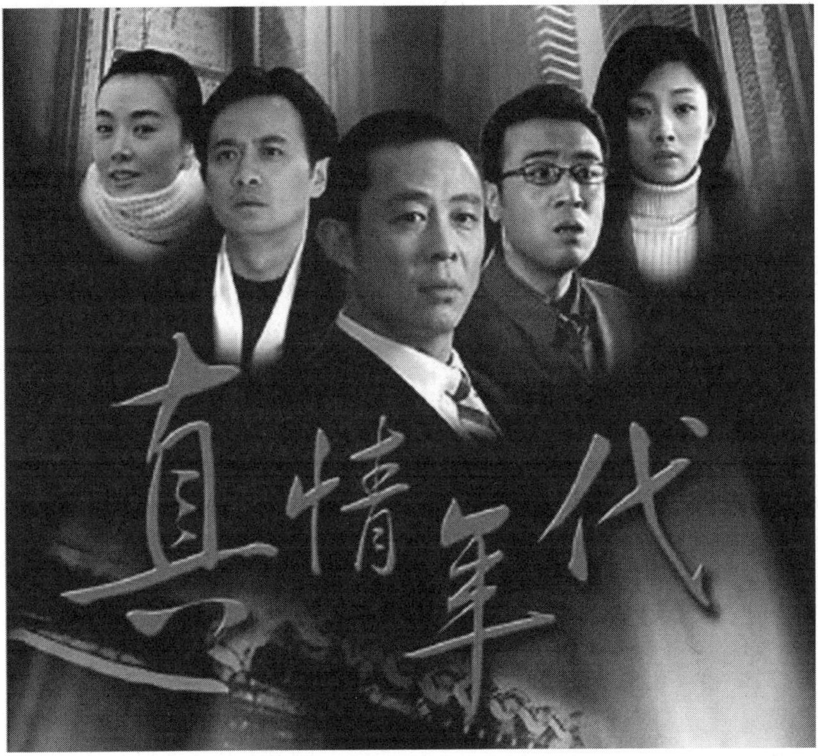


**Figure 4.3.** The five main characters in Age of True Feelings. *Age of True Feelings* (http://image.baidu.com)

and Li Heping, the other two young men who were trapped in the mine with him. Not long after the Cultural Revolution, all of them return to the city, only to have the first fissure occur amongst the four friends when He Ying decides to marry Zhao Penghui instead of Hao Jiefang.

From there on, the drama shows how the lives of these four Mao era youths drastically change in the post-Mao era. Zhao Penghui becomes a rich businessman. Not long after, his wife He Ying divorces him on account of an alleged affair on Zhao's part with Fan Xiaojie (which, as the drama indicates, did not really happen as she thought). Zhao ends up marrying Fan Xiaojie, who subsequently becomes a drug addict. Meanwhile, Hao Jiefang harbors hatred toward Zhao, who apparently "stole" two women from him (Fan Xiaojie, Zhao's second wife, was at first also Hao's girlfriend). The two men also compete in business deals. Li Heping, portrayed as being more intellectual than the others, tries to remain true to his own beliefs while also trying to stay loyal to his friends. His own marriage disintegrates after his wife goes abroad and decides to stay in America, and he refuses to join her there. At the very end of the story, Hao

Jiefang gets killed. The final scene shows his three oldest friends, with He Ying carrying his ashes, on their way to the countryside where they once lived; the drama ends with them aboard an open-cover jeep driving toward their village (presumably to either bury or scatter Hao's ashes).

The drama begins and ends with the four friends together and with their connection—in terms of love, friendship, and their sense of themselves—to the countryside where they lived as "educated youth." If we recall how the drama begins—when the three young men were trapped in a mine—the message of their "reunion" at the end is an attempt to refocus the meaning of their friendship in relation to the early part of their youth. At the same time, it is not altogether clear if such a retracing entails a better understanding, on their part, of the roots that inform and shape their friendship. This kind of retracing can easily be labeled as nostalgia. Indeed, during the 1990s, especially around 1998, there occurred a wave of self-representations to commemorate the thirtieth anniversary of the "rustication" movement. Scholars have questioned many of the positive representations of the educated youth's experience during the Cultural Revolution and considered them to be "nostalgic," reacting against the present by sentimentalizing and idealizing a not so ideal past.[32] While I recognize the validity of this critical assessment, I also question such a quick and ready dismissal without fully acknowledging the complexity that exists precisely because of the present situation.[33]

The complexity stems, first, from the critical perspective of the present and, second, from an uncertainty about and a desire to rethink the meaning of the past, namely, the meaning of a youth that straddles two very different historical periods. The result of this uncertainty and desire to rethink is manifested in the focus on *zhenqing* (true emotions/genuine feelings), which appears in the drama as the emotive domain in which the characters locate the positive meaning of their past. Indeed, throughout the drama, what connects the two eras is none other than their friendships—their true feelings for one another—which were formed during their years in the countryside as "educated youth" and whose near-disintegration is dramatized after their return to the city, where much of their life comes to be consumed by their constant efforts at getting ahead materially.

The implicit critique of the present manifests itself in the dramatic representation of conflicts that constantly bring their friendships to the brink of disintegration. For example, Zhao Penghui and Hao Jiefang enter into competition to make money and, more important, are willing to sacrifice their friendship in order to win. Entangled within the tensions in their friendship, additionally, are two women, He Ying and Fan Xiaojie. The latter, incidentally, is blatantly portrayed from a male point of view and in an overly melodramatic way. She is shown to be willing to give up her own dancing career in order to marry Zhao Penghui, to be ready to throw away her independence once she moves in with him, and to lead a daily existence where her greatest hope is that Zhao will come home on time and have dinner with her. Her lonely existence culminates when she is hospitalized, supposedly having (temporarily) gone mad, after she turns to drugs, first involuntarily and then voluntarily. These details are reminiscent of the representations of contemporary China found in many of the other dramas I study in this book.

By situating Mao era youth within the contemporary desire economy, the "postyouth" youth dramas inevitably raise questions about the changing values their characters have to confront and about the implications of their various choices. By emphasizing the importance of friendships formed during the Mao era, these dramas nevertheless stop short of exploring the significance of the historical context in which such friendships were formed and shaped. The "true feelings" (*zhen qing*), in other words, are cut adrift from any specific political or social linkages. As a result, it is not always clear what the word "true" entails. Li Heping is the only character whose role in the drama functions to locate conscience and, by extension, "true feelings."

Everyone in the drama changes with time except for Li Heping, who remains principled and unmoved by the desires and greed around him. From time to time, the drama suggests that his "goodness" is in essence egotistic and for self-protection. Most of the time, however, he is portrayed as an individual who is determined to resist taking the direction of so many other people toward money and power. He almost commits a corrupt act when he debates whether or not to sign, as an official, a contract to an unqualified company so that he can use bribe money to save Hao Jiefang, who has been arrested for squandering large loans he is unable to repay. When Zhao Penghui comes through with money to save Hao, Li is spared becoming another corrupt official. But even in his possible act of corruption, he is motivated by an intention to help his friend, not by a desire for self-gain. The question is what motivates his principled way of being. The drama offers no explanation except for setting him up as being different. This unidentified "virtue," I would argue, echoes most of the dramatic representations in television drama in that, ideologically, mainstream culture does not quite know how to identify a "positive" message except with seemingly universal terms such as "virtuous," "ethical," and "good." Like the *zhen, shan, mei* in Hai Yan's dramas, the goodness in Li Heping is mainly assumed but never explored. But if we remember the historical linkage that informs this set of dramas, that is, youths' lives set in both revolutionary and postrevolutionary times, Wendy Larson's recent discussion of the "Lei Feng spirit"—"for Lei Feng... no opposition between matter and spirit exists"—helps illuminate one cultural legacy, namely, that of the Mao era's revolutionary culture, that informs the representation of Li Heping.[34]

To sum up, by way of showing how Mao era youths' lives have unraveled in the reform era, these postyouth dramas offer a critical perspective on the social and cultural changes embodied and symbolized by the lives of various characters. Although their positive protagonists do not have a clear set of political ideals to subscribe to, the representational ambivalence toward the Mao era's idealism and the post-Mao era's desire economy that accomplishes the depoliticization of youth nevertheless indicates the role of historical experiences and the ways in which they are "remembered." Such ambivalence informs the melodramatic representations of the friendships, conflicts, and reconciliation between the characters. In this sense, we wonder what the very end of the drama means: why do they bring Hao Jiefang's ashes back to the countryside? Does their return to their collective "past" mean to further bury or to renew its meaning? The drama does not provide a clear answer. It echoes most of the other "postyouth" dramas in ending on a somber note, which indicates, on the one hand, a desire for larger meanings and, on the other, a continuing uncertainty about both the present and the past.

## *Shibing tuji* and the Yearning for New Idealism

If Li Heping is too one-dimensional to generate excitement as a "positive" character, a more recent drama—which I refer to as a "counteridol" youth drama—manages to generate excitement about a "good" character on a different level.[35]

In 2007, word of a new television drama spread like wildfire, fanned by enthusiastic viewers' response wherever the drama was shown. Like many other hit shows, this drama generated responses on the Internet in chat rooms, blogs, and various other vehicles, but, unlike most hit shows, the responses to this drama emphasized how "different" it was. Indeed, to many viewers, the drama was like a fresh breeze blowing out of their television screens.

The drama was *Shibing tuji* (Soldiers, be ready; hereafter, *Soldiers*).[36] Scripted by Lan Xiaolong and directed by Kang Honglei, the appearance of *Soldiers* quickly captured the imagination of millions of viewers, who marveled at the "newness" of the show. What was new about it and why was its "newness" exciting to so many viewers? First, in terms of content, unlike most youth dramas, its story is exclusively about the lives of soldiers away from the civilian world and does not have a single female character. Unlike other militarily themed dramas, *Soldiers* does not include love interests or marriage issues in the personal lives of its soldiers and officers. The only family-related content appears in the beginning, when the protagonist Xu Sanduo is urged to join the army by his widowed father (who has three sons, none of whom are married), and then sporadically in two other moments later in the story, both having to do with Xu's all-male family. While the heavily homoerotic and masculinist dimensions remain invisible to almost all viewers in China, the exclusively male cast and their stories do set the drama apart from its counterparts in the category of military-related dramas and in youth-related ones.

Also refreshing or new is the protagonist Xu Sanduo. The story of Xu Sanduo is about how a poor rural young man, who is forced by his father to join the army and who is almost rejected, is transformed from a clumsy, clueless, but stubborn person into a well-trained but still clumsy, clueless, and stubborn soldier. The "transformation" of Xu Sanduo in the drama is informed by a desire to celebrate someone who can be "heroic" without any of the "normal" traces of a hero. As a "hero," Xu Sanduo differs from traditional Mao era heroes, cynical Wang Shuo–esque youths, contemporary Chinese glamour-oriented middle-class youth idols, or white-collar *chenggong renshi* (successful professionals). Xu Sanduo's difference from these mostly young cultural icons stems from his own version of antihero characteristics. One of his key characteristics is his single-minded way of doing what he believes to be the right thing and his supposed lack of the worldliness to know when to stop. Because of his unique personality, the drama is full of humorous moments brought about by Xu Sanduo's seemingly unsophisticated behavior, including the questions he asks and the dialogue he has with other characters.

The drama begins ominously with a flashback in which Xu Sanduo, in a military exercise, falls from a fourteen-meter height to the ground. As he falls, his voiceover declares: "I made another mistake. They'll laugh at me again." In the midst of his fall, the drama flashes back to the moment in Xu Sanduo's home village when his father tries to get this son accepted by the recruiting officer Shi Jin. The function of the episode is to show the kind of family Xu is from—a widowed father who mistreats his third son, Sanduo (which literally means "the third who is one too many"), and forces him to join the army because the old man believes that is the only way out of poverty for a rural boy. When Shi Jin, the military recruiter, comes to their home, the father clumsily tries to persuade him to take his son, whom Shi Jin knows does not quite fit the normal profile of a soldier. After a round of rather comical exchanges, Shi Jin feels compelled to turn what he sees as a weak but promising young man into a soldier.

Before becoming an acceptable soldier, however, Xu Sanduo has to endure an additional rejection when the battalion commander above Shi Jin refuses to accept him after the first three months of training. Indeed, Xu Sanduo is not "desirable material" to be made into a qualified soldier, and, as such, the only place for him is an outpost where a squad of five soldiers is stationed with very little to do. Xu Sanduo's arrival at that outpost is to change the entire place without his knowing that he is doing so. Before his arrival, owing to a lack of regular supervision, the squad has been reduced to a card-playing, wise-cracking place ruled by cynicism. Xu Sanduo, however, stubbornly believes that, as a soldier, he must do what a soldier must do regardless of where he is. Every day, he gets up on time, makes his bed according to what he was taught as a new soldier, and helps make the others' beds because his fellow soldiers do not make theirs. He goes out for morning exercise alone while the rest of the squad remains in bed. He refuses to join card play, saying that it is meaningless (*meiyou yiyi*). He never seems to "get it" when his fellow soldiers sneer at him. His thickheadedness culminates when he accepts what he thinks is an order from his squad leaders to make a road in front of their post. When he starts the endeavor, the rest of the squad ignores him, believing that he will soon stop because of what they perceive to be the impossibility of the mission, only to realize that Xu is not going to give up.[37]

His sheer stubbornness finally moves the rest of the squad to join him in finishing the road. After that Xu Sanduo is "discovered" by the commander of his regiment and reposted to the battalion whose commander had refused to accept him and where Shi Jin is a squad leader. Xu Sanduo is placed in Shi Jin's squad, where he goes through another long ordeal owing to the disdain on the part of everybody except Shi Jin toward his seeming lack of skills and his seeming slowness and thickheadedness. This particular dynamic remains the major thematic thread carried through the rest of the drama as Xu Sanduo, in his thickheaded and stubborn way, manages to surprise and subsequently impress all his fellow soldiers and officers.

In short, the military environment in which a civilian is supposed to be made into a well-trained soldier makes life doubly difficult for Xu Sanduo, a not particularly clever, savvy, or quick-minded individual. From the very beginning, he is looked down upon by those around him with a sense of incredulous bemusement, and he takes everything said to him so seriously that many exchanges become very funny. The others marvel at how he has one less or one more *jin* (literally "tendon," which means "clue" here) than others and how he is like a "dog that always runs in the opposite direction" (*ni zhe pao de gou*). Ironically, of course, the seeming silliness on the part of Xu Sanduo always succeeds in turning the tables and makes others appear silly for underestimating him. In the end, as his battalion commander Gao Cheng finally remarks, Xu Sanduo is someone who, "although clearly a strong person, is born to appear like a nobody" (*mingming yige qiang ren, tiansheng yifu xiongyang*).

What is interesting about all of this is that Xu Sanduo does what he does based not on a particular doctrine, but on what he feels is the right thing to do.

What he feels is right has to have "meaning" (*yiyi*), and once he starts something that has "meaning," he "never gives up" (*bu paoqi, bu fangqi*). Whenever he is asked what it means to have meaning (*you yiyi*), he always gives what seems to be a circular answer, "to live well is to do meaningful things, and to do meaningful things is to live well" (*you yiyi jiu shi haohao huo, haohao huo jiu shizuo you yiyi de shi*). Xu Sanduo, needless to say, is an idealized character. In many ways, so is the military environment that he finds himself in—every man in his own way is a good man. The idealism Xu Sanduo represents hinges on the desire to revive a kind of "spiritedness," or *jingshen*, whose predominant characteristic is to do what is "meaningful." The key question here is what to Xu Sanduo is "meaningful" and why his circular answer, in addition to the idealistic nature of this character, can generate such popular response. I will return to this Xu Sanduo philosophy shortly.

The combination of Xu Sanduo's inner strength and his outward cluelessness is what endears him to his "brothers" in the army and also to millions of viewers. When Baidu, the Chinese search engine, set up a page to select, on an annual basis, the ten most influential individuals in China, Wang Baoqiang, the actor who played Xu Sanduo, was chosen by Chinese "netizens" as the most influential person (born after 1980) for the year of 2007, topping other celebrity figures including Yao Ming (the basketball player for the Houston Rockets) and Han Han, a so-called born-in-the-1980s (*ba ling hou*) young writer.[38] Wang's presumed influence comes from playing the character Xu Sanduo, so, in essence, the most influential young person in China for the year 2007 is a fictional character created for a television drama. It is interesting to note that many online discussions about Wang Baoqiang, the actor who plays Xu Sanduo, make references to his life story as being like that of Xu Sanduo. The expectations placed on a real person based on a character he or she once played may not be news, but the extent of the identification has turned the actor into an unlikely youth idol in the popular culture. This viewer-imposed idol status and especially the expectations implied are surely daunting to the actor, but as a cultural phenomenon the status also poses interesting questions.

Shortly after the airing of *Soldiers*, responses began to show up on the Internet. Among them were comments to the effect that Xu Sanduo was a Chinese version of Forrest Gump. Counterarguments pointed out that Gump is a man of low IQ, while Xu Sanduo is not. While the counterarguments are on target, a more interesting and relevant question is why Xu Sanduo readily evokes Forrest Gump and how to understand the difference between the two. One of the key differences, I believe, is that, while both play the role of an "other" in society, their representations are nevertheless informed and shaped by very different historical and sociocultural logic. If the role of Forrest Gump is in part to celebrate American small-town values and in part to celebrate the individual, Xu Sanduo's "otherness" is meant to question existing norms, assumptions, and the lack of confidence to challenge them. Jokingly or endearingly described as a "dog that likes to run in the opposite direction," Xu Sanduo's responses to "common-sense" questions, statements, and assumptions create both numerous moments of comical release and moments of reaffirmation of certain (forgotten or marginalized) virtues and values. To be sure, like Forrest Gump, Xu Sanduo is not an antisocial rebel, and, as such, he may not appear to be a radical enough character to be taken seriously by critics. But the fact that the character Xu Sanduo has generated a tidal wave of responses from ordinary viewers sets him apart from the Gump-type characterization and compels us to take the character's "otherness" seriously.

The editorial commentary on Wang Baoqiang having been chosen as the number one "most influential person of the post-1980 generation" for the year 2007, states that "it was a surprise when netizens supported Wang Baoqiang so strongly, but their support is also understandable. Wang Baoqiang represents the majority of the grassroots [in the society]. A great number of hardworking young people can find affirmation, hope, and strength in him."[39] It goes without saying that Xu Sanduo (and, by extension, the actor who played him) is inspirational. It also goes without saying that, if we unpack this "Xu Sanduo package" and analyze its composition, we can find layers of (most likely) conflicting meanings and in the end find the character deeply "mainstream."

Played by Wang Baoqiang, an unlikely actor whose "career success" itself is reflective of the changes and contradictions in the era of economic reform,[40] the character Xu Sanduo must first be understood in relation to all the other characters in the drama—his father, brothers, covillagers, fellow soldiers, and officers—and the military setting, and in relation to the larger historical context in which the mainstream culture has been undergoing a significant transformation. During the Mao era, the military was where revolutionary heroes and models—Lei Feng, Huang Jiguang, Dong Cunrui, and Zhang Side, to name the best-known ones—were created.[41] These heroes comprised a mixture of heroism, revolutionary ideals, and revolutionary values that were translated into such virtues as altruism, bravery, and a willingness to "serve the people" (*wei renmin fuwu*) and to sacrifice oneself for the greater good. The Mao era's official ideology that encouraged young people to cultivate a "revolutionary youth" (*geming de qingchun*) was embodied in these soldier-heroes. All of this, especially the idealism attached to these heroes, collapsed after the Cultural Revolution when, the entire revolution was thrown in doubt and when many young people became disillusioned in the face of subsequent rapid social and economic change. China entered an age of the "antihero," symbolized by the rise of glamour-oriented youth idols, nihilistic and self-interest-based philosophies of life, and Wang Shuo–esque characters whose function was mainly to poke fun at the revolution and its ideals. In the midst of all of this, along with the "bath water" went the "baby," namely, the need for a fuller understanding of the meaning of China's modern history in relation to revolutionary ideals, to a value system that combines spiritedness (*jingshen*) with a not too self-centered sense of the world, and to the question of why the revolutionary ideals have been marginalized if not completely jettisoned.

When, nearly three decades later, *Soldiers* unabashedly brings a kind of "heroism" and idealism back, it does so in response to a much-changed society. Unlike the Mao era's soldier-heroes whose stories were dramatized in larger-than-life fashion, the protagonists in this television drama are "humanized," with their flaws and personal quirks becoming a focus of narrative representation. What is more, with his lack of self-confidence and "worldliness," his stubbornness, and his seeming slowness in getting the point, the main character Xu Sanduo is far from either an idealized revolutionary hero or a macho and clever antihero. And yet, this protagonist, along with all the individuals who come into contact with him, have turned the character and the actor who played him into a new kind of youth idol in today's China. The question, however, remains: how do we understand this counteridol's circular answer to the question of what is meaningful, or *you yiyi.*

### Beyond Romance: Idealism in Postrevolutionary Youth

Xu Sanduo's circular answer is symptomatic of the ideological ambiguity in contemporary China. While there is a desire for meaning that is more than material success and possessions, the society as a whole is unsure about what should constitute that meaning. On the one hand, the desire for meaning is produced via criticism, which explains the critical implications found in the Chinese-made youth drama (and in other subgenres) identified above. Social injustice, corruption, moral decay, and ambivalence represented in these dramas are meaningful especially when they generate responses from active viewers to the social ills that are televisually represented. However melodramatically they are rendered, or precisely because of the reorganization of the melodramatic elements, these mainstream cultural texts can be provocative enough to be meaningful to viewers. Their recognition and responses, in turn, help contribute additional meanings to these dramas. On the other hand, Xu Sanduo's circular answer is also symptomatic of a void—indeed uncertainty—in the very notion of *yiyi,* or meaning itself. Meaning needs constantly to be searched for, symptomatic of the coexistence of ideological uncertainty and the possibility for discursive struggle in contemporary China. In these dramas, meaning exists and is promoted in such ideal notions as "purity" (*chun jie*) and "goodness" (*shan*), loyalty to friends, or a willingness to persevere (*bu paoqi, bu fangqi*). "Meaning," in this sense, corresponds to a collective desire for that which is considered to be "good," which at the same time also leads us back to a similar circular question and answer: what, then, is "good"? When Xu Sanduo's slogan *bu paoqi, bu fangqi,* or never give up and never give in, was picked up and took on a life of its own during the rescue and recovery operation immediately after the Wenchuan earthquake in 2008, this transference seemed to crystallize a moment of general selfless concern for those affected by the disaster. It also seemed to indicate that "goodness" is always contingent on when it is evoked.

The ideological implications, coming back to the dramas in question, lie precisely in the circular nature of this desire for meaning whose agency, often manifested melodramatically, functions to simultaneously expose and criticize as well as suture the social, cultural, and ideological discordance. The constant evocations of such "personal" virtues as purity, goodness, beauty, loyalty, friendship, and perseverance, simultaneously manifest a lack of such virtues and a desire to promote them, constituting a structure of feeling that is sentimentally meaningful while also symptomatic of an ideologically weakened awareness of the structural issues of the social changes—a quintessential postrevolutionary idealism. As such, televisual representations of youth in contemporary Chinese mainstream culture are symptomatic of the ideological uncertainties in the postrevolutionary era, but at the same time, to echo a point made at the beginning of the chapter, they are also indicative of a collective desire and search for ideals and idealism and of the cultural and ideological forces—and the tensions within them—that inform that desire and that search.

CHAPTER FIVE

# Also beyond Romance

## Women, Desire, and the Ideology of Happiness in "Family-Marriage Drama"

❑ ❑ ❑ ❑ ❑

Nowhere in the post-Mao reform era has the rise of the idea and pursuit of *xingfu,* or "happiness," by women in China been better manifested than in popular culture representations of such themes as love, marriage, and family, including television drama. What does "happiness" mean in gender terms in the post-women's-liberation age? Why is it assumed to be particularly important to women? How are we to understand the changing socioeconomic conditions and cultural values that direct (especially) women's attention toward a search for personal "happiness" in such domains as love or heterosexual romance, marriage, and family? What is the relationship between women's pursuit of "happiness" and discontent?

Western feminist scholarship in literature and film studies has long argued for the importance of understanding the relationship between melodrama and women's and gender issues because, in melodrama's "emphasis on the domestic sphere and its resistance to rationalism, feminists have become interested in its subversive tendencies."[1] In addition to valuing melodrama "for its resistance to 'highbrow' literary standards," feminists also value "its foregrounding of women's issues." "Especially, in the family melodrama, generational and gender conflicts and issues of sexual difference and identity are presented. This opens up a large space to the domestic sphere and for female protagonists" and a space where "melodrama's narratives are frequently motivated by female desire."[2] While it is important to guard against the essentialist tendency to equate the "domestic space" with women, feminist attention to (earlier) European and American literary and filmic melodramas helps shed light on representations of a certain social sphere and women characters that "highbrow" criticisms tend to dismiss out of hand or ignore.[3] Within the post-women's-liberation context of contemporary China, much about the relationship between melodrama and women's and gender issues awaits scholarly attention and critical analysis. Xie Jin's and Zhang Yimou's films, for example, come to mind (despite their seeming differences).[4] What also come to mind are television melodramas authored or scripted by women. It is important to note that while, owing to lack of financial support, women writers and directors have been decreasingly represented in filmic production, many of them have been compelled to cross over to television, where they have made themselves and their works highly visible. The gender divide here continues to indicate the existence of a gender hierarchy in what certain elite circles consider to be "highbrow" and "lowbrow" cultural forms. At the same time, "lowbrow" cultural forms such as television open more space for women writers (and women script writers) to tell their stories to an even wider audience.

This chapter examines the relationship between women and their desire for happiness as represented in the "family-marriage" drama (*jiating hunyin ju*), especially those scripted or adapted from stories by women writers. As indicated in the Introduction, many television dramas are adaptations from literary works, and writers to varying degree involve themselves in the adaptation process. The same has been true with women writers. I have chosen televisual adaptations from three well-known women writers, in part because those dramas were popularly received and generated interesting discussions both online and in the print media.[5] More important, however, the fact that the writing careers of these three women writers straddle both the 1980s and the two decades after that, and the fact that their literary-televisual crossover has allowed "women's perspectives" to be popularly represented captured my attention. The evolution in their writing career and the issues they address seem to dovetail with the changes in gender politics in what I call the post-women's-liberation era of the last three decades.

In relation to the televisual adaptations of their works, I am specifically interested in the fact that, in the last three decades of economic reforms in China, pursuit of "happiness" has become a major cultural metaphor for "female identity" and "womanhood" has become a "natural" goal in women's lives in the postrevolution era. At the same time, I am also interested in televisual representations of discontent and the fact that, when consumer-culture-defined happiness becomes the major, at times, the only, goal in life, especially for women, it is often problematized in the very act of trying to achieve the goal. In relation to this paradox, I examine the gendered social and ideological implications in the relationship between urban women and consumer-culture-defined "private" domains such as love, marriage, and family. Pursuit of happiness and related discontent, needless to say, are also symptomatic of the social changes and ideological tensions, manifested in gendered terms, in the reform and post-women's-liberation era. Given that the dramas I study in this chapter are based on women's writings, my discussion will also explore the pursuit of happiness and its related discontent in relation to the difference between women's writings in the decade of the 1980s and televisual dramas based on women's writings popularly received in the 1990s and beyond. Three decades since the start of the economic reform, the "happiness"-informed female identity has generated new questions, challenges, and problems when it comes to gender politics in contemporary China. While the ideology of happiness is powerfully advertised and subliminally alluring, it has also redrawn social domains for women in which they tend to find themselves being identified mainly with sexuality, love, marriage, and family.

### Engendering the Ideology of Happiness in the Post-Women's-Liberation Age

By the "post-women's-liberation age," I refer to the post-Mao era (1976 to the present) with a focus on changes in women's and gender issues and also with an understanding that those changes have been specific to different phases within this period. In the 1980s, the women's liberation movement led by the Chinese Communist Party came under intense critical scrutiny. The Mao era's women-related and "gender-equality" policies were not only criticized for their alleged indifference and neglect of "sexual difference" between men and women, they were also held responsible for the supposedly abnormal *yin sheng yang shuai* phenomenon, or the phenomenon of the ascendance of the yin (feminine) and the decline of the yang (masculine).[6] Criticisms of the party-led women's liberation movement and the Mao era's gender policies, along with the gradual retreat of the state from people's bedrooms, helped change the cultural discourse on gender issues.

At the same time, unexamined assumptions within these criticisms also gave rise to a discourse of sexual essentialism that articulated a desire for men and women to "return" to their "proper" (gender) roles and "real" sexual identities.[7] Corresponding expressions were found in the new culture movement of the 1980s in male intellectuals' preoccupation with (the lack of) "male potency" in relation to a male-centered nation–self-identity and in female intellectuals' preoccupation with issues of "female identity."[8] One of the unintended consequences has been a redirecting and narrowing of what it means to be a woman (and a man), identifying such issues as love, sexuality, marriage, and family as naturally female-oriented and others like *guojia* (state), *gonggong* (public), *shehui* (society), and *jiti* (collective) as gender neutral or masculine.[9] Indeed, the flip side of the efforts to "restore" male and female identities to men and women, and the critique of the supposed lack of "feminine" identity in revolutionary women is the foregrounding of an unexamined notion of "femaleness" and "womanhood." The sexual essentialist assumptions developed in the postrevolution and post-women's-liberation era have thus enabled a "logical" union between women's identity and their life's destiny centered on an unexamined notion of "happiness." The bifurcation between the "private" and the "public" and the feminization of the former and masculinization of the latter, in other words, has functioned as an ideological preparation for the consumer culture's new definition of happiness.

As a new cultural construct within the context of globalizing consumer capitalism, the notion of happiness has quickly become something women are encouraged to identify with. Identifying women's "natural" space with such "private" domains as marriage and family has, in turn, narrowed the meaning of the relationship between women and "happiness." Within this narrowed meaning of happiness, women have increasingly come to be dependent on external factors, as opposed to their own inner strength and independent spirit, for their sense of happiness. The "feminization" of the notion of happiness is, in both specific and essentialist terms, connecting women with such roles as being a wife and a mother, and with specific (and often unexamined) ideas associated with these roles. The limited social roles that connect women with their sense of "happiness" are symptomatic of the gendered ideological paradigm shift in post-women's-liberation China.

Perhaps not ironically, then, "happiness" within this context, though discursively constructed as a personal matter, is in effect collectively imagined and collectively pursued. Tensions and struggles represented in television dramas are indicative of the contradictions within this collective desire whose object is socially and economically conditioned and ideologically defined, and yet whose cultural articulations and manifestations orient the masses around the belief that it is up to an individual to achieve her happiness.

All of this constitutes the larger historical context and the social and ideological conditions in which we encounter the meeting between the ideology of happiness and gender politics in contemporary China and the ways in which that meeting is manifested in popular cultural representations of women, love, marriage, and family. Family-marriage dramas penned by women writers are one such cultural manifestation. They examine, often via such melodramatic elements as coincidence, excessive emotion, and sentimental pathos, the ways in which women's pursuit of "happiness" in love, marriage, and the family is a double-edged sword that leaves many marriages in ruins and love in doubt along the way. Women writers' attention to themes of love, marriage, and family accentuates the irony and discontent involved in this pursuit.

In what follows, I will focus on dramas based on works by three women writers: *Lailai wangwang* (Comings and goings, 1999) by Chi Li, *Zhongguo shi lihun* (Divorce Chinese style, 2004) by Wang Hailing, and *Kong jingzi* (Nothing in the mirror, 2002) and *Kong fangzi* (Empty house, 2004) by Wan Fang. Though different, these dramas are essentially about the failure of women's pursuit of "happiness" as defined by consumer culture and about an interesting dialectic that occurs between women's pursuit and their ultimate "unhappiness" or their realization of the need to move beyond the confines of this (illusive) goal. I focus on representations of the female protagonists in these dramas in conjunction with the following shared issues: (1) tensions within the changed and changing social roles and gender identities in men and women in face of the rising dominance of the consumer-culture-defined ideology of happiness, (2) the ways in which women's lives come to be associated with (their pursuits of) "happiness" and the corresponding uncertainties in such pursuits, and (3) women's understanding (or lack thereof) of the gendered "self" in imagining "happiness" and in face of the collapse of their pursuits.

I explore the notion of the "female self" in conjunction with some of the most influential women's writings of the early 1980s and with the rise of the ideology of happiness in women's lives since the early 1990s. An understanding of the connection and difference between the two bodies of women's writings indicates a renewed significance in revisiting women's writings of the early 1980s, especially with regard to issues of women's sense of the self. I am interested in this comparison for the purpose of bringing out a neglected component in our understanding of post-Mao literary expressions of female awareness of their "feminine" identity in relation to their sense of independence. Such awareness, although also full of ambivalence and tension, continues to function as an undercurrent that informs today's representations of women both in literature and in television drama.

## Two Unhappy Female Characters and Their "Comings and Goings"

Duan Lina and Lin Zhu are two female characters in *Comings and Goings*, a drama based on the novella of the same title by Chi Li.[10] *Comings and Goings* is chronologically bracketed between 1975 and the late 1990s, seemingly oriented around the transformation of the life of its male protagonist, Kang Weiye, while also capturing the rapid and profound changes taking place within those two and half decades. Because the story focuses on the changes in Kang's personal life, especially in relation with two women, his wife, Duan Lina, and his extramarital lover, Lin Zhu, the drama is in effect also about these women characters and their relationships with Kang. At the same time, however, following the original story that uses Kang's life—especially his eventual unhappiness—as the major thread of its narrative structure, the drama assumes a sympathetic perspective toward its male protagonist. This sympathy is manifested, in part, in the fact that the relationships Kang has with women characters are clichéd: the wife is loudmouthed, unreasonable, and unpleasant, while the lover is young, pretty, college-educated, and yet self-centered, representing what are believed to be typical characteristics of white-collar female professionals. But our exploration of an otherwise clichéd drama and its representations of women characters becomes more meaningful if we understand both the sympathy toward Kang and the seemingly clichéd representations of the two female protagonists dialectically, as manifestations of uncertainties and ambivalence within the ideology of happiness and changes in social and gender relations and identities. The drama (inadvertently) shows that, for these women, the domestic sphere does not appear to be where their imagined happiness resides.

Duan Lina appears early in the drama when she is introduced to Kang Weiye as a potential spouse. At the time, in 1975, Kang is back from the countryside, where he had been sent as an "educated youth," only to find himself assigned to work in a meat-processing factory. Kang's life back in the city is portrayed as a dead end. He is young and good-looking, but his daily routine in the factory is the antithesis of everything a "happy" life is supposed to be. What finally gets him out of the rut of the meat-processing factory is Duan Lina, then a female military cadre from a high-ranking military official's family, who takes a liking to Kang after being introduced to him. As a woman from a more powerful social background and enjoying a stronger social role than Kang, Duan's power is demonstrated in pushing herself onto him despite his misgivings and in finding him a job in a governmental bureau. Thus, from the beginning, the drama sets up an explanation for why this marriage will eventually fail—the relationship is built on an "unnatural" power relation, *yin sheng yang shuai* (ascendance of the feminine and decline of the masculine). The drama also sets up a difficult transition in a woman's life, from being a cadre steeped in a position of power and in the mode of revolutionary discourse to being a wife and mother, a transition, as we shall see, unsympathetically represented through the portrayal of Duan Lina.

As the drama fast forwards to the 1990s, a series of social and structural changes begin to affect the relationship between the two negatively: the drastic reduction in the state's military spending results in Duan Lina's father's retirement and the subsequent lessening of his influence, and results in Duan's demobilization and subsequent transfer to work in the city's Fulian (a municipal branch of the All China Women's Federation, an official organization for women). Meanwhile, feeling stuck in a bureaucratic rut, Kang leaves his government job and, "jumping into the sea of commerce" (*xia hai*), he eventually has a company of his own in the garment industry. The power relation between husband and wife begins to shift when Kang succeeds in his endeavors and becomes a successful businessman, while Duan no longer has her father's position to rely on, nor does she have a job from which she can derive much power, an apparent "correction" of the so-called *yin sheng yang shuai* phenomenon.[11] This narrative detail is important to note, for it is at this point that the drama becomes increasingly unsympathetic toward Duan as a woman. She is unable to adjust to the changing power relations in her life in general and in her marriage in particular, and becomes everything a "reasonable" and "pleasant" woman is not. Here Chi Li is perpetuating the negative view of "strong" women for their having supposedly enjoyed more power than men (in the Mao era) and for their supposed lack of "femininity" and "feminine" sensibilities. In Duan Lina's case, the drama makes sure that she is the one responsible for causing her marriage with Kang to fail.

After she leaves the military and does not have a powerful father to depend on, Duan Lina is loudmouthed and "nasty" in just about everything she does. On the one hand, she remains the same despite the rapid changes taking place around her and in her life; she is merely turned from an "articulate" military cadre mouthing revolutionary slogans to an equally ridiculous-sounding "Fulian" cadre. On the other hand, however, stripped of the power from the social roles she used to enjoy, she is forced to realize that her "happiness" now depends on whether or not she is able to defend her marriage and family. Her role as Kang's (alienated) wife thus comes to the fore when the drama shows her trying to be more "feminine" in her looks and, failing that, in her various schemes to prevent her husband from divorcing her and to sabotage his extramarital affairs. In a not so subtle way, these narrative details suggest that Duan is pursuing a lost cause despite her efforts at defending her marriage, for she simply does not possess the "necessary feminine quality" to begin with.

The seemingly clichéd and melodramatically predictable representation of Duan Lina thus takes on several layers of negative symbolic implications. First, it shows her as a woman deriving her sense of power from a (once) powerful father. Such a characterization is symptomatic of the negative view of women's liberation because it is a top-down liberation in which women derive their power from their "father"/the state.[12] Second, now that she can no longer depend on the "father"/state for power, Duan is predictably forced to turn to her husband, her marriage, and her family for a sense of self. The problem, thirdly, is that she is not "womanly" enough to guarantee a successful "transition" into a "domestic" space. In short, the drama implies that, in the changed social milieu, "happiness" remains illusive to Duan mainly because she does not possess the "proper" feminine qualities supposedly necessary for maintaining what she wants. But it is the reference to female power in conjunction with the Mao era and its "unsuitability" in the post-Mao era that is most pronounced.

Representations of the Duan Lina character, therefore, not only continue to echo the widely held view in the 1980s that women had become too powerful and that this was a phenomenon in need of correction, but also and more importantly make a direct connection between ("unfeminine") women like Duan Lina and their inability to find "happiness" in their marriage and family life. The lack of "femininity" in Duan's case, to summarize, is the "missing link" between a happy marriage and her self, and the underlying assumptions make Duan a lost cause. I will return to the implications of this kind of negative portrayal of women later in the discussion.

Lin Zhu, Kang Weiye's lover, in contrast, is everything that Duan is not. Portrayed as a Westernized Chinese white-collar professional, Lin Zhu is a petty-bourgeois (*xiao zi*) woman who is pretty, Westernized, and capable of being practical and accepting "reality." Her attractiveness to Kang accentuates "youth and beauty" as the key component of "femininity," precisely what Duan does not possess. The portrayal of Lin Zhu also manages to capture the changes in different generations of women's sense of their own identity and of what they imagine is needed—a successful man to depend on—in order to secure "happiness" in life. Both textually and subtextually, tensions between Duan and Lin in the drama mirror the structural logic of a traditional patriarchal society in which different generations of women are pitted against one another in competing for men as guarantors of their happiness. "Femininity," once again, is essential within such logic.

Ironically, the drama also demonstrates that "femininity" does not really lead to the "winner's" happiness. When Lin Zhu succeeds in winning over Kang, the drama does not offer her a "happily-ever-after" ending. Once Lin leaves her job and moves into the house that Kang buys for her, she becomes "a bird in a cage." Everyday, she waits for Kang to come back from work on time, constantly craving his company, constantly failing to have it. Eventually, she becomes fed up and decides to leave Kang.

Between the time when Lin Zhu becomes Kang's mistress and when she disappears from his life, the drama offers three moments when she is directly confronted by Duan. The apparent melodramatic nature of these confrontations points to the tension, contradictions, and silliness manifested in these women's desire to find "happiness" through a man. In fact, in the third "meeting," when Duan Lina bursts into the house Kang has secretly bought for Lin, the latter is already going through a period of loneliness owing to Kang's constant preoccupation with his business and his inability to decide what to do with his marriage. This last confrontation between the two, therefore, though predictably clichéd, is a melodramatic moment making visible the fact that, when the two women fight over this man, neither of them seems to do so based on a conviction that she will find "happiness" in a marriage with him.

The Duan-Lin conflict and its ambivalence and tension indicate that "happiness" is an object in life that women pursue with much confusion. Even though Chi Li's story inevitably reveals her own biases (against the Fulian, for example), her representations manifest her ambivalence toward the mindless pursuits of "happiness" by women. Such pursuits do not allow them to both look out (into the society to understand the social construction of their desires) and look in (to themselves to explore what such pursuits would entail on a psychological level). While older women who grew up during the Mao era are ridiculed for not knowing how to be "feminine" and for being ill-prepared for the changing gender politics in the era of market reforms, younger women of the "new era" are also critically represented for failing to understand the limitation of depending on their "femininity," "youth," and "beauty" as means for finding "happiness." Chi Li's portrayals of these characters are informed by her ambivalence, which is itself a mixture of stereotypes and an unwillingness to fully accept "femininity" as the only path for women to find "love," which in turn leads to their "happiness."

### Lin Xiaofeng in *Divorce Chinese Style*

If Chi Li's representations of women are somewhat stereotypical, Wang Hailing's penetrate the surface of stereotypes into the messier psychological domain of women's desire for "happiness," their inability to face and deal with the rapid changes happening around them, and, especially in *Divorce Chinese Style*, the negative consequences of that inability.[13] More than Chi Li's, dramas based on Wang's stories ask women to look into themselves when they are seeking or believe that they are defending their own "happiness."

*Divorce Chinese Style* was a 2004 hit television serial with twenty-three episodes. Its popularity put the author Wang Hailing back in the spotlight six years after the first drama based on her story *Qian shou* (Holding hands, 1998) became popular. However, unlike *Holding Hands,* which tells a story similar to *Comings and Goings* with the exception that the wife is a much kinder and gentler woman than Duan Lina and in the end becomes determined to leave her marriage, *Divorce Chinese Style* tells the story of a woman, Lin Xiaofeng, whose obsession with wanting her husband to earn more, whose ill-founded suspicion of her husband's supposed extramarital affairs, and whose inability to act "rationally" drive her from the "happy" marriage and family that she wants to keep. Indeed, in this drama, it is Lin's "irrational" behavior that constitutes the major source of the drama. However, instead of using Lin's "irrational behavior" as a form of resistance (as has been suggested by Western feminist studies of melodrama and women), the drama, as we will see, employs it ambivalently.

Lin Xiaofeng and her husband Song Jianping, like many well-educated couples of their generation, met in college and got married afterwards, each working in the job assigned to them. Lin Xiaofeng is a high school teacher and Song a surgeon. They have a son and live in an apartment assigned to Song. Together with their little boy, they have lived a relatively peaceful life, until, of course, the wife wants more. Lin becomes conscious of her desire after she witnesses what happens in the hospital's cafeteria to the former chief of the state-owned hospital where her husband works. The old chief, who is upset that he has to pay the same price for what he tries to buy regardless of size, is mocked by a young migrant worker for being obsessed with prices and, worse, for taking more napkins than others every time he buys his food. The humiliation is too much for the old man's heart, and he dies of a heart attack right in front of Lin and others in the cafeteria. This melodramatic moment functions as a rude awakening for Lin, who concludes that "there is no use being known as an honest person (*mingsheng hao you shenme yong*). These days if you don't have money, nothing matters." Thus, the drama proceeds to unfold how Lin is driven, first, by her desire for a more financially secure and comfortable life provided by her husband and, then, by her sense of insecurity and jealousy (of imagined lovers of her husband's) after he becomes a successful surgeon in a private hospital.

The opening episode dramatizes a sociocultural logic widely accepted in today's China: money is increasingly becoming the only tangible value with which an individual's worth is measured (if you are smart and good, why aren't you rich?). The former head of the hospital is thus assumed to be a "nobody" when he is found buying his meals in the cafeteria and even quarreling over the size of a dish. Narratively, this melodramatic detail is intentional in that it points to a central and cynically accepted "new" value system at work: money is the embodiment of one's social worth and, by extension in Lin's case, what she will connect her personal "happiness" with. The "dollar sign" and its assumed social values, as the rest of Lin's story demonstrates, will function as a major driving force underlying her pursuit of what she believes to be her personal and familial happiness. Thus, from the very beginning, the drama sets Lin on a collision course with her self-interest and sense of well-being: Lin pins her hopes for happiness on the development of her husband's career and decides to resign from her teaching job when her husband's career takes off. She then spends her life trying to make sure that her husband does not "stray." More than one-third of the twenty-three episodes that ensue will be devoted to the battles between Lin and Song as the former becomes increasingly paranoid to the point of, as the many melodramatically rendered events in the drama show, being "hysterical."

There is a major difference between this drama and *Comings and Goings.* Lin Xiaofeng's story is not a typical one in which a male protagonist's affair causes the female counterpart to react "irrationally." Instead, Lin's behavior stems from her inability to understand the changing world at large and her desire that is generated by the changes; as a result, in her own everyday life, she becomes increasingly paranoid and "hysterical." The story focuses on how, while pushing her husband away, she at the same time takes his distance to be evidence of affairs and in turn becomes obsessed with trying to uncover them. The drama, in other words, tells the story of a woman in a vicious cycle of irrational behavior that gradually spins out of control.

It meticulously shows Lin as someone who does not allow interpretations other than her own, and she sees nothing but negative possibilities. To secure future happiness, according to Lin, a woman must fight in the present. And "fight" she does. The list of what she does is long, from assuming a punishing attitude toward her husband whenever he fails (and later refuses) to answer her obsessive phone calls, to following him around secretly and eventually taking pictures of what she believes to be an affair, to physically and psychologically hurting her son to the extent that the child resorts to cutting himself in the hope that it will prevent his parents from fighting, to putting sleeping pills into the wine she prepares for her husband and for the woman she imagines to be his lover, and, last but not least, going to her husband's hospital to denounce him in front of his co-workers and then breaking a window and threatening suicide. The dramatic escalation to this final moment, when she stands on the sill of the broken window with Song kneeling behind her while his subordinates look on, is both striking and ridiculous. It shows how this woman eventually comes unraveled and how that unraveling is both much ado about nothing and self-destructive.

When critics and viewers questioned this negative or "blame the woman" portrayal, Wang Hailing reportedly replied that she wanted women to learn to transcend their limitations and to learn to be responsible for the consequences of their own actions.[14] This expectation is directly written into the drama (although not the novel itself), when, at the end, the female protagonist, Lin Xiaofeng, is given an opportunity to make a speech in which she is shown to have somehow gone through a 180-degree change and is able to offer a self-criticism detailing why her marriage has failed. Lin shows up at the farewell party Song's hospital holds for him before his trip to Tibet (where he will serve for a year as a volunteer doctor) and requests a chance to speak in front of everyone at the party. After relating a fable that advises women to treat their marriages with wisdom, she says, "The more you want to hold on to your love, the more easily you will lose your own self.... Everyone wants to have love and a happy marriage, but love requires an ability to let the one you love also love you back.... When I saw Song Jianping walking around the streets not wanting to go home, I realized that our marriage had failed. Unfortunately, it was too late for me to realize that." Whether or not an irrational individual like Lin, as she is so drastically portrayed, can change into such a rational being overnight, the point of the speech can be understood as an (add-on) message from the producers stipulating the moral lesson of the drama. But what does this moral lesson mean, exactly? I will return to this question.

## Engendered Enlightenment? "Nothing" in the "Mirror" or in the "House"

There are three television dramas based on Wan Fang's stories, all of which have the word *kong* in their titles, *Kong jingzi* (Nothing in the mirror, 2002), *Kong fangzi* (Empty house, 2004), and *Kong xiangzi* (Empty alleyway, 2005). Even though *Kong xiangzi* was made last, it is a story about two young women living through the 1970s and 1980s. Based on a novella by Wan Fang with a different title, its televisual version received the name *Kong xiangzi* mainly because the producers hoped to ride on the success of the other two *kong* dramas. As a result, a loosely combined trilogy based on Wan Fang's stories came into existence. Of these three dramas, the first two are more closely related to my discussion here.

The word *kong* carries with it a Buddhist connotation that refers to an enlightened state of mind capable of recognizing the meaningfulness of "nothingness." *Kong*, therefore, can mean something as specific as a state of "nothingness" after something (or somebody) is gone, but it can also refer to the state of spiritual epiphany (when, for example, one is able to let go of worldly worries, recognizing the dialectic between permanence and impermanence). As such, *kong* embodies a paradox that refers to something simultaneously absent and present. Its Buddhist implications notwithstanding, as a piece of wisdom passed on through lived experiences, *kong*, when positively understood, symbolizes moments of realization when individuals come to accept paradoxes in life and then learn to start anew from there.

When it comes to the dramas in question, the significance of the word *kong* lies in the historical and narrative contexts in which the dramas are produced and received. When *kong* is combined with "mirror," "house," and "alleyway," all of which suggest domesticity, the word carries with it a connotation that questions, in part at least, the social reality and cultural imaginary in which women desire and pursue "happiness." The word *kong* indicates a woman writer's interest, on the one hand, in examining different women's choices in their pursuit of happiness, the various assumptions contained in those choices, and the consequences that result, and, on the other hand, in demonstrating a critical intervention that helps destabilize the seeming seriousness of these pursuits. But more important, I see Wan Fang's dramas as efforts at imagining alternatives for women to find "happiness" in their lives. In this sense, the word *kong* echoes a desire to transcend the confines of "happiness," defined, in this case, by consumer culture. Whether such a desire will lead to alternative ways of being and whether those alternatives are viable socially and politically remains a question, but at least in the case of Wan Fang's dramas, the notion of *kong* centers more on questioning reality than on merely finding a way to escape it.

In *Nothing in the Mirror,* the story follows two sisters, their (different) pursuits of "happiness," and the consequences of their choices. In the room that the two of them share, a mirror is prominently placed, suggesting a symbolic relationship between their sense of self (as women) and what they imagine their happy life to be. At the same time, they each serve as the other's "mirror." Sun Li, the older sister, is the pretty one, but she is also vain. In relation to her, the mirror symbolizes her illusions that, as the story unfolds, lead her to be the one who comes up empty-handed. The younger sister Sun Yan is not as pretty but is much more kind-hearted and down to earth. In relation to the mirror, however, she is someone with less confidence in herself, and she has to go through several rather painful relationships before she returns to a man she did not choose but who is equally kind and down to earth and therefore is the right one for her. Even though the representations of the two sisters appear to follow stereotypes—the pretty one is always self-centered and vain while the plain-looking one is always kind although somewhat lacking of self-confidence—the implication of the nothingness in the mirror complicates the issue.

Symbolically, the "mirror" embodies social and gender meanings based on which these young women (and, by extension, young women in general) relate to one another and to the world. If they are not careful, women can become captives of the "meaning" of the reflection unless they learn to see beyond it. The author does not have the illusion that most women will be able to do that, but at least, with the notion of *kong jingzi,* she is suggesting that a realization may be the first step toward that possibility. Although the two sisters and their differences manifest a familiar bias, the metaphor of the mirror allows a degree of self-reflection on the part of the sisters regarding their search for "happiness." In Sun Yan, especially, one senses a degree of self-awareness because she is more level-headed when it comes to her own desires and to what it means to be happy. In the last episode, Sun Yan has a brief exchange with her second husband, who, like her, is an ordinary worker in a hospital. "Is there still happiness when people grow older?" she asks. "What do you think?" the man asks. "I think so," Sun Yan replies, "for example, right now, when two people are able to share their thoughts and understand each other." As the entire drama ends, a family, all the adults having faced the consequences of their own choices, reunites to celebrate the Chinese New Year. There, we see Sun Yan, who is divorced and remarried to a man with a daughter; her mother, whose husband has just died; Sun Li, who is divorced and whose American boyfriend has just left her; Pan Shulin, who is Sun Yan's second husband and whose first wife also died a few years ago; and Sun Li's son and Pan Shulin's daughter, the two children whom Sun Yan will take care of after her sister leaves. Over the visual image of the happy family and the music comes Sun Yan's voice for the last time:

> Seeing everybody around me, I am feeling very happy. Sun Yan, oh Sun Yan; isn't life quite, quite good? The blue sky is so clean, serene, and bright that it looks just like a mirror. Even though we are unable to see ourselves in this mirror, I know for sure that this mirror captures each one of us and all that happens to us. I really want to tell everyone: let us live well, help each other, and care for one another. Don't you think this would be nice?

In contrast to the desires dramatized in the dramas discussed earlier, through Sun Yan, *Nothing in the Mirror* celebrates a woman who chooses not to follow blindly what the outside world urges her to pursue. At the same time, Sun Yan's choice and voice also reflect a somewhat conservative turn in contemporary China in celebrating a woman who is "pure at heart," willing to sacrifice, and not driven only by self-interest. In this sense, albeit in a less dramatic way, Sun Yan reminds us of Liu Huifang, the female protagonist in *Yearnings* whose character generated much critical response that questioned a woman who remains good and pure despite unkind and unfair treatment.[15]

In *Empty House*, the author follows the structure of *Nothing in the Mirror* by representing two close friends who, though following different paths and at times turning against one another, learn to realize that in the end it is their friendship, as opposed to their homes and the men in their lives, that ultimately helps sustain them. The quest in life for these women is no longer simply to search for a materially desirable man, especially when life has taught them that such a pursuit will end up making them feel *kong*—empty and unfulfilled. In this sense, Wan Fang's stories differ from the previously discussed dramas in that hers give substantial narrative attention to relationships and friendships between women (including between the two sisters in *Nothing in the Mirror*). Even though the melodramatic story lines sometimes overwhelm the significance of this attention, it is nevertheless written into the plot and narrative

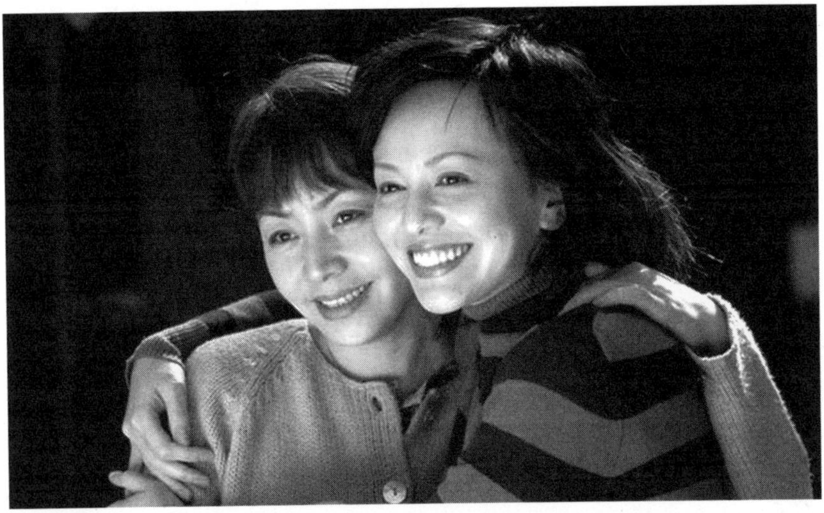

**Figure 5.1.** Ding Yalan and Yang Hongying. *Empty House* (http://image.baidu.com)

structure in such a way that, in the end, especially in *Empty House,* the female protagonists can no longer be pigeonholed according to stereotypes.

Reportedly, after this drama completed its first run, many viewers were disappointed by its supposed lack of drama compared to *Nothing in the Mirror.*[16] It is true that, unlike the latter, this drama does not focus on moments of conflict. When Ding Yalan's husband dies in an accident, for example, the drama does not exploit the tragedy. When Yang Hongying's marriage deteriorates, the decline is represented somberly. Many viewers did not like the touch of sadness both suggested in the title *Kong fangzi* and conveyed in the drama's somber mood. Indeed, even though the absence of a husband is not something to celebrate, the sadness in this story is not a cause for pity. The sadness stems from the women's own realization, as opposed to self-pity, that they must move on and do so on their own and with the help from each other. This harks back to the point made earlier, that *kong* is not necessarily emptiness but the beginning of a different state of mind in which the individual is not burdened with as many illusions as before. For women, especially, such a state of mind has the potential of being more liberating than being bogged down in constant battles in an unhappy marriage and trying to defend what may be an empty promise to begin with, the promise of "happiness."

The irony lies in the author's comments about why she chose to use the idea of an "empty house" to tell the story of these two women. She has been quoted as saying: "The most important things for a woman are love, marriage, and family. . . . A house represents home. . . . Women cannot live without love."[17] Therefore, even though the drama represents women who have lost their husbands through divorce or death but who have learned to become strong in the process of dealing with the aftermath, the author herself nevertheless suggests that this does not make a woman happy and is therefore sad. For the author, then, the house stays "empty" even though the woman still lives in it. So, while the two dramas based on Wan Fang's stories demonstrate a degree of disillusionment with women's mindless pursuit of "happiness," it does not follow that this sense of "emptiness" transcends into an "enlightened" way of thinking. Still, Wan Fang opens the "investigation" of women's pursuit of "happiness" by entertaining the possibility of resistance to the ideology of happiness. An "empty" house may not be desirable for a woman, but Wan Fang's story also suggests that it does not necessarily entail an emptiness of the heart. The drama's focus on the friendship between the two women characters is what makes the representations of the two women appear less clichéd than the characters discussed above.

In these dramas and in the family-marriage subgenre as a whole, in sum, we hear different voices in dialogue with one another in the representations of the relationship between women's desire and the ideology of happiness. While these dramas all share a focus on women's efforts to find and secure "happiness" in love, marriage, and family, some are more critical than others and each perspective reveals a degree of ambivalence that conditions the ways in which their stories are told.

## The Ideology of Happiness and Post-Women's-Liberation Gender Politics Revisited

This ambivalence is key to exploring further the relationship between the ideology of happiness and the gender politics represented in these dramas and, by extension, within the context of rapid social and economic changes in reform-era China. To do so, I would like to refer back to Wang Hailing's response to viewers and to discuss some of the larger implications that exist both within her response and within the dramatic representations discussed above. I will then compare representations of the female protagonists in television drama with those in literature by women writers of the early 1980s. I explore what they share, how they differ, and why revisiting the earlier female voices in light of the more recent ones can help us (1) understand better the shared legacy of the women's liberation movement and (2) recognize how that legacy informs an ambivalence in questioning the mindless pursuit of happiness and in establishing a critical sense of "self."

Wang insists that her critical portrayal of Lin Xiaofeng is meant to help women not to become victims of the blind pursuit taking place in the society at large. I find her point worth exploring. Women like Lin Xiaofeng have socially benefited from the women's liberation movement under the Communist Party—they are "modern" women who receive equal education to men and work at their own jobs—and their "difficulties" do not stem from the historical conditions that existed before women's liberation. And yet today many of them desire to return to a materially "modernized" cocoon in which they expect themselves to be well provided for and well protected by their husbands. Within that context, women's happiness becomes increasingly linked to whom they marry and what their husbands can provide for them. While some Western feminists might support such a possibility in the name of women's choice, in the United States this "choice"-based argument tends to operate on a dichotomy that privileges the "individual" and deemphasizes the social and structural limitations within which women make their choices. The same is true when such a discourse of choice is translated into China without the necessary critical understanding. The privileging of "individual choice" not only turns women's sense of their happiness into a narrowly focused husband-securing mission, but also downplays the importance of developing a structural understanding and critical awareness of the "choice discourse." Such a tendency weakens women's social sense of who they are. In this sense, one cannot but wonder whether "female awareness" (*nüxing yishi*) necessarily equals female "gender consciousness" (*nüxing xingbie yishi*).

Wang Hailing further states that she wants to show that women need to increase their ability to "reason" (*you lixing*). Otherwise, she argues, they will find themselves in a situation similar to that of Lin Xiaofeng in which they sink into a kind of madness that no one except themselves can save them from. "Don't keep saying that you have sacrificed your youth," she says. "It is going to be 'wasted' anyway regardless of whom you marry."[18] While Wang accepts that increasingly there are women who choose to be stay-at-home moms, and her focus in fact orients around a small privileged group of urban women who can afford to make such a "choice," her critical representation of Lin Xiaofeng does not just target this particular social group. Unlike *Comings and Goings*, Wang's drama does not merely stereotype and caricature women. Instead, it relentlessly stays on track to indicate the danger that arises when women fail in their ability to understand others' and their own humanity and instead blindly follow the doctrine of "happiness." Instead of blaming men for women's "unhappiness," therefore, Wang Hailing's drama challenges the public, especially women, with her critical portrayal of Lin Xiaofeng. In a limited way, it managed to generate much-needed (and yet not nearly enough) public debate about what women in the post-women's-liberation era need to do to move beyond the confines of the unreasoned pursuit of happiness and to learn to be reflective as individuals capable of standing on their own.

The drama offers a hopeful note in the last episode by having Lin Xiaofeng deliver a speech that does not quite fit her character up to that point. Although Wang's original story does not end on such a hopeful note, still, one can argue that the narrative as a whole makes a connection between the critical representation of women like Lin and the need for another round of "consciousness raising" in face of a much changed social, cultural, and economic reality. The fact that Wang Hailing herself does not end her story on such a positive note indicates that the author does not believe in a didactic approach and that she remainss uncertain and ambivalent about the ways in which women like Lin Xiaofeng choose their life's path. Wang's critical representation of and her ambivalence toward women like Lin, in this sense, is not that dissimilar from the Chinese Enlightenment discourse in which part of the debate has always been how to turn the "Chinese people" into "rational" individuals capable of handling both freedom and the responsibilities that come with it. But are women writers like Wang Hailing guilty of sharing the project's epistemology in blaming women for being irrational?

Given the rapid social and economic changes taking place in China, where a popular slogan is that for women "it is better to marry well than to do [one's job] well" (*gan de hao buru jia de hao*), criticizing Wang's critical representation of Lin misses an important point. That is, Wang Hailing shares with many other Chinese women writers an effort to represent the struggles women wage in life, while at the same time she explores the structural and ideological implications of what appear to be women's own limitations. It is to women's benefit to learn to understand the social and cultural changes in today's China and to recognize what is at stake for them under such conditions. In this sense, we can say that not only is what unfolds narratively in *Divorce Chinese Style* more about a Chinese style of marriage than about divorce, but also, and more important, we should note that what is "Chinese" about this portrayal of marriage and divorce is more temporal (historically related) than cultural (intrinsically Chinese). In this context we can also say that the most uncondescending way of representing the lives of contemporary (urban) Chinese women is to place them in the midst of major social contradictions and represent their desires, their struggles, and their limitations.

On this note, I would like to turn to some of the women's writings of the early 1980s that also focus on love, marriage, and family but in a different way. This comparison demonstrates the extent to which the ideology of happiness has morphed its way into conditioning women's sense of self and sheds light on the corresponding ambivalence on the part of women writers. But more important, it helps frame a discussion exploring the question of female agency and, perhaps, the development of a critical sense of the ideology of happiness.

While critics have focused on the extent to which women's writings of the early 1980s strongly expressed a desire for "female identity," they have not recognized that women writers of the time did not readily assume that love, marriage, and family life were to be the only places where "female identity" belonged. In writing about women and their inner conflicts, that is, many women writers at the time continued to value women's independence. The social and economic condition of the time produced ambivalence on the part of the writers about how to understand women's desire for "female identity," to be sure, but such ambivalence was not geared toward putting women writers in a position to cede women's social position, identity, and their sense of who they are to the domains of love, marriage, and family.

Zhang Jie's "Love Must Not Be Forgotten" (*Ai, shi buneng wangji de*) (1979) was the first story after the Cultural Revolution to discuss the subject of love and marriage. It was also the first story by a woman writer that reconnected the identity of women back to love and marriage. But reading it again more than three decades later and against the changes in gender politics within the same period and against the difficult transitions portrayed in the dramas discussed above, I find the female voice in this story refreshing because she refuses to give up her identity for love and marriage just because the rest of the society would have her do so. Indeed, Shanshan, the first-person narrator who tells of her mother's tragic experience in love and marriage, rejects Qiao Lin, the young man who fits every social norm of the time, and claims that she would rather remain single if she does not find someone she really loves. Additionally, she also declares that she will not love the way her mother loved by worshiping a man whom she in fact hardly knew. Despite the romantic ideal of a "manly man" that underlies Shanshan's unwillingness to accept Qiao Lin, at least two things remain important for her, namely, her willingness to remain single and to not be pressured into marriage by social norms and her unwillingness to emulate her mother in "worshiping" a man. As a young woman, in other words, Shanshan holds her ground and does not want to connect her entire identity to love, marriage, and family, and she expresses pride in not doing so.

In the early 1980s, Shanshan's voice was not unique. Characters in Zhang Jie's other stories as well as in Zhang Xinxin's, Chen Rong's (Shen Rong's), and Zong Pu's fiction struggle with their identity in relation to love, marriage, and family, but none of them ties herself to this realm. In Zhang Xinxin's "How Did I Miss You?" (*Wo zai na'r cuoguo le ni?*) and "On the Same Horizon" (*Zai tongyi dipingxian shang*), for example, the female protagonists ponder the issue of "female identity" when, in each story, a strong woman comes into contact with a strong man whom she likes but who does not know how to respond to a woman who stands on the same ground and who does not behave in a "feminine" manner.

Such women characters are also found in Zhang Jie's "The Ark" (*Fang zhou*), in which three middle-aged professionally successful women face a challenge from men and younger women who use "femininity" as a weapon against them.

Contrary to the hope expressed at the end of Zhang Jie's story that younger generations of men (and women) will "know better," the history of the last three decades has shown in fact that the challenge and difficulties facing Zhang Jie's female characters were just the beginning of the culture's subsequent "success" in turning "femininity" into a social, economic, and ideological weapon against women. Shortly after the Cultural Revolution, femininity was used as a weapon against strong-minded women, who have long been negatively equated with images of "androgynized" or "masculinized" women of the Mao era, an image that is said to have made women unhappy. It then defined new social roles and a new cultural image for women, channeling women's sense of their "self" into the consumer-culture-defined notion of "happiness."

The literature by the women writers of the early 1980s did not limit female identity and social roles to the designated domains of love, marriage, and family. Those stories often end by questioning men's position and with their affirmation of women's own choice. While these women writers believed that a woman's happiness would be furthered by finding "a good man," they did not operate on the assumption that it depended solely on finding him. With the hindsight of three decades, I suggest that much of this resistance on the part of women writers at the time had to do with their affirmation of the more socially oriented positions that women occupied in the immediate decade after the Cultural Revolution. But this resistance began to erode when the 1980s preoccupation with a return to women's "real" gender identity went from challenging the limitations of the women's liberation promoted by the Communist Party to advocating essentialized gender roles and identities as China quickened its speed in "joining the international track" of globalizing capitalism.

Some of the consequences of this development appear in contemporary television dramas' representations of women's pursuit of happiness and their discontent in relation to love, marriage, and family life. Like their counterparts in women's literature of the 1980s, the contemporary dramas are concerned with the ways in which women stake out their positions in society, but unlike earlier voices, in portraying women's dilemma in their search for "happiness," women writers in the 1990s and beyond face a larger uncertainty regarding how a woman can learn to be strong and independent. Many are reluctant to consciously revisit the issue of women's social roles beyond the dichotomy of "womanly" roles such as lover, sister, daughter, wife, and mother versus not-so-womanly ones, including various kinds of professionals, implicitly reinforcing the appeal of the popular slogan that "it is better for a woman to marry well than to do her job well." Like many other cultural texts, these dramas can leave one feeling ambivalent. On the one hand, some of these writers resort to traditional virtues still operative in contemporary gender politics, keeping "strong women" either out of picture or portraying them as not particularly desirable individuals. On the other hand, they help put the ideology of happiness in question, especially with regard to its impact on women and the ways in which women's sense of self needs to move beyond their increasingly narrowly defined gender roles. In different ways, dramas based on Wang Hailing's and Wan Fang's stories, as discussed above, exemplify efforts in recognizing women's attempts and ability to move beyond the confines of the ideology of happiness.

❑ ❑ ❑

To conclude, while these women writers do not always share with one another the same view of women in relation to rapid social changes, the televisual representations of their stories indicate that, in contemporary China, where the logic of consumer capitalism has come to dominate, *xingfu,* or happiness, has permeated mundane everyday life while manifesting itself in a deeply gendered way. It is deeply gendered because, as part of consumer culture's ideology, it is produced as a "natural" sociocultural domain where women are expected to find themselves—their sense of "self" and of self-worth—and where, as the dramas demonstrate, they are in effect confined by two things, social status and material possessions, both of which are dependent on marriage. The linkage between a woman's happiness and love, marriage, and family is thus realized and also comes to carry with it the logic of consumer capitalism.

Precisely because of such embedded tension, these dramas provide grounds for further discussion and debate. They continue, in the tradition of twentieth-century Chinese literature and culture, to represent the changes that have taken place in women's lives in relation to their historical context and to address a wide range of issues, revealing along the way their own biases, prejudices, and preoccupations. From their writings and the dramas adapted from their stories, we find that, from modern struggles for women's liberation to post-women's-liberation gender politics, the meaning of Chinese women's social positions and their personal identities continues to be contested. The dramas offer insight into the lure of the modern that Chinese women face on an unprecedented global scale in the name of "happiness." It remains to be seen what lies ahead as the lure of the modern continues to be a strong force.

CHAPTER SIX

# Listening to Popular Poetics

## Watching Songs Composed for Television Dramas

❑ ❑ ❑ ❑ ❑

This chapter switches gears to focus on a ubiquitous but little noticed phenomenon: songs—especially their lyrics—composed for television dramas. In an age when poetry reading has become a marginalized activity, popular songs, among them those composed for television dramas, have, for better or for worse, become (popular) poetics of the age.[1] Together with the exponential increase in the production of television dramas in the last three decades, the bulk of songs composed for them has also accumulated into a phenomenon of its own. Some of them have become part of the regular repertoire of popular music, often heard independent of their original dramas.[2] Although they have existed under the radar of critics, as part of television drama and popular culture, their musically conveyed expression nevertheless manifests a range of sentiments, indeed the pathos of the age. As such, they offer another point of entry into understanding contemporary Chinese mainstream culture and the social and ideological implications within it. What is sung and how it is sung, whether the lyrics complement or contradict a particular drama's theme, in what ways they do so, whose voice the lyrics represent, what the music and visual images say about the lyrics, and what some of the recurrent tropes are constitute some of the questions I will explore in the following.

Before addressing these questions in conjunction with specific songs, let me take a step back and offer a brief discussion of what I mean by "popular poetics." Today, a textual definition of "poetics" has to take into consideration the contributions of recent theoretical developments in literary theory and criticism, especially in terms of understanding how and why definitions of "poetics" have now become part of "theory" itself and why they have been expanded beyond the traditional understanding of poetry. Jonathan Culler, conscious of the influence of poststructuralist theory, for example, defines poetics as "linguistic acts of all kinds."[3] Speaking of "acts," Culler points out one aspect of poetics that is especially relevant to my discussion at hand:

> A poem is both a structure made of words (a text) and an event (an act of the poet, an experience of the reader, an event in literary history). For the poem conceived as verbal construction, a major question is the relation between meaning and the non-semantic features of language, such as sound and rhythm. How do the non-semantic features of language work? What effects, conscious and unconscious, do they have? What sorts of interaction between semantic and non-semantic features can be expected?... For the poem as act, a key question has been the relation between the act of the author who writes the poem and that of the speaker or "voice" that speaks there.... In thinking about lyric, it is crucial to *begin* with a distinction between the voice that speaks and the poet who made the poem, thus creating this figure of voice.[4] (emphasis original)

As "act," Culler continues, the "figure of voice" can be both a personal utterance and an extravagant exaggeration. Lyrics, in the latter case, "strive to be an event."[5] If we expand the distinction between semantic and nonsemantic features to include the use of music and image, we can easily recognize popular songs, including those composed for television dramas, in poetic terms.

When it comes to poetics, additionally, we must note that notions such as "figure" and "metaphor" themselves have been reexamined and understood anew, especially, as Culler states, when literary theory has "embraced the paradoxical conclusion that language is fundamentally figurative and that what we call literal language consists of figures whose figurative nature has been forgotten." What this means "is not that there is no distinction between literal and figurative but rather that tropes and figures are fundamental structures of language, not exceptions and distortions."[6] Our everyday—literal—language, in other words, can be made "anew" and thereby reexamined when we try to recover the "forgotten" figurative origins within it. In this sense, in studying lyrics that appear to use "literal" language and, as a result, that are read as "ordinary" or conventional (which in Chinese is referred to as *da bai hua,* a term commonly used to dismiss lyrics in certain kinds of poetry and contemporary popular songs including songs written for television dramas), our reading should become an act that aims at recovering, as it were, the "figurality" that is forgotten and taken to be ordinary. Examining "poetics" in a "popular" sense entails paying attention to what appears to be *da bai hua,* or literal and everyday language, something that is generally assumed to be the defect of songs composed for television dramas.

"Popular poetics" thus defined can be further understood in conjunction with the notion of "social poetics" developed by Michael Herzfeld, who emphasizes (popular) poetics as a social act, stating that "social poetics recognizes that people deploy the debris of the past for all kinds of present purposes" and that "social poetics is about the play through which people try to turn transient advantage into a permanent condition in this socially comprehensive sense. It links the little poetics of everyday interaction with the grand dramas of official pomp and historiography to break down illusions of scale."[7] What is meant by "social poetics" is an approach or a way to understand the dialectics within (and sometimes across different) cultures in ways in which, in Herzfeld's examples, national identities are constantly challenged but nevertheless continue to be evoked and maintained. The fluidity that Herzfeld recognizes in poetic "figure of voice" as social acts echoes the notion of "significance" in the study of poetics, identified by Culler as an act of interpretation that "depends not just on the convention of unity but also on the *convention of significance,*" and where "the rule is that poems, however slight in appearance, are supposed to be about something important, and therefore concrete details should be taken to have general significance. They should be read as the sign... for important feelings or intimation of significance" (emphasis mine).[8]

## Musical Lyrics as a Convention of Significance in Visual Narratives: From Film to Television

Part of the significance in studying the musically conveyed lyrics of songs composed for television drama stems from understanding popular poetics as social acts of meaning making that play with different "conventions of significance." In reading such songs, therefore, we need to take into consideration the relationship between music, imagery, and lyrics as poetic "figures of voice" that help "intimate signification" in visual narratives. Indeed, in addition to being mediated through words and instead of being read aloud, part of the meaning in songs is organized through a melodic convention of significance and interpretation of the lyrics, including the use of different musical instruments and the different ways in which a song is sung and "stitched" or "sutured" together with images.

A related "convention of significance," then, is the way in which music and songs were developed in the history of the making of such visual texts as, first, film and, then, television drama. In filmmaking, whose history is much longer than the making of television drama, the use of music or songs has played an important role in meaning making, and, as such, it has long been blended into filmic narratives. Today, even though filmmakers experiment with films without much or any music (as a way of resisting it as a familiar norm of meaning making), music continues to be a major part of cinematic poetics or filmic composition.

Musically, the impact of filmic songs often exceeds the visual texts themselves. Throughout the history of Chinese cinema, for example, many songs composed for films have become so popular that they continue to be passed on independent of their original films as part of the modern Chinese popular music repertoire.[9] Songs from films made in the 1930s, especially, have contributed to Chinese culture, including the national anthem of the People's Republic of China and other popular musical classics.[10] Films from the Mao era and the early 1980s, additionally, contributed to the development of a musical tradition, combined with Western, Soviet, and Chinese styles of singing. Within this "convention of significance," with its underlying ideology of modernization that today is better than yesterday and tomorrow is going to be better than today, filmic songs are always upbeat and their lyrics grandiose and idealistic. Since the late 1980s, however, the role of music or songs in film has significantly changed along with filmmaking as a cultural practice. Other than such early experimental films as *Yellow Earth* and *Red Sorghum*, the "fifth-generation" directors and their younger counterparts appear to have "purged" songs from most of their films.[11] With the decline of the popular impact of the film industry in China, contemporary Chinese culture has witnessed nearly two decades in which there has been an absence of songs popularized by films (with the exception of the one from *Titanic* and a few from Hong Kong films).[12]

During the same period, television dramas came to replace films as a major cultural outlet for which songs are written and performed, and through which they are heard and spread. Songs composed for television dramas emerged along with the socioeconomic changes that both inform and are informed by changes in cultural production in general and in visual-narrative-related "conventions of significance" in particular. Indeed, in China today, along with the rise in the dominance of television drama as a major popular visual form of storytelling, television dramas have become the only visually featured narratives that have continued to include in their total composition one or two songs.[13] In television drama, early examples of musically rendered popular poetic "acts" or "events" include songs from such Hong Kong dramas as *Huo Yuanjia, Chen Zhen,* and *Old Shanghai,* as well as ones composed for such mainland productions as *Journey to the West, Ji Gong,* and *Yearnings.* The film, *Still Life,* which I discuss in Chapter 1, used music from some of these well-known dramas to enhance a sentiment, indeed a paradoxical sense, of nostalgia and hope (against hope). If we take a closer look at the context in which these early dramas came about and emerged as "cultural events" and also at the ways in which their music is reevoked and employed in a different context as in *Still Life,* we are able to see the extent to which the songs and music composed for these dramas can function sociopoetically to effect additional meanings in face of a new social reality.

In the case of the three Hong Kong dramas, their popular reception on the mainland in the early 1980s had more to do with the timing of their broadcast than their quality as television drama. China in the early 1980s was hungry for anything from outside. That cultural hunger conditioned the development of a "convention of significance" that helped the rapid spread of all kinds of imported cultural products, among them television dramas (and the songs that came along with them).[14] The cultural sentiment of the time (in the immediate aftermath of the Cultural Revolution) was actively "stitched" into the reception of both the visual narratives and the music and lyrics of the songs composed for them in such a way that they continue to be remembered as a cultural event symbolizing an important moment of recent Chinese history. As such, their signification can be reevoked and made anew with additional social and ideological implications when the same songs are heard in a different context and shown from a different perspective.

In the case of *Yearnings*, the first broadcast of this fifty-episode-long narrative in 1990 helped mark the sentiment of another moment of change in contemporary China and did so, among other things, with two songs that have since become popular classics: "Haoren yisheng ping'an" (literally, "a good person deserves a life that is safe and sound"; "Bless Good-Hearted People" hereafter) and "Youyou suiyue" (literally, "those long years that are life"; "Long Ago Years" hereafter). The popularization of the drama became a cultural event, marking the turning point between the decade of the 1980s and that of the 1990s within the reform era. Inevitably, the poetics of these two songs became an event of sorts themselves.

The year 1990, when *Yearnings* first appeared on television, signaled symbolically the end of the 1980s after the turbulent year of 1989. Chinese intellectuals as a whole found themselves at a crossroads from which different groups were to embark on different paths, including some who would join with other forces to stake out a space in popular culture. As mentioned in the Introduction, with the involvement of a group of well-known writers including Zheng Wanlong and Wang Shuo in the creation and production of *Yearnings*, and with this first Chinese fifty-episode "indoor television drama" (*daxing shinei ju*)[15] receiving unprecedented public fanfare and generating considerable controversy, the creation of this drama marked the moment at which many writers and intellectuals were to turn to popular culture for expression.[16] Indeed, it is not far-fetched to suggest that, as a cultural event in which a group of writers joined efforts in creating a television drama, the success of the drama *Yearnings* signaled the end of a phase and the beginning of another within the reform era.[17] On the cultural front, what was ending was the so-called *wenhua re*, or "culture fever," an intellectual movement that attempted to be another round of (modern) Enlightenment. What was beginning was the shifting of writers and intellectuals in their role as "social actors" into dispersed positions, with some entering the domain of popular culture, including the making of visual narratives such as television drama. The sentiment expressed by the two songs in *Yearnings* helped mark such a shift and a turn to popular culture in search of meaning and value.

Sung by two of the best-known singers of the time, Mao Amin and Li Na, the two songs—their lyrics and melody—help set not just the mood of the entire drama but, more important, the poetic tone, indeed a "yearning" sentiment, of its theme. With one song placed at each end of an episode and being repeated in each new episode, these songs, like most television-drama songs, function as a modern version of the commentaries found in traditional theater, storytelling, and vernacular fiction in which the third-person narrator surfaces to offer, through poetic lines, commentaries and expressions of moral inquiry beyond the melodramatic narrative of the story itself. We hear such lines in the song "Bless Good-Hearted People" (roughly translated; the emphasis is mine) as "who will drink with me; in the years that we know each other, wherever we are, close or far away, it is *this feeling* (*ci qing*) that warms human existence";[18] or in the song "Long Ago Years": "throughout life, we search far and low, yearning for a genuine way of being; who can tell me, if I was right or wrong... let us put the past in the past; let us keep the *genuine feelings* (*zhen qing*) and start anew."[19] Together with the musical composition and imagery, these lyrics help bring out the theme of the drama (*dian ti*), indicating that what is being yearned for is *zhen qing*, or true feelings, which in essence means "genuine kindness." This repeatedly expressed yearning for "genuine kindness" thus became a sentimental figurative voice of the time in which *Yearnings* was conceived, produced, and received, marking the beginning of yet another change that was quietly but surely occurring in Chinese society and culture.

Along with this change, popular culture became an arena where struggles for ideas and values take place. The success of *Yearnings* and the two songs composed for it signaled the beginning of a shift in the relationship between intellectuals and "popular culture" and a change in cultural production that would, in turn, effect changes in popular poetic "conventions of significance." Expressed through melodies that were composed to enhance the "yearning" sentiment and were carried nationally first through television and later through radio and other electronic means, independent of the drama itself, these songs were to become part of contemporary Chinese popular and social poetics whose "figure of voice" can be made anew whenever it is reevoked at the "right" moment (as in *Still Life*, for example).

In what follows, I will focus on two major poetic themes—that of "history" and that of a sense of (seemingly sentimental) "longing"—one that recurs mainly in history/emperor dramas and the other, in all of the other subgenres, such as anticorruption, family-marriage, and youth dramas, that I have studied in this book. I will explore the lyrical and musical deployments of poetic conventions, the question of figure of voice, the ways in which these poetic "acts" either reinforce or destabilize conventional meanings, and the ways in which we can understand their implications. After thus discussing each group of the lyrics, I will briefly consider the "suturing" effect of such popular poetics and the ways in which to understand such effects within the larger context of social transformation.

## The Trope of History: Singing a Modern Chinese Ambivalence

One thing that characterizes songs composed for television dramas is that, unlike ordinary pop songs, songs composed for television dramas convey meanings that are simultaneously abstract and specific or detailed. They are part of a specific narrative for which lyrics are supposed to be composed accordingly, and they are abstract in the sense that some kind of general significance is implied. On the surface, especially when it comes to such subgenres as the history drama, songs—lyrics and music—are composed to correspond to the genre. Most of the emperor dramas (of the *zheng shuo,* or serious, type), for example, open to a symphonic orchestra that suggests something grandiose and serious, and they are often accompanied by lyrics that are composed with "history"—or historical sentiment—as their main theme. On a first-impression level, the lyrics, music, and images—the three components of television-drama songs—are all synchronized to set the tone for the drama to come (or to enhance what has just been shown). What they "do," in other words, follows a familiar structure of expectations that habitually associates the meaning of history with what is grandiose, what is magnificent, what is violent, and what is "sublime." They strive, in other words, to be an "event," which, in the case of the best-known emperor dramas, fits their theme. But more interesting in all of this is the fact that the imagery, music, rhythm, and other nonsemantic features complicate the words or lyrics; the "figures of voice," in other words, complicate both semantic and nonsemantic meanings.

In Chapter 2, I identify the television glut in representations of emperors as both a form and an act of "re-collecting," not so much collecting "history" as collecting modern and contemporary imaginaries of "history." When it comes to the songs composed for these dramas, one hears additional "figures of voice" that complicate such acts of re-collecting. To identify these figures of voice, let me first bring in the television drama version of the well-known historical novel *Sanguo yanyi* (Romance of the three kingdoms), a drama that can be considered as an earlier version of what was to become the subgenre of the history/emperor drama (of the "serious" type). Adapted from a well-known and long popularized "history" novel, the television drama version was yet another addition to the versions of this legendary work of literature. Put on the air in 1994, a few years before the onslaught of emperor dramas on television, this eighty-four-episode serial was expensive in terms of production costs and expansive in scale. Part of the extravaganza is the music composed for the drama, which, together with the imagery of fire, battlefields, and legendary figures, sets in motion the drama that tells the stories of well-known historical figures, their personalities, their relationships, and their personal and political skills that are imbued with the contradictory implications regarding heroism that *Romance of the Three Kingdoms* is well known for. In this sense, the adapted drama continues the narrative tradition of the novel, which is more about human relationships and human drama played out in a historically known period than the history of the period itself.

What is interesting, however, is that the song composed for the drama has something to say about (the concept of) "history" itself:

> On and on rolls the Yangtse River, charging eastward
> Like heroes, billows upon billows they contend but
> All fallen in the end: gain or lose, right or wrong
> Everlasting are only the green hills
> Time and again the sun sets lonely in the west
>
> Fishermen and woodsmen still comb the beach, hair grey
> Watching the autumn moon and spring wind
> Life's happiness lies: a wine jar, good company
> Past events still hang on the lips of people present.[20]

"History," as the lines suggest, may be more than stories of the past that people chat about in their leisure time. Like traditional storytellers' opening remarks, these lines tell the viewer not to take the dramas of these characters too seriously; compared with the natural world, human glories come and go.

Juxtaposed in contrast to the "natural world," "human glories" become a metaphor for "(human) history" and are set up in problematic terms as something not to be taken seriously, especially when seen in relation to the natural world. At the same time, given the serious tone of the music and imagery that accompany these words, this contrast reveals what I would call an ironic double figure of speech, which is commonly used as a rhetorical device in poetics; in suggesting that there is no need to take past events seriously, these lyrics in essence are saying precisely the opposite: they are asking in what ways we should take "history" seriously and based on what should we do so.

This ironic double figure of speech, in other words, is a rhetorical marker through which we can explore what these few lines actually say. Ostensibly, by evoking the Yangtze River, the green hills, the autumn moon, and the spring wind, and by juxtaposing the ephemeral nature of human beings' earthly concerns including their heroic deeds with the everlasting cycles of the natural world, these lines evoke a familiar (Chinese?) cultural convention that resorts to a sense of irony by placing human desires against the long view of history. Juxtaposing "nature" and the "human world," the speaker is essentially asking: compared with the natural world that tirelessly continues its cycle, isn't it laughable that humans fail to realize that they are just mere mortals in that world? But if we understand this question as a double figure of speech, its real implications lie elsewhere. To explore this issue further, let me continue with a few additional textual examples drawn from emperor dramas.

The four "serious-type" emperor dramas mentioned in Chapter 2, *Emperor Kangxi, The Yongzheng Court, The Qianlong Court,* and *Emperor Wu of the Han Dynasty,* are all accompanied by one or two songs. In the lyrics, one hears "commentaries" on the meaning of those "pasts" that are at times ironic and at times entirely serious. On the one hand, past glories, no matter how magnificent they once were, are now understood as always destined to end; on the other hand, they are defiantly celebrated even though they appear to have indeed ended up in the "dustbin of history." This double figure of speech with regard to history occurs differently in different emperor dramas, with emphasis falling on one side or the other, indicating the existence of different perspectives in the representation of past emperors. In the last lines of the opening song for *The Qianlong Court,* we hear:

> Endless stretches of wealth
> Suddenly disappear like the setting sun, like the tail end of smoke
> Like a dream are those one hundred years of efforts for prosperity
> In a split of second, it rises and falls.[21]

The sentiment underscores the drama's emphasis on the ways in which a seemingly prosperous time under the reign of Qianlong gradually weakened and the ways in which human weaknesses contributed to the decline of a prosperous age. Whether or not the lines are intended to warn against present pursuits of wealth and glory, this is a historical view not unfamiliar to most Chinese. By supporting the theme of this particular drama, these lyrics echo the lyrical sentiment found in the song for the drama *Romance of the Three Kingdoms,* both emphasizing the ephemeral nature of "human glories" but both also asking the same implied question: in what ways should we take history seriously?

By comparison, the opening song for *The Yongzheng Court* strikes more of a celebratory and defiant tone:

> In judging heroes from the past, success or failure
> Who is to say they are in the know
> Thousands of years of crimes and accomplishments
> Let others judge
> Against all odds you travel alone
> Wanting to leave behind a strong country
> Still, you cannot stop a bad name from being attached to you when
> you are gone.
>
> People say the worst suffering in life is human suffering
> You still have no regrets
> People say those who win over hearts win over earth under heaven
> Let us see who rules over it.[22]

Even though the original Chinese version does not have pronouns such as "you" or "they," some kind of a pronoun is in fact implied. In this translation, I have made the "speaker" an interlocutor speaking directly to the emperor Yongzheng, the subject of this drama. But one might also make the speaker assume the position of "I," in which case the speaker would be the (imagined) voice of the emperor speaking defiantly toward a historical record that has not been particularly kind to him. The changeable or unstable nature of the pronouns in this case is interesting. On the one hand, using "you" or "I" changes the identity of the speaker in the lyrics. But, on the other hand, the different pronouns do not necessarily suggest there is a different "figure of voice" in each speaker. To be sure, with the speaker addressing the emperor as "you," a modern individual is singing about Yongzheng, the emperor, wondering what he might say after more than two hundred years, during which time he has come to be known as a cruel and ruthless ruler. It is a sympathetic voice that echoes the one in the lyrics of the song in *Romance of the Three Kingdoms*—historical judgment is always subject to change, coming and going in cycles beyond the control of mere mortals. With the speaker speaking from the position of "I," the voice becomes a defiant one. Either way, it does not really change the implications of the lyrics. When sung in the Chinese original, neither "you" nor "I" is specified; the "speaker" in effect sings with both of these voices implied. The real signification here lies with the figure of voice. But before I explore the question of figure of voice in these songs, let me bring in one more example, from the 2004 hit *Emperor Wu of the Han Dynasty,* without which my discussion here would not be complete.

The lyrics of its opening song go as follows:

> In the midst of a long rolling river, you are a little drop
> Among the rolling mountains, you are a unique peak
> You hide loneliness in the cracks of dark clouds
> You write dreams on the sky and grassland
> You warm the earth by burning yourself to ashes
> Dancing fires reveal your last innermost feelings.[23]

Unlike the song in *Romance of the Three Kingdoms* in which nature is set up in contrast to the human world, in these lines the "everlasting" nature of the natural world is employed as a metaphor for human history, and, as such, the natural world carries with it a sense of glory, of something sublime. Unlike the ironic sentiment expressed in the two examples given earlier, these lyrics deploy nature to personify a "glorious" past. How do we understand this (albeit subtle) shift in voice with regard to (representations of) China's past? Is there still an ironic double figure of speech at play in these lines? My answer is yes.

Words and terms like "loneliness," "dream," "ashes," and "dancing fires," for example, continue to suggest the ephemeral nature of human glories. Even if they are "written" into history (symbolized by the natural world), from the long point of view of history, such glories are still like "a little drop" in a long rolling river. At the same time, what is powerfully written into history is not so much glory as rather universal human feelings and failures. Hence, "glories" have become part of the dark clouds, sky, and grassland, and, indeed, the "debris of history" accumulated like ashes burned from human desires that are constantly dancing like fires. Here, the ironic double figure of speech has become more complicated, suggesting an ambivalent (more than ironic) point of view toward history.

This ambivalent point of view is not particularly new in relation to modern Chinese history. In fact, it is largely a product of modern Chinese history. As such it can explain why ambivalence abounds in critics' responses to the late twentieth and early twenty-first century emperor-drama craze in general and to the drama *Emperor Wu of the Han Dynasty* in particular. Some view the drama as the latest Chinese display of cultural conservatism and nationalism, while others, as I mentioned in Chapter 2, celebrate the drama for signaling a "new historical consciousness," a consciousness, I suppose, that may not be imbued with as much ambivalence. Most critics outside of China, I dare say, would tend to feel uncomfortable with any kind of display of the glory of past (Chinese) rulers, let alone the elaborate and extravagant displays found in emperor dramas. In this sense, one might suggest that there is something provocative in the phenomenon of emperor dramas that can even generate a moment of cultural intimacy among critics. These critical responses, positive or negative, however, indicate less about "Chinese history" than about historical point of view, or historical consciousness, and its contemporary implications. What is "contemporary" within the Chinese context is the ever-present specter of the "Chinese quest for modernity," by which I, following Marshall Berman's definition, refer to the collection of modern Chinese experiences and all the attempts or efforts at trying to make sense of them.[24]

From the ironic double figure of speech identified earlier to the seemingly earnest tone in this last song, there continues a shared sense of history whose manifestation is ambivalently modern. Manifested in the ambivalence in question are the tensions within this collection of modern experiences and intellectual endeavors in which the notion of history itself and the question of how "historical China" should be understood and how it relates to modern China continue to be contested, both in China and elsewhere. Put differently, what we actually hear in these songs, returning to the ironic double figure of speech described earlier, is yet another moment of intimation of a modern (Chinese) sentiment, an ambivalent one to be exact, that characterizes part of modern Chinese experience.

Even though in the West there is a habitual reflex to dismiss such sentiment as potentially nationalistic and therefore conservative (Western media, for example, tend to discount nationalist sentiment in China by attaching the label of "official" propaganda to it), I would argue that this ambivalence manifests more than a desire for past glories or a desired national identity. It is also a cultural act of negotiation with the dominant "modern" historicist or teleological view of history within which (premodern and modern) "Chinese history" simply has not been able to find a place to sit well.[25] The popular poetics expressed in these lyrics demonstrate, albeit in their limited ways, yet another attempt at presenting history and its understanding in a different light. If anything structurally "Chinese" is reinforced by the poetic act of double figure of speech in these lyrics, it is the ways in which they intimate a nonlinear, circular, and ephemeral sense of history. Indeed, the poetic acts and poetic voices, though realized through familiar conventions of signification (such as evoking tropes of nature, evoking a Daoist sensibility about being resigned to nature's forces, and evoking a sense that the universe is cyclical by nature), nevertheless point the question of modern Chinese experience back to its own historicity. Measured against the linear and teleological view of history, where does the significance of Chinese history lie? Why does it matter? Or, for that matter, does it matter at all?

The lyrics of the songs indicate an uncertainty in relation to these questions. The trope of history figured in these songs continues to manifest uncertainty and ambivalence, once again, not really about history as such but about how history is perceived and evaluated. In this sense, so long as China's path to modernity continues to be littered with this kind of uncertainty, one can expect more such ambivalent singing of "history."

## The Social Poetics of *Shang Gan* (Sentimental Longing) in the Midst of Roaring Economic Development

The lyrics discussed above, when musically rendered in conjunction with images, convey a touch of emotion that is sentimental. In the age of postmodernism, sentimentality has been discredited for its alleged nostalgic psychic orientation that is deemed conservative by nature. Perceived from this perspective, the songs I examine in this section could easily be dismissed as being even more sentimental than the ones discussed above. And yet, although modernist and postmodernist aesthetics have rejected sentimentalism, its persistent presence in popular culture in general and in Chinese television drama in particular is worth noting and still demands explanation. In song after song composed for dramas ranging from anticorruption dramas to family-marriage dramas to youth-drama subgenres, we hear lyrics filled with emotions of longing, hope, or despair and about loss, times past, loneliness, love, and friendship.[26] Depending on the context, such lyrics function, sociopoetically, as cultural expressions that, to be sure, resort to "melodramatic conventions" to question social reality, but, precisely because of that, also help reveal where the social tensions and cultural uncertainties reside from which such sentiments stem, informed by a range of layered cultural and historical legacies. It is with this understanding that I turn to songs from a number of different subgenres that are composed and sung in a range of different styles. Despite their stylistic differences, however, they tend to share what can be identified as a sentimental figure of voice.

Earlier I mentioned the songs in *Yearnings* and identified the sentiment for "genuine feelings" expressed in those songs. Let me pick up where I left off on this point and explore other songs that evoke a similar sentiment. First, from the opening song of *Yingxiong wuhui* (Heroes have no regrets, 1996), an anticorruption and anticrime drama:

> Besides true feelings, what else can I give you?
> Besides kindness, what else do I love you for?
> Besides courage, what else can I leave behind?
> Besides heartache, what else can I forget?

Dreams allow us to choose, again and again
And also make us miss one another, again and again
True feeling keeps us together
Besides having no regrets, what else can we say?[27]

In relation to the drama, this song refers to the failure of a love relationship between the male protagonist and his girlfriend because the latter does not want him to continue to work as a policeman and yet he, after leaving the police force for a while to work in business, decides to return to the force. Their relationship fails, but in these lyrics we hear, again, the yearning for "true feelings" and "genuine kindness" that human beings both long for and are prone to destroy. A relationship that is difficult to realize in real life "poetically" becomes the basis for a sentiment where "true feelings" reside. The times may have changed in that corruption, crimes, and danger abound, but human longings have not changed. "True feelings," however, are never enough in the face of the complexities of the social world. This song reveals a contradictory feeling of wanting to have no regrets for one's choice while feeling helpless in the face of its consequences. What prevents the lyrics from being too sentimental is an insistence on recognizing that which is positive in face of loss, thereby preventing the figure of voice from being dominated by a sense of self-pity.

A second example is the only song composed for *Xingjing bense* (Good cops and bad cops, 1999), another anticorruption and anticrime police drama:

At dawn on my way, nothing can keep me from stepping forward
Kind-hearted people wish me good luck
Dusk falls like a curtain
But I am not lonely
I am willing to suffer even more
I surge forward in wind and rain, looking for the road ahead
I must conquer this darkness; that is why I will not give in
I must conquer this darkness; that is why I must not cry.[28]

In these lines, we hear from someone who is lonely and faces a "dark curtain," but he must conquer both loneliness and darkness regardless. We hear a mixture of despair and courage that, ironically, reminds me of the imagery of history, as described by Walter Benjamin, in which history "flairs up briefly," shedding light on what underlies it (in this case, the mixture of despair and courage).[29] Although narratively this drama focuses on the struggle between a group of "good cops" and their corrupt superior officer, the formers group's eventual triumphant is not expressed in this song. What is revealed, rather, is once again a seemingly sentimental feeling about an individual living in a not so pretty social reality who is still determined to press ahead.

The third example comes from *Yu Guanyin* (Jade goddess of mercy, 2003), a Hai Yan (youth) drama discussed in Chapter 4:

> Please remember what I said on those wintry nights
> Please leave me my hope expressed under the moonlight
> Please let me kiss your name
> Please let me remember your kindness deep in my heart
> I look up at the starry sky
> Calling out to heaven for you to appear.[30]

There is a permanent sadness to the longing expressed in these lyrics because, at the end of the drama, the male protagonist knows that not only will he never be together with the woman he loves, he also will never know where she is and what her life is like. This is the case not because his loved one has died or married someone else but because, after many tragedies, she chooses to become an undercover police officer assuming a different identity. Metaphorically, her change of identity symbolizes an unconventional loss for the young male protagonist, who is yet to come to terms with what his loss means. Once again, the sentiment of longing voiced in the song points to a social reality that is both harsh and unrelenting, and also to psychological challenges individuals have to confront.

In addition to the lyrics, the sentimental feeling in each of these three songs is expressed musically in what is generally referred to as *tongsu yinyue,* or popular music. This musical convention of significance contributes to both the ways these songs convey a sentiment and the ways they are received. Its origin can be traced to the late 1970s and early 1980s when Deng Lijun, a Taiwanese singer, was introduced to China and her songs were popularized there, when Taiwanese "university campus songs" (*Taiwan xiaoyuan gequ*) were all the rage, and when Su Xiaoming, the first Chinese to try to sing in the *tongsu* manner, caused controversy.[31] Each of these constitutes part of the "cultural event" of the development of *tongsu gequ,* or pop songs—both in terms of music and lyrics—in the early post-Mao era. With music thus going "light" and lyrics becoming more vernacular, this cultural event in the early 1980s carried with it a "mind-altering" cultural function and ideological implications.[32] Despite some initial discomfort and resistance on the part of the elite, by the 1990s, the popular style of singing had gone mainstream. All the songs that I have just mentioned and most songs from television dramas are composed in the style of pop music. The speaker in these songs often assumes the position of "I," talking directly to someone, baring his or her heart and revealing emotions with a touch of sentimental longing.

As my interpretations above indicate, the "sentimentality" in these songs is of a contemporary variety. It expresses a sense of longing, to be sure, but there is not a particularly strong indulgence in sentimentalism. Mixed with the longing is hope and a determination to move forward regardless. Past and present, good and bad, darkness and brightness, loneliness and togetherness, kindness and indifference are not necessarily paired in binary oppositions but accepted as things that coexist in life whether one likes it or not. At the same time, there is a strong desire for what is "good," what is "true," and what is "genuine." The feeling behind this is not Pollyannaish but is symptomatic of a society uncertain of its values and struggling to reclaim acceptable ones.

This uncertainty is most interestingly manifested in the song—lyrics and music—composed for *The Police Chief* (2002). I discuss aspects of the drama in Chapter 3, but for the sake of this discussion, let me briefly review the story. Zhong Liuyi, a supposedly highly intelligent criminal who has had a rags-to-riches life experience, vows, as an act of vengeance, to corrupt all officials who may be potentially useful in his future business dealings. When the new police chief arrives in town, Zhong tries his usual scheme but fails. From then on, the two are locked in a struggle until Zhong finally has had too many run-ins with the law and arranges to have himself killed by, of all people, his girlfriend, who is also the daughter of the police chief. She defies her father and first allows herself to be seduced by Zhong and then falls in love with him. The moral ambiguity throughout the story of this drama is expressed in the theme song of the drama as well. Sung by the actor who plays Zhong Liuyi, the lyrics go as follows:

> Is there a past event still worth remembering?
> Memory continues to pierce through my aching heart
> Is there still a past event that I can wave away?
> Silence has taught the lonely you to find excuses to forget
> Are there still friends to trust?
> Wishing time could be reversed so that I could find that first
>     genuine love
> Is there still gentleness I can feel?
> A kind heart I can still trust and a promise worth remembering.
>
> No complaints, no regrets
> True love never changes
> Loyalty is my life's companion

Even if there are dangers ahead and I am lost in a fog
A future hand is holding you
You will continue your endless journey ahead, do not stop
I have nothing else to desire.[33]

This is another example of lyrics in which the speaker expresses a longing for something that exists only in memory. Who is the speaker here? If it is Zhong Liuyi, the sentiment expresses a contrast to his portrayal in the drama. There, he is a ruthless criminal full of hatred and vengeance. But the drama represents him with a twist: it reveals, as part of its plot, why a fine young man ended up being so ruthless and so vengeful. This background information is particularly worth noting for it is related to what is expressed in the song.

Those familiar with contemporary Chinese history know the significance of the resumption of college entrance examinations in 1977 shortly after the end of the Cultural Revolution. Zhong belongs to the first group of young (and not so young) people who passed the examinations and entered college. The drama specifically notes that, unlike most of those people, Zhong is originally from the countryside (as opposed to "sent-down youth," who were originally from cities). Even though much of this information remains in the background of the story, all of it is significant in that it leads to the "life-changing" moment when Zhong is betrayed by his first love, a woman who comes from the family of a high-ranking official. Her family connections help him start out in business. In historical terms, this refers to early liaisons in post-Mao China between power and capital: individuals connected with a level of power enjoyed opportunities to start commercial or business ventures (in the 1980s). In the drama, Zhong becomes part of such a venture thanks to his girlfriend, only to be sacrificed by her kind of people when their illegal business transactions are discovered. Zhong is persuaded to take the blame and is sentenced to jail. After he is released from prison, Zhong strives to become rich so that he can help the poor but also seeks revenge. Thus, we are given moral ambiguity: he helps children in the countryside, on the one hand, and schemes to corrupt as many government officials as possible, on the other. The social implications of this moral ambiguity surface in the lyrics of the song.

Reading the lyrics against this narrative background, we sense something beneath the thin cover of sentimental-sounding longing. That is, the "sentimentality" expressed in this song is socially rather than individually oriented. When we situate what appears to be personal—such as "memory continues to pierce through my aching heart," "silence has taught the lonely you to find excuses to forget," "wishing time could be reversed so that I could find that first genuine love," and "a kind heart that I can still trust and a promise worth remembering"—within the context that I have just described, the figurality of these sentimental-sounding terms becomes less "sentimental" and more critical. What is "remembered," in Zhong Liuyi's case, is not something to be nostalgic about; the figurality of his memory denotes a mixture of past events that is not easily absorbed or easily forgotten.

Such sentiments are repeatedly expressed in songs written for other anticorruption dramas including *Black Money*, *Absolute Power*, and *Red Carnations*. In *Black Money*, for example, the lyrics of the opening song read as if someone is repenting, wishing for life to start over differently and yet knowing that all that has been done will remain part not only of his or her memory but also of his or her reality. In the lyrics, the line "give me one more chance" is repeated six times, followed by "I thought I could" four times. It is not clear which character in the story this song is written for specifically; it could be written for any or all of the characters and, by extension, for all who care to listen.

Mixing regret, longing, and the knowledge that what is done cannot be changed or forgotten, these lines echo the sentiment and criticism that I have identified in all of the songs I have discussed here. Looking at these songs together with other songs in family-marriage and youth dramas in which the longing for love and the regret for lost love are strongly expressed, one cannot but sense that the popular poetics in contemporary China is preoccupied with a sense of loss in the face of a society udergoing rapid change. But the predominant sentiment expressed through the seemingly sentimental longing is, once again, nostalgia juxtaposed with hope.

❑ ❑ ❑

This dialectic of hope constitutes part of the continuing sociocultural search for meaning and values. At the same time, this dialectic—along with the tensions, contradictions, and political implications within it—is symptomatic of the suturing function of the mainstream culture. Sentimental longings are critical of the present, but, depending on how such emotions are rendered, their expressions can at the same time be informed by a sense of helplessness. It is this sense of helplessness that entails an implicit acceptance of the reality that can be manipulated by different social and ideological forces. For further understanding of televisual songs and their poetic and ideological implications, more remains to be watched, listened to, debated, and examined. Stay tuned.

# Epilogue

## Intellectuals, Mainstream Culture, and Social Transformation

❑ ❑ ❑ ❑ ❑

In arguing in my Introduction for the need to focus on mainstream Chinese culture, I contended that mainstream culture is where discursive or ideological struggles take place. The previous chapters demonstrate more specifically what I mean in saying that various cultural and historical legacies inform such types of cultural production as the television drama and its representational mode. In television drama, different ideological positions and perspectives coexist, manifested, melodramatically, via representations of different ideas and competing values in response to social change and the tensions and problems that follow. This characteristic is shared by subgenres I am unable to include in this book, but it is to be hoped that further studies will continue to explore the complexity and implications demonstrated in those genres.

I would like to conclude by highlighting a theme that implicitly runs through this book, namely, the changing relationship between mainstream culture and the role of intellectuals in the postrevolutionary socioeconomic transformation in contemporary China. Future studies of Chinese mainstream (popular) culture need to take into consideration the formation and development of, for a lack of a better word, a "cultural ecosystem" in the last three decades in China with four major forces or groups dominating meaning production, namely, *guan, mei, chan, xue,* or officials, the media, industry, and the academy.[1] It is no longer accurate to assume a monolithic entity called "Chinese intellectuals" independent of these forces when the cultural production of meaning has become multifaceted and tension-filled. Nor is it accurate to apply ready-made labels to voices from within these forces without fully understanding their contextual, dialogic, and ideological implications.

Indeed, to reiterate, since the early 1990s, the role of Chinese intellectuals has become more diverse and complex than before. In the 1980s intellectuals appeared collectively to share an oppositional position vis-à-vis the "state," a position that was largely informed by a readiness to say good-bye to revolution (*gaobie geming*) and an impatience for China to pursue (what turned out to be an American style of) "modernization." The irony within this "oppositional" stance was that when it came to the desire for modernization, intellectuals were in fact not so oppositional after all. The majority shared with the reformers in power a developmentalist (*fazhan zhuyi*) oriented modernization imaginary and contributed to a delegitimization of the revolution led by the Chinese Communist Party by associating it with "traditional culture" (*chuantong wenhua*), which, as indicated in the famous television essay serial *He shang* (River elegy, 1987), was represented as being responsible for China's being *luo hou*, or lagging behind in "modernization."[2] More than two decades later, this frame of argument has been proven historically unsophisticated. The social, environmental, cultural, and human costs of rapid economic development and the much increased polarization between the rich and the poor have compelled a new understanding of "development" and "modernization" and generated heated debates among intellectuals themselves.[3]

Indeed, around the year 2000, when I began to pay attention to the phenomenon of television drama as a dominant form of storytelling in contemporary China, the turn of the century had already witnessed debate, among intellectuals in China regarding different assessments of the economic/market reforms, legacies of Chinese socialism and the communist revolution, and the ideological positions that inform the different assessments. These new debates, as I have noted in the book, are manifested in television dramas when writer/critic/scholar intellectuals engage with this major form of storytelling, either in creative or in critical terms. Such participation (and its lack) is itself part of the yet to be fully explored story of the changed and changing relationships between mainstream culture and intellectuals and between the power structure and its critics, and of the discursive struggles among the increasingly divergent groups of intellectuals and the cultural elite in China.[4]

On one level, if, to echo Yin Hong, there is an "accomplice," or *gong mou*, relationship between the state and the market, the interests of the aforementioned power groups are deeply entangled. By identifying these four groups as "accomplices" I do not suggest that this is a phenomenon particular to China. It may well have been the structural and cultural consequences of China joining the "tracks" of globalizing capitalism and adopting its cultural logic that resulted in the formation of a new cultural elite whose positions and perspectives both inform and are informed by the socioeconomic structural changes and by their shared "modernization" imaginary emphasizing mainly wealth and power. The development of contemporary Chinese "mainstream culture" is closely related to such reformation within the larger structural and cultural logic of global capitalism. Recognizing that Chinese intellectuals' positions are implicated is an honest assessment and a first step toward recognizing different kinds of entanglements with globalizing capitalist power in China's postrevolutionary reform era.

On another level, against the backdrop of the rapidly changing socioeconomic system in the name of market reform and the corresponding reformation of the cultural system, the formerly (in the 1980s) shared "oppositional" stance by intellectuals rapidly became transformed into different and even conflicting responses to the "new" social, economic, and political circumstances. Various articulations of these different perspectives constitute genuine ideological struggles among different worldviews both in response to and as part of the changing cultural system in contemporary China. As a result, the relationship between mainstream culture and intellectuals, as I have tried to indicate in this book, is itself troubled, layered, tension-filled, and carries multiple implications.

China's cultural and historical legacies and the social and economic problems that the developmentalist pursuit of modernization has created have generated and will continue to generate serious debates about the direction of China's economic reform, the Chinese "modernity" imaginary, and the role of intellectuals in such ideological struggles. These debates are not only symptomatic of ideological tensions both within and among the aforementioned four groups, but are also part and parcel of the "cultural ecosystem" in today's China.[5]

The fact that intellectuals are themselves deeply entangled with the existing cultural system in China will continue to manifest itself in the ongoing debates about different intellectual perspectives and positions and about the nature of China's economic reform and China's path to modernization. Such debates will also continue to influence mainstream (popular) cultural production of meaning. It remains to be seen in what ways Chinese intellectuals' role in meaning production will affect the discursive struggles to imagine a society that is not dominated by the logic of globalizing capitalist culture and a society that dares to imagine a different path to social equality and justice.

# Notes

## Introduction

1. *Kewang* was well received among the population when it appeared around 1990 and 1991. It was hailed as the first Chinese *shinei ju* (literally, "indoor drama," which refers to the way in which the drama was shot). The popularity of the drama also generated critical attention. In English writings alone, critical responses include Jianying Zha, "Yearnings"; Lisa Rofel "*Yearnings:* Televisual Love and Melodramatic Politics in China"; and Wu Di and Lisa Pola, eds., *Class and Gender Debates over the Television Soap Opera "Aspirations."* After *Yearnings,* dramas such as *Beijingren zai Niuyue* (A Beijinger in New York, 1993), *Yangniu zai Beijing* (Foreign babes in Beijing, 1995), *Yongzheng Wangchao* (The Yongzheng court, 1998), and *Zouxiang gonghe* (Marching toward the republic, 2004) have generated critical attention outside of China. See for example, Sheldon Lu, "Soap Opera in China: The Transnational Politics of Visuality, Sexuality, and Masculinity"; Lydia Liu, "*Beijing Sojourners in New York:* Postcolonialism and the Question of Ideology"; Xueping Zhong, "Multiple Readings and Personal Reconfigurations against the 'Nationalist Grain'" (an essay partially about *A Beijinger in New York*); and Ying Zhu, "*Yongzheng Dynasty* and Chinese Primetime Televsion Drama." In China, much more critical attention has been given to television drama, be it individual hits or various "new" trends. I will describe some of the major responses when discussing specific subgenres and dramas.

2. There have been sporadic publications on Chinese media and television in the last two decades, but not until very recently have there been book-length publications on the phenomenon of television drama. Most of them are studies by media studies scholars. See James Lull, *China Turned On: Television, Reform, and Resistence;* Mike Chinoy, *China Live: People Power and the Television Revolution;* Michael Curtin, *Playing to the World's Biggest Audience;* Ying Zhu, *Television in Post-Reform China: Serial Dramas, Confucian Leadership and the Global Television Market;* Ying Zhu, Michael Keane, and Ruoyun Bai, eds., *TV Drama in China*; and Ying Zhu and Chris Berry, eds., *TV China.*

3. Examples of other English writings on Chinese television drama include Y. Chen and X. Hao, "Conflict Resolution in Love Triangles: Perspectives Offered by Chinese TV Dramas"; Kathleen Erwin, "White Women, Male Desires: A Televisual Fantasy of the Transnational Family"; Michael Keane, "By the Way, FUCK YOU! Feng Xiaogang's Disturbing Television Dramas"; Michael Keane, "Television Drama in China: Engineering

Souls for the Market"; Xiaokang Sun, "A Chinese in the New World: Television Dramas, Global Cities and Travels to Modernity"; and Haiyan Lee, "Nannies for Foreigners: The Enchantment of Chinese Womanhood in the Age of Millennial Capitalism."

4. For a discussion of "codes," see, for example, Robert Allen, "On Reading Soaps."

5. It was not until I had completed the first drafts of this manuscript that most of the publications mentioned in note 2 on Chinese television drama came out. My book treats television drama as a complex cultural form within the larger contexts of both contemporary and modern Chinese history.

6. Wang Hui, *China's New Order: Society, Politics, and Economy in Transition.*

7. Haiping Yan, *Chinese Women Writers and the Feminist Imagination, 1905–1948.*

8. Recent articles on individual dramas have analyzed and interpreted layers of complex social, cultural, and ideological meanings and contradictions. See notes 2 and 3.

9. It is important to acknowledge here that postmodern theories, developed in the postindustrial West, have made the questioning of the high-low cultural hierarchy possible. The study of ethnography and of "everyday life" informed by cultural anthropology has offered a significant contribution to scholarly recognition of the importance in understanding "mainstream popular culture."

10. Slavoj Zizek, "Introduction," in *Mapping Ideology;* Carla Freccero, "Chapter One," *Popular Culture: An Introduction.*

11. Some Chinese critics are beginning to argue that this tendency is indicative of tensions in the West in which cultural struggles between nobility and the bourgeoisie continue, with the latter overtaking the former in power position while also inheriting the former's hierarchical sense of culture. See, for example, Cheng Wei, *Zhongchan jieji de haizimen* (Children of middle class); Wang Xiaoyu, "Yichang wenhua de guangrong geming" (A glorious revolution of culture).

12. Freccero, "Chapter One," 4–5.

13. Zizek, *Mapping Ideology,* 9.

14. Ibid., 9.

15. See Cheng Wei, *Zhongchan jieji de haizimen,* and Wang Xiaoyu, "Yichang wenhua de guangrong geming."

16. I must emphasize that I do not mean there has been no scholarly attention paid to mainstream popular culture. What I refer to is the tenacious tendency, or discomfort, on the part of scholars in the humanities when it comes to mainstream popular cultural texts.

17. On the one hand, the dominant class' ideology is transmitted via a populist-appearing trajectory thanks to the commercialization of the technology-aided mass media. What appears to be populist, at the same time, is in actuality hegemonic, controlled, and manipulated via commercialized mass media governed by the interests of capital. Mainstream (popular) culture, in other words, is simultaneously populist appearing and yet hegemonic. On the other hand, starting from the early twentieth century, the various avant-garde—modernist—arts and literature emerged as resisting forces against the rising power of mass-produced popular media and their representations, only to be canonized later back into the mainstream (elite) culture. Thus the formation of "mainstream popular culture" in the West has itself always been full of tensions and contradictions.

18. In Bauman's discussion, he does not seem to be concerned with the "teloes" of cultural structure and praxis. Zygmunt Bauman, *Culture as Praxis.*

19. I quote Williams extensively here not only because he is one of few major cultural theorists in the West who ventured into discussions of television and television drama and offered valuable observations, but also because of his interest in understanding the structural implications of this cultural form.

20. Raymond Williams, *Television: Technology and Cultural Form,* 50.

21. Ibid., 50.

22. Ibid., 53.

23. Ibid., 50.

24. Ibid., 53.

25. Ibid., 53.

26. Exceptions include media-study scholars and media critics such as Bill Moyers, whose program can be seen on PBS.

27. Numerous discussions of television culture (including television drama) have been published in China. So far, however, most remain in the form of short critical reviews or essays in which critics offer shorthand commentaries on either a phenomenon or a popular drama. In recent years, some scholars in the field of communication and media studies have approached the study of television culture from perspectives informed by Western communications and cultural studies.

28. Ruoyun Bai, "Media Commercialization, Entertainment, and the Party-State: The Political Economy of Contemporary Chinese Television Culture."

29. Ibid., 4.

30. Ibid., 14.

31. I notice a change in Bai's view in her recently published article "'Clean Officials,' Emotional Moral Community, and Anti-Corruption Television Dramas." There she notes the role of writers in television drama production in China. At the same time, however, the state-market dichotomy remains a dominant view in her discussion. See Ruoyun Bai, "'Clean Officials,' Emotional Moral Community, and Anti-Corruption Television Dramas."

32. Yin Hong, "Chongtu yu gongmou—lun zhongguo dianshiju de wenhua celüe" (Conflicts and collaborations: on the cultural strategies of Chinese television drama). The English version is Yin Hong, "Meaning, Production, Consumption: The History and Reality of Television Drama in China."

33. Ibid., 8.

34. Jing Wang, "Introduction."

35. Jing Wang, ed., *Locating China,* 28.

36. Wang Hui, "Depoliticized Politics: From East to West."

37. *Fazhan shi ying daoli* is a famous slogan attributed to Deng Xiaoping, allegedly made during his famous *nan xun,* or tour of the south, in 1992 against the backdrop of the fallout of the 1989 Tiananmen Square Incident and its political aftermath. On both concrete and symbolic levels, this slogan became the motto for the subsequent economic "takeoff," as the Communist Party–led state embarked on a "development" oriented market reform while leaving political reform on the sidelines.

38. Lin Chun, *The Transformation of Chinese Socialism.*

39. Wang Hui, *China's New Order.*

40. Though intellectual debates in China in the last decades have been simplistically labeled as being between the "new left" and "liberals," a fuller understanding of the issues debated requires us to look beyond mere labels. See the discussion in Chaohua Wang, ed., *One China, Many Paths;* Wang Ban's review of *One China, Many Paths,* in *Modern Chinese Literature and Culture;* Mark Leonard, "China's New Intellegentsia"; Qin Hui, "Dividing the Big Family Assets"; Xudong Zhang, *Whither China?;* and Wang Hui "Depoliticized Politics."

41. *Zhongguo dianshi hongpishu, 2001* (The red book of Chinese television, 2001), 161.

42. Ibid., 175.

43. *People's Daily* (overseas edition), December 23, 2002, 8.

44. *Zhongguo dianshi hongbishu,* 181.

45. Because of the lack of television sets, access to television broadcasting was a privilege in China throughout the 1960s. Television remained a highly limited medium through the end of the 1970s. Starting from the early 1980s, as possession of a television set became a popular "obsession," content production including commercials for television was poised to become a major cultural industry.

46. *Zhongguo dianshi hongpishu,* 162.

47. Ibid., 179.

48. Lu Di, ed., *Jiexi zhongguo mingying dianshi* (Analyzing China's private television industry).

49. *Zhibo fenli* (separation of production and broadcasting) refers to television stations no longer being the only content producers (as most used to be). The practice of "separation" began in the 1990s in China, although media critics in China today continue to debate what it means, how it has been practiced, and what problems it has caused. See Li Peng, "Guanyu zhibo fenli" (About *zhibo fenli*).

50. In the late 1970s and early 1980s when television industry was being jump-started, television stations in China were organized into a four-level structure: national (CCTV), provincial (including Beijing and Shanghai), city, and county. That structure, known as *siji ban dianshi,* or, roughly, four-level governments making television, was set up mainly to expand coverage. Stations at the lowest level have functioned mainly as transmitting stations and rarely make programs of their own except perhaps local news. From the early 1990s, there have been increasing calls to restructure the system, and the result has been a variety of new structural models such as the so-called Beijing, Shanghai, and Hunan models.

51. Lu Di, ed., *Jiexi Zhongguo mingying dianshi,* 5.

52. For further understanding of how private production companies work and do not work, see *Jiexi Zhongguo mingying dianshi.*

53. The notion *zhuxuan lü* is said to have been coined by photographer Song Haiyan in 1987. Shortly after that, debates followed concerning the notions of *zhuxuan lü* and *duoyuanhua* (multiple-ism). It was not until 1994, when Jiang Zemin, the then secretary-general of the Chinese Communist Party, put forward the notion *hongyang zhuxuan lü, tichang duoyuan hua* (literally, "to expand the main melody and promote diverse subject matter") at the one hundredth anniversary of the birth of Mei Lanfang (http://blog.sina.com.cn/S/blog-4cc721ef01000anj.html).

54. The notion of *wenyi wei gongnongbing fuwu* originated in Mao Zedong's "Talks at the Yan'an Forum on Art and Literature" in 1942.

55. Li Zehou and Liu Zaifu, *Gaobie geming: huiwang ershi shiji zhongguo* (Farewell to revolution: a retrospective on twentieth-century China). The notion of "farewell to revolution" had circulated before the publication of Li and Liu's book. There have been periodic debates on the notion ever since. See Jianmei Liu, "Farewell or Remember Revolution?" 193–209; Jianmei Liu, "Conclusion," 210–216.

56. There have been continuing criticisms leveled at the realist tradition in Chinese literature. My discussion here is fully aware of the existing arguments.

57. *Hexie shehui,* or (build a) harmonious society, is a slogan created, promoted, and upheld by the Hu Jintao and Wen Jiabao leadership when it came into power in 2002. For more information on this leadership, see John Wong and Lai Hongyi, eds., *China into the Hu-Wen Era: Policy Initiatives and Challenges;* Sujian Guo and Baogang Guo, eds., *China in Search of a Harmonious Society.*

58. Since the rise of television drama as a major cultural phenomenon, there has been constant state censorship to curb the popularity of certain subgenres. Attempts at curbing the popularity of anticorruption dramas and police-crime dramas and decisions to remove imported dramas from prime-time slots are examples of the tensions between the official controllers of cultural production and those who produce cultural texts. The constant censoring acts on the part of the official cultural authorities at the same time indicate that there have been constant attempts, either driven by the market or caused by a mixture of factors, at breaking official controls, rules, and boundaries in the making of television drama.

59. There is often tension among certain groups of practitioners—writers, directors, and actors—whose artistic sense continues to be oriented to still-prevalent hierarchy-oriented value judgments. Ambivalence toward popular culture continues to be shared by scholars in certain circles of academia.

60. After I wrote this, I noticed the similar point made by Jing Wang using the phrase *deng xia hei.* She ends her introduction to *Locating China* with some cautionary remarks: "I would caution us against treating all organized and planned spaces in contemporary China as devoid of transformative potentials. This is not just a theoretical issue. In real life, Chinese have a saying 'The most invisible place is the spot right underneath a light.'" *Locating China,* 28.

61. In the 1980s, television dramas that were adapted from well-known contemporary authors' works, including *Jinye you baofengxue* (Upcoming storm tonight, 1985) by Liang Xiaosheng and *Cuotuo suiyue* (Times idled away, 1983) by Ke Yunlu. Throughout the 1990s and into the twenty-first century, writers whose names are closely (and controversially) related with television drama include Chi Li, Wang Hailing, Wan Fang, Lu Tianming, Zhang Chenggong, Zhou Meisen, Zhang Ping, and Hai Yan. To a lesser extent, well-known writers such as Zhang Kangkang, Tie Ning, Ah Lai, Wei Ren, and others have also seen their works adapted to television drama.

62. There have been periodic discussions in China about the role of writers in television drama. See, for example, Xie Xizhang, "Dianshiju 'Zhang Damin de xingfu shenghuo'de wenhua pingxi" (A cultural analysis of the television drama *Zhang Damin's Happy Life*); Du Qingchun, "Zouxiang wenhua shengchan de jingdian wenben zai

shengchan" (The popular cultural industry's reproduction of classics); Zhang Yi, "Shashibiya hua yu dianshiju jingping" (Shakespeare-ization and good television drama); and Shu Jinyu, "Remen dianshiju: ming zuojia men bu maizhang" (Television drama as big hits: famous writers' cool responses). The writer of the last piece reports that, despite their expressed contempt toward television drama, writers like Chi Li, Wang Shuo, and Liang Xiaosheng, have all directly or indirectly participated in television production.

63. The perennial debates on "realism" in the Chinese context are indicative of academic critics' anxiety over the impact of "mainstream" culture and its alleged conservative ideological tendency.

64. Examples of the consideration of television as an art form can be found in articles and books published in the 1980s and 1990s in China. They include such magazines as *Zhongguo dianshi* (Chinese television), *Dianshi yishu* (Television art), *Yingshi yishu* (Art of film and television), *Dangdai dianshi* (Contemporary television), and *Dianshiju* (Television drama), and such books as Song Jialing, *Dianshiju yishu lun* (Theory of the art of television drama); Yang Tiancun, *Dianshiju chuangzuo lun* (On creating television drama); Lu Haibo, *Dianshiju meixue* (Aesthetics of television drama); Zeng Qingrui and Lu Rong, *Zhongguo dianshiju de shenmei yishu* (The aesthetics of Chinese television drama); Zhong Yibing, *Zhongguo dianshi yishu fazhanshi* (History of Chinese television art); Wu Suling, *Zhongguo dianshiju fazhan shigang* (A historical outline of Chinese television drama); and Xu Hong, *Dianshiju shenmei tezheng tansuo* (An exploration of the aesthetics of television drama).

65. Examples include such premodern classics made into television dramas as *Honglou meng* (Dream of the red chamber, 1987) and *Xiyou ji* (Journey to the west, 1986) as well as modern classics such as *Sishi tongtang* (Four generations under one roof, 1985; original novel by Lao She).

66. Like the movie-related magazines of the 1920s and 1930s, contemporary television-related magazines must be recognized as a major component of television as a cultural industry and cultural form. By "television guilds" I refer to organizations that call themselves *dianshi yishujia xiehui* or *dianying dianshi gongzuozhe xiehui* (association of television artists or association of television and film professionals). Some of the major television magazines are sponsored by one such association but funded by a particular television station. In fact, most of these magazines are published by a television station. This has to do in part with the control of publication in China, where no business can form an independent publishing house without being attached to a state-owned or state-sponsored publishing entity—hence the collaborations between "associations" and television stations. Even with such controls in place, there are at least fifty-odd television-related magazines, ranging from magazines purely for entertainment to somewhat scholarly ones.

67. Imported dramas from the United States, Mexico, Brazil, Japan, and Hong Kong were among the first seen on television that aimed mainly to entertain. For discussion of imported foreign television dramas in the 1980s, see Junhao Hong, *The Internationalization of Television in China: The Evolution of Ideology, Society, and Media since the Reform;* Junhao Hong, "China's TV Program Import 1958–1988: Towards the Internationalization of Television?"; and Junhao Hong, "Penetration and Interaction of Mass Media between Taiwan, Hong Kong and the Mainland China: Trends and Implications."

68. Generally speaking, a series refers to a collection of episodes whose stories begin and end within one episode; only the characters and their professions remain the same. A serial, in contrast, is a collection of episodes with a developing central story. Raymond Williams gives a clear definition in his discussion of television drama in *Television: Technology and Cultural Form*," 54.

69. By the end of 2002, in major cities in China, through cable and depending on which city one is in, a household can have access to twenty-five to forty channels, including the eleven specialized channels from the CCTV, several channels from local and provincial stations, and many more satellite channels from other provinces. Since then, the number of the channels on CCTV alone has increased to sixteen. In some regions, many households now receive more than fifty channels on average.

70. Since television programming in China is not divided by "seasons" as it is in the United States, showing television dramas is a yearlong business, punctuated by what are deemed to be important anniversaries, which in turn are followed by dramas with related subject or themes. The restructuring of television stations in recent years has created additional time slots to be filled, and many are being filled with none other than television drama, either new shows or reruns. On CCTV alone, at least four of its sixteen specialized channels show television drama daily with Channel 1 (Zhongyang Yitai) and Channel 8 (Dianshiju Pingdao) having the privilege of the first run of a new show in prime time (6:00–10:00 p.m.). The other two channels show reruns outside prime time, with a few additional channels also including drama in their programming. In any given location, many households have access to dozens of local and satellite channels in addition to CCTV that also show television dramas. Pirated copies of hit shows or shows that promise to be popular are readily available on various street corners in cities where small-time vendors of pirated DVDs and VCDs lurk. Though according to surveys many—particularly students and young and middle-aged professionals—do not bother to watch most of the television dramas, television dramas are still the second most watched type of program in China (next to television news and "news magazines"), and surpass film as the major source of visual dramas.

71. Zhong Chenxiang, "2000 nian Zhongguo dianshiju chuangzuo gaikuang" (A brief summary of Chinese TV drama and its creation in 2000), 13.

72. This piece of information came from some of the people—script writers, directors, and producers—I interviewed in Beijing in 2003 and 2004. It is difficult to find an official figure, and most likely there is none, for not only do companies come and go, but there is no official entity that keeps count.

73. According to those I interviewed, one of the fears in producing a television drama is that a finished product may never be broadcast even if it is purchased by television stations. This happens all the time, often for unpredictable reasons, some political, some commercial, and some simply whimsical.

74. A few studies make direct reference to "melodrama" in the contemporary Chinese cultural context. See, for example, Yuejin Wang, "Melodrama as Historical Understanding: The Making and Unmaking of Communist History," and Lisa Rofel's "*Yearnings:* Televisual Love and Melodramatic Politics." My study resembles these discussions in recognizing the complexity of "melodrama" but argues for a more focused understanding of melodrama as a narrative mode.

75. For fuller discussions on "melodrama and modernity," see Ben Singer, *Melodrama and Modernity: Early Sensational Cinema and Its Contexts.*

76. Given the limited scope of this book, I am unable to explore the relationship between Chinese melodrama and Chinese modernity, but the issue remains a viable one for future investigation.

77. Peter Brooks, *The Melodramatic Imagination: Balzac, Henry James, Melodrama, and the Mode of Excess.* For additional discussions on melodrama, see Christopher Prendergast, *Balzac: Fiction and Melodrama;* Daniel Gerould and Jeanine Parisier Plottel, eds., *Melodrama;* Jacky Bratton, Jim Cook, and Christine Gledhill, eds., *Melodrama: Stage Picture Screen;* Michael Hays and Anastasia Nikolopoulou, eds., *Melodrama: The Cultural Emergence of a Genre;* Ben Singer, *Melodrama and Modernity: Early Sensational Cinema and Its Contexts;* and Hon Mercer and Martin Shingler, *Melodrama: Genre, Style, Sensibility.*

78. Peter Brooks, "Preface to the Original Edition," in *The Melodramatic Imagination,* xvii.

79. Ben Singer, *Melodrama and Modernity,* 131.

80. Ibid., 37–47.

81. Roland Barthes, "Rhetoric of the Image," 37.

82. Ibid., 38–39.

83. Ibid., 51.

84. I do not mean to say, however, that there has been no experimentation with the visual. Li Shaohong, a female director of both film and television, has produced two television dramas, *Daming gongci* (Palace of desire, 1999) and *Juzi hongle* (As tangerines turn red, 2002), in which she has experimented with such visual elements as costumes, the use of color, makeup, and other components of the mise-en-scène. Such experimentation, however, is rare.

85. For the earliest mentions of *zhuxuan lü* in China, see Ai Zhisheng, "Jinyibu duanzheng chuangzuo fangxiang, fanrong dianshiju yishu" (Continue to follow the correct direction in flourishing the art of television drama); Chen Zhiang, "'Zhuxuan lü' yijie" (One interpretation of "main melody"); and Liu Xiliang, "Hongyang zhuxuan lü, tichang duoyang hua" (Promote main melody and encourage variation). For an early discussion in English of "main melody," see Claire Conceison, "The Main Melody Campaign in Chinese Spoken Drama."

86. Almost every Chinese article or book I have seen that names and lists television drama subgenres names them differently. While some list "history drama" (*lishi ju*), costume drama (*gu zhuang ju*), martial arts drama (*wuxia ju*), and emperor drama (*huangdi ju*) separately, for example, others list all of them under either the rubric of *guzhuang ju* or *lishi ju.* Depending on the focus of a critical piece, some would disdainfully identify all dramas set in the Qing dynasty as *bianzi ju,* or pigtail dramas (in reference to the Qing male hairstyle). Some critics list *hunyin jiating ju* (family-marriage drama) and *shenghuo ju* (everyday-life drama) separately; others further separate *nüxing wenti* (women's problem) dramas, depending on how a story is organized. Some dramas are grouped under *jingfei jun/pian* (cop drama), and others are not because they devote their narrative focus mainly to the inner workings of different levels of officialdom, thereby exposing various types of (relatively) higher-level corruption. Last but not least,

while dramas about the former Communist Party leaders or military "heroes" from the various phases of the Communist revolution (known as *hongse jingdian,* or red classics) and those about the "positive" aspects of everyday life have generally been labeled as *zhuxuan lü,* a close examination may raise the question of what "main melody" really means. The list of inconsistencies continues.

87. As already noted, during much of the 1980s, most popularly received dramas shown on television came mainly from two sources: (1) imported dramas from such countries and regions as Japan, Brazil, Mexico, the United States, and Hong Kong; and (2) domestically produced adaptations of classic novels. The political upheavals in the late 1980s and early 1990s and the subsequently accelerated economic reforms changed, among other things, the landscape of the production, broadcasting, and consumption of television drama. Genre expansion in television drama is indicative of this change.

88. Jeffrey Kinkley, *Corruption and Realism in Late Socialist China: The Return of the Political Novel.*

89. There have been studies in English on *Kewang* (Yearnings, 1990), *Beijingren zai Niuyue* (A Beijinger in New York, 1993), *Yangniu zai Beijing* (Foreign babes in Beijing, 1995), *Yongzheng wangchao* (The Yongzheng court, 1998), and *Zouxiang gonghe* (Marching toward the republic, 2004). See also note 2.

90. For example, a crime drama can be identified as a *jingfei ju/pian* (literally, "cop and criminal drama") but can also be identified as a *she'an ju* (drama of legal cases). In the latter case, some of the dramas may be identified as anticorruption dramas.

**Chapter One: Looking through the Negatives**

1. David Wittenberg, "Introduction: Extreme Mainstream"; Carla Freccero, *Popular Culture: An Introduction.*

2. Discussions of *Ermo* in English include Anne T. Ciecko and Sheldon H. Lu, "*Ermo:* Televisuality, Capital and the Global Village"; Ping Fu, "*Ermo:* (Tele)Visualising Urban/Rural Transformation"; and Shuqin Cui's brief mention in "Screening China: National Allegories and International Receptions. "

3. There is a "past-looking tendency" in many of the fifth-generation films in which the filmmakers examine such issues as "tradition," "modernity," and "revolution." Critics have viewed their choice of topics as "allegorical," and most of the readings have been in that vein, regardless of whether the critics agree with Fredric Jameson or not. For studies of the fifth-generation filmmakers, see Chris Berry, ed., *Perspectives on Chinese Cinema;* Rey Chow, *Primitive Passions: Visuality, Sexuality, Ethnography, and Contemporary Chinese Cinema;* Jerome Silbergeld, *China into Film: Frames of Reference in Contemporary Chinese Cinema;* Xudong Zhang, *Chinese Modernism: Culture Fever, Avant-Garde Fiction, and the New Chinese Cinema.*

4. See Ciecko and Lu, "*Ermo:* Televisuality, Capital and the Global Village," for additional discussion on the implications of "spectatorship."

5. Jason McGrath, "The Independent Cinema of Jia Zhangke: From Postsocialist Realism to a Transnational Aesthetic," 104.

6. It is interesting to note that, on commenting on *Ermo,* many of my students see the "harmful" effects of television on rural China. What they tend to miss is the contradiction in the representations of Ermo the character, including the fact that, as a

rural woman, Ermo does not seem to fit their stereotypes of Chinese women, who are supposed to be submissive, homebound, and not interested in making money. What is missing in this kind of reading is a historical knowledge that recognizes and understands (even if critically) the changes brought about by the socialist revolution and postsocialist reforms to the lives of women, in this case, in rural China. As in most cultural texts on contemporary China, the "revolution temporality" is unavoidably present regardless of whether or not it is intended.

7. As one of the best-known contemporary "urban generation" or "new generation" filmmakers in China, Jia Zhangke has been reviewed, interviewed, and written about internationally. Examples include Shuqin Cui, "Negotiating In-Between: On New-Generation Filmmaking and Jia Zhangke's Films"; Kevin Lee, "Jia Zhangke"; Xiaoping Lin, "Jia Zhangke's Cinematic Trilogy: A Journey across the Ruins of Post-Mao China"; Jason McGrath, "The Independent Cinema of Jia Zhangke: From Postsocialist Realism to a Transnational Aesthetic"; and Ban Wang, "Epic Narrative, Authenticity, and the Memory of Realism: Reflections on Jia Zhangke's *Platform*."

8. Among quite a few written mentions of Sun Wukong in Mao's works (including *On Contradictions* [*Maodun lun*], the best known is Mao's poem "A Reply to Guo Moruo" ("Qilü: he Guo Moruo"), written in 1961.

9. These two slogans were widely circulated throughout the 1990s. *Yu shi ju jin* was coined during the era of Jiang Zemin in the 1990s, a period marked by an explosion in economic development and a neoliberal ideology of "free market" and "modernization" in support of developmentalist social and economic policies.

10. Shelly Kraicer, "Chinese Wasteland: Jia Zhangke's Still Life"; Dennis Lee, "Jia Zhangke's Portraits of China's Convulsive Change."

11. *Shanghai tan* was later chosen as one of the ten best made-in-Hong-Kong television dramas of the 1980s.

12. I was revising this chapter when the Wenchuan earthquake occurred in Sichuan Province. As I was watching this film again two weeks after the earthquake, I was struck by the eerie similarity between the devastating scenes of the earthquake and the demolished sites shown in this film. The fact that both are located in Sichuan made the similarity even more striking.

13. It is interesting to note that in 2008 reruns of what are known as *jingping dianshiju*, or television drama classics, were programmed by many major television stations including Central Chinese Television (CCTV). See Huang Qing, "Weihe jingpingju chongbo yu yan yu lie?" (Why is there an increasing interest in reruns of television drama classics?).

### Chapter Two: Re-collecting "History" on Television

1. See Ying Zhu, "*Yongzheng Dynasty* and Chinese Primetime Television Drama"; Ying Zhu, "*Yongzheng Dynasty* and Totalitarian Nostalgia"; Ying Zhu, *Television in Post-Reform China: Serial Dramas, Confucian Leadership and the Global Television Market;* Gotelind Müller, *Representing History in Chinese Media: The TV Drama Zou Xiang Gonghe.* The latter is essentially a scene-by-scene synopsis of the drama with an introduction, which is titled "Blind Alleys and Royal Paths Towards the Republic: The Implications of the Chinese TV Drama *Zou xiang gonghe* as seen in the Public Discussion"

(1–27). The unique feature of this introduction is its attention to debates, carried out in China by Chinese critics about the drama.

2. "All history is contemporary (history)" has become such a frequently quoted and circulated statement that, like many frequently used proverbs, its origin appears to be irrelevant in its use. Nevertheless, the "dictum" is said to come from the Italian philosopher and historian Benedetto Croce (1866–1952). See Angelo A. De Gennaro, *The Philosophy of Benedetto Croce: An Introduction.* The following quote from De Gennaro's book makes the same point: "The practical need that is at the basis of every historical judgment gives history the character of 'contemporary history' because though facts are remote or very remote, history always refers to the need and to the present situation in which those facts propagate their vibrations" (46).

3. In the development of (what in English is termed) local operas in traditional China, over time many such operas developed repertoires about historical and legendary figures and borrowed textual materials from one another and staged them in their particular theatrical style. In modern times, the introduction of Western-style spoken drama (at the turn of the twentieth century) broke the dominance of traditional (musical) theater and their repertoires, and made it possible for dramas to deal with contemporary or modern issues. Both Beijing opera (a theatrical form that originated from two regional local operas and evolved into its own form in the Qing court in the eighteenth century) and many local operas have continued to enjoy a modern presence, and many of their repertoires continue to be based on legendary and historical stories, with a few even finding their way into film. Modern writers such as Guo Moruo and others have tried creating history drama for both traditional and modern-drama theaters. During the Mao era, especially toward the beginning of that era and during the Cultural Revolution (1966–1976), "history" as represented by *di wang jiang xiang* (emperors and their generals and ministers) and *caizi jiaren* (traditional scholars and beauties) was criticized for not representing the spirit of "socialist realism" and was subsequently forced to disappear for about a decade. But after the Cultural Revolution, "history drama" returned with a vengeance, mostly on television, where "history" will be repeatedly re-collected and put on display.

4. It was not until the development of Western-style drama, *huaju* or spoken drama, that Chinese theater became "traditional." "History drama," in this sense, is a modern phenomenon.

5. For discussions on transregional/transnational circulation of television drama in general, see Junhao Hong, *The Internationalization of Television in China : The Evolution of Ideology, Society, and Media since the Reform;* Michael Curtin, *Playing to the World's Biggest Audience: The Globalization of Chinese Film and TV;* and Ying Zhu, "Transnational Circulation of Chinese-Language Television Dramas."

6. Huo Yuanjia is a historical figure (1868–1910) known for his martial arts skills and for founding Jingwu Men (or Jingwu Tiyu Hui, a sports club emphasizing excellence in martial arts) in 1910 in Shanghai. Since his untimely death (presumably caused by poisoning), Huo Yuanjia has become a legendary figure in popular culture, especially in film and television: perhaps the two visual media best able to render martial arts in a way that attracts viewers' interest. There have been a number of films and television dramas bearing his name. The 1981 version of the Hong Kong–made twenty-episode

television drama was an instant success when it was shown on the mainland. Generations of Chinese today continue to remember the song that opened and ended each episode. For discussions of songs written for television dramas, please see Chapter 6 in this book.

7. Chen Zhen is believed to be a fictional character based on a number of people known to be related to Huo Yuanjia.

8. He Xiaobing, "Dianshiju 'bianzi xianxiang' guan kui" (A close look at the "phenomenon of pigtails" in television drama), 22–26. Conflicting dates have been given for the television dramas *Dream of the Red Chamber* and *Journey to the West.* He Xiaobing as well as Shao Qi, the author of *Zhongguo dianshiju daolun* (An introduction to Chinese television drama), date the two dramas as appearing in 1986 and 1987, respectively. The Wikipedia and *Baidu baike* on the Internet, among other sources, date the former as 1987. I follow the "popular" convention of dating it at 1987 (see http://zh.wikipedia.org/wiki and http://baike.baidu.com/view/2571.htm).

9. The Chinese search engine Baidu lists 208,000 entries about the 1987 production of the television drama *Dream of the Red Chamber.* The passing away in 2007 of Chen Xiaoxu, the actress who played Lin Daiyü in that production, and the recent publication of *Jiyi Honglou* (Remembering *Honglou*) by Ouyang Fenqiang, who played Jia Baoyu, are two of the latest events that have revealed detailed information about the making of the drama.

10. Wang Yichuan, "Wo kan dangqian Zhongguo dianshi de hou lishiju xianxiang" (Emperors and unofficial history: my view on the posthistory drama phenomenon in contemporary Chinese television).

11. The publication of "history novels," or *lishi xiaoshuo*, by Eryuehe (pen name of Ling Jiefang) in the 1990s would become another inspiration and source for making emperor dramas. Some of the "seriously told" emperor dramas are adaptations from Eryuehe's novels such as *Yongzheng huangdi* (Emperor Yongzheng, 1988), *Kangxi dadi* (Kangxi the great emperor, 1990–1992), and *Qianlong huangdi* (Emperor Qianlong, 1994–1996).

12. The former includes *Wu Zetian* (Empress Wu Zetian, 1995), *Yongzheng wangchao* (The Yongzheng court, 1998), *Da ming gongci* (Palace of desire, 2001), *Kangxi wangchao* (The Kangxi court, 2001), *Qianlong wangchao* (The Qianlong court, 2003), *Xiaozhuang huanghou* (Empress Xiaozhuang of the Qing dynasty), and, most recently, *Han wu da di* (Emperor Wu of the Han dynasty, 2004) and *Qin Shi Huang* (First Emperor of the Qin dynasty, 2003/2007). The playfully told dramas may or may not be titled after an emperor. They include *Huanzhu gege* (Princess Huanzhu) I, II, III (each is an independent long serial); *Kangxi weifu sifang ji* (Emperor Kangxi traveling undercover) I, II, III, IV, and V; *Tiezui tongya Ji Xiaolan* (Clever-and-sharp-mouthed Ji Xiaolan) I, II, III; *Fengliu caizi Ji Xiaolan* (Ji Xiaolan, the gifted talent, 2001); and *Zaixiang Liu Luoguo* (Prime minister Liu Luoguo, 1994).

13. See Susan M. Pearce, *Museums, Objects and Collections;* Susan M. Pearce, *On Collecting: An Investigation into Collecting in the European Tradition.* Quotation from Lydia Chiang, *Collecting the Self: Body and Identity in Strange Tale Collections of Late Imperial China,* 4–7.

14. Zhang Yiwu, in *China Daily,* February 2, 2005 (http://www.chinadaily.com.cn/english/doc/2005-02/content_414251.htm).

15. Examples of critical commentaries on the emperor-drama phenomenon in China can be found in such journals and magazines as *Zhongguo dianshi* (Chinese television), *Beijing dianying xueyuan xuebao* (Journal of the Beijing Film Academy), *Zhongguo guangbo yingshi* (Chinese radio, film, and television), *Dianshi yishu* (Art of television), *Dianshiju* (Television drama), and many more.

16. I presented a paper on this issue titled "From *Army Nurse* to 'Emperor Dramas': Gender, Cultural and Political Implications of a Woman Director's Career" at the annual meeting of the Association for Asian Studies, March 22–25, 2007, Boston.

17. *Jingying*, or elite, was a positive term during the 1980s, referring to the return and ascendance of intellectuals to the cultural center after the Cultural Revolution.

18. The heated nature of Chinese intellectual debates is said to have begun with Wang Hui's article "Dangdai Zhongguo de sixiang zhuangkuang yu xiandaixing wenti," or "Contemporary Chinese Thought and the Question of Modernity," published in 1997. The English translation of the article is included in Wang's *China's New Order*, edited by Theodore Huters. Although intellectual debates in China since then have been at times personal, the passion is indicative of the coexistence of different political positions and ideological persuasions among contemporary Chinese intellectuals and the fact that there is actually nothing "depoliticized" in their debates.

19. During the 1980s, market forces remained rather negligible compared with the state's role in the management of such media as television and film. There were also experiments by "elite" intellectuals using film and television for cultural criticism. *Heshang*, or River Elegy (1988), a six-episode television show, is a good example. Neither fiction nor a documentary, this show was a televisual version of intellectual musings about what intellectuals perceived to be the "ills" of the remnants of traditional Chinese culture and the need for China to modernize.

20. Xueping Zhong, *Masculinity Besieged? Issues of Modernity and Male Subjectivity in Chinese Literature of the Late Twentieth Century*.

21. Music, films, literature, and television dramas from Hong Kong and Taiwan were among some of the early cultural products imported into the mainland in the 1980s. From the early 1990s, in addition to exchanges of cultural products, an increasing number of artists started traveling between the three regions, and they generated more transregional cultural exchanges. On the mainland, such cross-regional cultural exchanges generated anxiety among elites and cultural critics over the *gang tai hua*, or Hong-Kong-and Taiwan-ization, of Chinese culture.

22. Wang Hui, "Depoliticized Politics: From East to West."

23. At times, scholars have chosen to identify this kind of transregional cultural exchange under the general term "transnational." See, for example, Sheldon Lu, ed., *Transnational Chinese Cinemas*; Sheldon Lu, *China, Transnational Visuality, Global Postmodernity*.

24. The actress Zhao Wei who played Xiao Yanzi became an instant household name after the first *Huanzhu gege* series. The fame also turned her into a public villain a few years later when she covered herself in a Japanese flag during a fashion show. As an actor, Zhao Wei has had trouble moving beyond her initial success. None of her subsequent roles in film or on television won her the kind of recognition that the character Xiao Yanzi did.

25. The notion of "cool" has remained an illusive term, but numerous books have the word in their titles, which helps indicate its evolution. See Thomas Frank, *The Conquest of Cool : Business Culture, Counterculture, and the Rise of Hip Consumerism;* Lewis MacAdams, *Birth of the Cool: Beat, Bebop, and the American Avant Garde;* Malcolm Gladwell, "The Coolhunt"; Alan Liu, *The Laws of Cool: Knowledge Work and the Culture of Information.*

26. The three television dramas about these three Qing emperors are rough adaptations of Eryuehe's (Ling Jiefang's) novels.

27. It is generally understood that the entire project of the *Shi ji* (which used to be called the *Taishigong shu, Taishigong ji,* or *Taishi ji—taishi* being the position of the officially appointed historian) was conceived by Sima Qian's father Sima Tan, who reportedly told his son that he must try his utmost to complete a history book. What Sima Qian completed was a book of 5,125,600 words (in classical Chinese) that covers about three thousand years of history all the way to the reign of Emperor Wu.

28. Unless otherwise noted, all translations are mine.

29. In Chinese: "他建立了一个国家前所未有的尊严。他给了一个族群挺立千秋的自信。他的国号成了一个民族永远的名字。"

30. In addition to Ban Wang's *The Sublime Figure of History: Aesthetics and Politics in Twentieth-Century China,* some of the most recent musings about this and related issues include Bonnie S. McDougall, *Fictional Authors, Imaginary Audiences: Modern Chinese Literature in the Twentieth Century;* Sabina Knight, *The Heart of Time: Moral Agency in Twentieth-Century Chinese Fiction;* and Wendy Larson, *From Ah Q to Lei Feng: Freud and Revolutionary Spirit in Twentieth-Century China.*

31. Given that this is a perennial issue in modern Chinese intellectual discourse, it is fair to suggest that all studies of modern Chinese history address the issue of how to understand modern Chinese experiences. Recent discussions that offer new interventions to Foucauldian-genealogy-informed historiography in the China field include Wang Hui, *Xiandai Zhongguo sixiang de xingqi* (The rise of modern Chinese thought); and Ban Wang, *Illuminations from the Past: Trauma, Memory, and History in Modern China.*

32. For an extensive discussion of this issue, see Ban Wang, *Illuminations from the Past.*

33. Ibid., 23.

34. Ibid., 24.

35. Ibid., 25.

36. There have been numerous critiques in China of the so-called emperor drama or history drama. Examples include Liu Ping, "Zai lishi yu xianshi de qihedian shang" (Between history and reality); Yue Peng, "Qinggong xi zouhong manshuo" (Some thoughts on the popularity of the Qing court drama); Liu Yan, "*Yongzheng wangchao:* lishi wenben de wenhua chanshi" (*The Yongzheng Court:* a cultural interpretation of a text of history); Wang Jinhe, "Fan'an yue fan yue luan: ye tan *Yongzheng wangchao*" (Confusion increased: also about *The Yongzheng Court*); Wang Wei, "Jiaowang guozheng de Yongzheng xingxiang" (Overly corrected image of Yongzheng); Zhang Dexiang "*Yongzheng wangchao* sanwei" (Three flavors of *The Yongzheng Court*); and Chen Mo, "Qingtingju jiazhi daoxiang toushi" (An examination of value guidance in the Qing court drama).

37. *Han wu da di* (Emperor Wu of the Han Dynasty) (sixty-four-episode television drama, dir. Hu Mei, 2004).

38. Zhang Yiwu, *China Daily*, February 2, 2005 (http://www.chinadaily.com.cn/english/doc/2005-02/content_414251.htm) (translation original).

39. Ibid.

40. Ibid.

41. Zhang Yiwu, "Bei 'zhuanhuan' he bei 'tidai' de xin wenxue" (New literature that has been transformed and replaced).

42. The fact that Lu Xun has remained one of the most studied modern Chinese intellectuals has not always sat well with a variety of groups both inside and outside of China. And yet this fact also conversely proves his importance precisely in continuing to provoke debate.

43. Xueping Zhong, "Who Is Afraid of Lu Xun? Politics of 'Lu Xun lun zheng' and the Question of His Legacy in the Post-Revolution China."

44. See Wang Hui, *Fankang juewang* (Struggle against despair); Qian Liqun, *Jujue yiwang* (Refuse to forget); Qian Liqun, *Yu Lu Xun xiangyu* (Encounter Lu Xun); Ban Wang, "Tradition, Memory, and Hope: Lu Xun and Critical Historical Consciousness."

45. For a short critique of Zhang Yimou's *Hero*, see Ban Wang, "Epic Narrative, Authenticity, and the Memory of Realism: Reflections on Jia Zhangke's *Platform*."

**Chapter Three: In Whose Name?**

1. *Cangtian zai shang* was written by Lu Tianming, already a well-known writer by then, who is also the script writer of the drama. It is said that it took quite some time before the script was approved and the drama was shot and produced. In addition to Kinkley's writing on Lu Tianming and his works, see Lu Tianming's blog for related information about the writer. Pieces in Chinese related to *Heavens Above* include "Fanfu zuojia Lu Tianming: wo jiushi yao xie zhege shidai de shiqing" (Anticorruption writer Lu Tianming: I insist on writing about things that happen in our own times); "Caifang Lu Tianming" (Interviewing Lu Tianming). See also Jeffrey C. Kinkley, "The Trendsetter: Lu Tianming's *Heaven Above*."

2. In 2004, the Guangdian Zongju (the State Administration of Broadcasting, Film, and Television) reportedly rejected 40 percent of the 308 crime-oriented television drama proposals and put out a new regulation that prohibited anticorruption dramas, cop dramas, and crime dramas from being shown in prime time slots (http://www.people.com.cn/GB/yule/1018/2421436.html).

3. In addition to Jeffrey Kinkley's *Corruption and Realism in Late Socialist China: The Return of the Political Novel*, Ruoyun Bai has also written on similar issues, specifically on the anticorruption televisual subgenre. See Ruoyun Bai, "'Clean Officials,' Emotional Moral Community, and Anti-Corruption Television Drama."

4. Kinkley, *Corruption and Realism in Late Socialist China*, 3.

5. Ibid., 4.

6. Ibid., 8.

7. Some of my discussion in this chapter overlaps with Kinkley's but I have a different perspective, mainly because much of the thinking in this chapter was developed independently before the publication of Kinkely's book. I presented an earlier version

of this chapter at the conference "Towards an Age of Rights: Chinese and International Perspectives," Center for Chinese Studies, University of Michigan, February 1–2, 2008.

8. Some of Zhou Meisen's novels are *Zhigao liyi* (The highest principle, 2000), *Zhongguo zhizao* (Made in China, 2001; renamed *Zhongcheng,* or *Loyalty,* when adapted for television), *Juedui quanli* (Absolute power, 2002), and *Guojia gongsu* (Sued by the state, 2003).

9. See Kinkley's discussion of the "fall" of the anticorruption novel in the section "The Fall" in his introduction to *Corruption and Realism in Late Socialist China,* 18–21.

10. Lu Xun, *Zhongguo xiaoshuo shilüe* (A brief history of the Chinese novel).

11. For discussions of the social conditions of the late 1980s, see, for example, Wang Hui, "The Historical Conditions of the 1989 Social Movement and the Anti-historical Explanation of 'Neoliberalism,'" in his *China's New Order,* 46–77.

12. "Marketism" is a translation of the Chinese word "*shichang zhuyi*" used by contemporary Chinese intellectuals who argue that the notion of a "free market" is itself ideological. See, for example, Han Shaogong's article, based on a speech at Suzhou University, "Lengzhan hou: wenxue yu xiezuo xin de chujing" (After the Cold War: new context for literature and creative writing).

13. The film was adapted from the novel *Jue ze* by Zhang Ping, one of the few writers in Zhou Meisen's league with regard to writing about politics and the corruption of officialdom. For a discussion of Zhang Ping in English, see Kinkley, *Corruption and Realism in Late Socialist China.*

14. Including a cynical realization that, instead of helping lessening corruption, the officially organized promotion of anticorruption films such as *Shengsi jueze* helped benefit the creators and producers of the film, illustrating that "socially correct" and politically acceptable cultural products can also enjoy market benefits. The box-office total from the film reportedly exceeded 1.165 hundred million RMB (http://ent.sina.com.cn/film/chinese/2000-10-14/19263.html).

15. It is a pity that, other than reviews and spontaneous online debates, which tend to be abrasive and not conducive to thoughtful discussion, most televisual texts do not receive adequate critical attention. In addition to a few books written in Chinese on the history of television drama, scholars like Yin Hong have begun to write more about the subject. See, for example, "Yin Hong, Yang Daihui: Zhongguo dianshiju yishu chuantong" (Yin Hong and Yang Daihui on the artistic tradition of Chinese television drama) (http://medial.people.com.cn/GB/5258393.html).

16. Indeed, I would argue that if aspects of these dramas were to be studied, examined, and discussed—critically analyzed—they could well function as cultural texts for furthering critical examinations of the social, political, and ideological issues in contemporary China. The fact that critics dismiss them as lowly popular cultural entertainment along with media's promotion of such dramas as pure entertainment constitutes a Chinese version of hegemony that prevents the complexities of the issues in such dramas from being fully examined and discussed.

17. See *Corruption and Realism in Late Socialist China* for Kinkley's discussion of Zhou Meisen, which is less extensive than his discussion of Zhang Ping.

18. It is interesting to note that the new regulation regarding the status of anticorruption dramas states as a criticism that some "anticorruption" dramas were really not

about corruption but about the inner workings of officialdom, treating corruption only as a tangible example of a problem (http://www.people.com.cn).

19. No official count exists. The unclear definition of related subgenres including cop dramas, crime-related dramas, and anticorruption dramas also makes it difficult to count.

20. Among these dramas, the best known include (1) several Zhou Meisen dramas such as *Zhongcheng* (Loyalty, 2001), *Zhigao liyi* (The highest principle, 2002), *Juedui quanli* (Absolute power, 2004), and *Guojia gongsu* (Sued by the state, 2003); and (2) crime-oriented dramas such as *Daxue wuheng* (Snow-covered, 2001), *Hongse kangnaixin* (Red carnations, 2001), *Gongan juzhang* (The police chief, 2002), and *Hei dong* (Black hole, 2001). Those of the second type were so popular that their successes generated imitations such as *Lanse matilian* (Blue lilies), *Gongan juzhang II* and *Gongan juzhang III* (The police chief II and III), and the so-called *hei xilie,* or black series—there are no less than ten dramas with the word *hei* (black) in their titles; examples include *Hei jin* (Black money), *Hei fen* (Black powder), *Hei bing* (Black drug), *Hei qiang* (Black guns), and *Hei wu* (Black fog). Many in the "black series" were penned by Zhang Chenggong.

21. There are still reruns of old anticorruption dramas outside the prime-time slots and mostly by local or satellite stations that are not watched by the majority of viewers.

22. For discussion of "good" officials in contemporary popular anticorruption narratives, see Kinkley's book and Ruoyun Bai, "'Clean Officials,' Emotional Moral Community, and Anti-Corruption Television Dramas."

23. See, for example, Yu Xingzhong, "Qiangshi wenhua, eryuan renshi yu fazhi" (Hegemonic culture, binary-oppositional epistemology, and rule by law).

24. There are numerous articles on issues regarding China's SOEs. Some recent writings include Yashang Huang, *Selling China: Foreign Direct Investment during the Reform Era,* and Liu Rixin, "Guoyou qiye de guoqu, xianzai he jianglai" (SOEs' past, present, and future).

25. *Daxue wuheng* has been translated into English under several titles including *Pure as Snow* by Ruoyun Bai and *The Blizzard Leaves No Trace* by Kinkley. My own translation, "Snow-Covered Traces," though it has a different emphasis is closer to Kinkley's in meaning.

26. This drama is based on a novel of the same title by Zhang Chenggong.

27. *Jidushan bojue* is both the Chinese title of the French novel *Le Comte de Monte Cristo* and the name of its main character (the title of the book is also translated as *Jidushan enchou ji*). It is among the nineteenth-century French, English, and Russian novels popular with young Chinese growing up during the Mao era.

28. In addition to official corruption, there is a newly coined term in Chinese that refers to other kinds of corruption, *ya fubai,* or subcorruption (or derivative corruption). It usually refers to the abuse of power by those whose profession allows them to seek personal gain. They include those in the medical, teaching, and media professions.

### Chapter Four: Beyond Romance

1. For discussions of the evolution of the category of youth in modern China and on its various implications, please see Frank Dikotter, *Sex, Culture and Modernity in*

*China,* and Mingwei Song, *Long Live Youth: National Rejuvenation and the Chinese Bildungsroman, 1900–1958.*

2. Liang Qichao, *Shaonian Zhongguo shuo* (On Young China) (1900).

3. See Dikotter, *Sex, Culture and Modernity in China;* Mingwei Song, *Long Live Youth.*

4. For information about what went on at Versailles, see standard texts on modern Chinese history including John Fairbank, *China: A New History,* and Jonathan Spence, *The Search for Modern China.*

5. Since the mid-1980s, questioning May Fourth has been one of the major scholarly trends in Chinese studies circles in the West. Like all historical movements, May Fourth may be subject to critical reevaluations for a long time to come, all the reevaluations informed by their own historical conditions and ideological stance. This latest round of critical attacks on the May Fourth movement stems from a shift in Western academia toward revolutions and radical social movements including non-Western nations' struggles for national independence.

6. For a recent discussion of "revolutionary spirit," see Wendy Larson, *From Ah Q to Lei Feng: Freud and Revolutionary Spirit in Twentieth-Century China.*

7. See, for example, Xueping Zhong, Wang Zheng, and Bai Di, eds., *Some of Us: Chinese Women Growing Up in the Mao Era;* Xueping Zhong "'Long Live Youth' and the Ironies of Youth and Gender in Chinese Films of the 1950s and 1960s"; and Guobin Yang and Ming-Bao Yue, eds., *Collective Memories of the Cultural Revolution.*

8. For more discussion of youth in the 1980s and 1990s, see James Farrer, *Opening Up: Youth Sex Culture and Market Reform in Shanghai;* and Jieying Xi, Yunxiao Sun, Jing Jian Xiao, eds., *Chinese Youth in Transition.*

9. Pan Xiao, "Rensheng de lu a, zenme yuezou yuezhai" (Why life's path is becoming narrower and narrower).

10. It is important to note that many of the same writers and critics, such as Zhang Chengzhi, Han Shaogong, Ah Cheng, and Li Tuo, to name just a few, have begun to reevaluate their own thinking and writing in the 1980s. Three decades of economic reforms and rapid "modernization" in China have generated new questions that have prompted many of them to rethink their earlier views. See for example, Zha Jianying, *Bashi niandai fangtanlu* (Interviews about the 1980s). Many of these and other writers' additional reflections can be found on the Zuoan website http://www.eduww.com.

11. For a discussion on "eating a bowl of youth" (*chi qingchun fan*), see Zhang Zhen, "The 'Rice Bowl of Youth' in Fin de Siècle Urban China."

12. Even though not all of the dramas from Korea are strictly of the "youth-idol" type, the television (together with the film) industry in Korea, nevertheless, has established itself as a powerhouse for generating shows that are not only popular in Korea, but also in other parts of East Asia (Japan, mainland China, and Taiwan). Most of these shows center on young characters and star some of the most well-known young Korean actors and actresses, whose beauty, though often the result of skilled cosmetic surgeries, has defined the most desired look for young people in these countries and regions.

13. The phenomenon of the "youth-idol drama" began in the early 1980s with importations of dramas from outside of China. The most notable example is the 1982 broadcast of the Japanese drama whose Chinese title is *Xueyi* (Blood in question). Its success

not only inaugurated what would later be known as *qingchun ouxiang ju,* or youth-idol dramas, but also made the young actors Yamaguchi Momoe and Miura Tomokazu two of the earliest youth idols in post-Mao China.

14. Qiong Yao's fiction was introduced into mainland China around 1981 and generated the so-called *Qiong Yao xianxiang,* or Qiong Yao phenomenon. Early-twentieth-century "middle-brow" literature refers to the so-called Mandarin Duck and Butterfly literature and other similar writings popular among city dwellers in Shanghai. Qiong Yao's "romance" novels, incidentally, can be set in either modern or unspecific "premodern" settings. When her *gege* novels (*gege* is a Manchu word for female, which tends to be translated as "young women, misses" in Chinese and today is often used in Chinese to refer specifically to daughters born into the Qing court or royal families) are adapted into television dramas, because of their settings and their "playful nature," they are categorized as emperor dramas of the *xishuo* type. For a discussion of Qiong Yao in English, see Miriam Lang, "San Mao and Qiong Yao, a 'Popular' Pair."

15. For a discussion of the DVD market for television drama, see Rong Cai, "Carnivalesque Pleasure: The Audio-Visual Market and the Consumption of Television Drama."

16. Regulations issued in 2000 by the State Administration of Radio and Television (Guojia Guangbo Dianshi Ju) stipulates that only 15 percent of prime-time slots should be devoted to imported television programs. See Zhu Guoliang, "Huangjin shiduan 'fengsha' yinjin ju" (Limiting imported dramas in prime time).

17. See, for example, Yu Bing and Wen Ye, "Zhongguo qingchun ouxiang ju weishenme re bu qilai" (Why Chinese youth-idol drama does not attract viewers' interest); Ni Xueli and Zhang Cui, "Gan'ga de Zhongguo qingchun ouxiang ju" (The embarrassing Chinese youth-idol drama). For a discussion in English of a related type of drama, see Ya-chien Huang, "Pink Dramas: Reconciling Consumer Modernity and Confucian Womanhood."

18. This claim mainly refers to the imitations produced in the late 1990s. *Fen dou* (Strive for success, 2007) is one recent example that is said to be "realistically" dealing with the lives of the young white-collar workers who were born after 1980 (the post-1980 generation).

19. See part 3, "Production, Reception, and Distribution," in Zhu, Keane, and Bai, *TV Drama in China,* for discussion, in English, of some aspects of the reception issue. Also see *Zhongguo dianshi guanzhong xianzhuang baogao* (Reports on the viewership of Chinese television); Liu Yan and He Ru, "Dianshiju bianpai celüe yu guanzhong manyidu" (Television drama programming and viewers' satisfaction).

20. Zhao is the director of a few hit television dramas, including *Guo ba ying* (Play to the fullest, 1993), *Dong bian ri chu xi bian yu* (East sunshine, west rain, 1996), *Yong bu mingmu* (Eyes forever open, 1999), *Xiang wu xiang yu you xiang feng* (Like fog like rain also like wind, 2000), *Na shenme zhengjiu ni, wode airen* (With what to save you, my loved one, 2001), and *Biele, Wengehua* (Good-bye, Vancouver, 2002). His meticulous attention to mise-en-scène and other visual elements to provide an up-to-date "modern" glamour has helped establish him as a *weimei* (beauty for beauty's sake) type of director.

21. The two of them have also collaborated from time to time (on *Eyes Forever Open* and *With What to Save You*), but dramas based on Hai Yan's fiction, including the ones directed by Zhao, are usually identified with the writer (as opposed to the directors).

22. Born as Si Haiyan in 1954, Hai Yan is a self-claimed amateur writer, working as an upper-level manager of the Beijing Jinjiang Hotel Group (among other business titles). He is reported to have joined the army at the age of sixteen and later worked in the line of public security before becoming a manager. Through writing, he has become a famous figure in popular culture, and his success is uniquely symptomatic of the era in and about which he writes—few writers in China have had a writing career like that of Hai Yan, who owes his literary success (in terms of popularity) solely to the success of the television drama adaptations of his novels, a success that has in turn secured him celebrity status both in the print media at large and on the Internet. Because of his success, he has also become a legendary figure with a life experience that in part reflects the Chinese history of the past sixty years. Since first publishing *Plain-Clothed Cops* (Bianyi jingcha) in 1985, Hai Yan has written nine more novels, seven of which have been adapted into television dramas. He is also known to have participated in the planning (*ce hua*) of other dramas.

23. Hai Yan has participated in some of the adaptations of his novels, including *Jade Goddess of Mercy* and *With What to Save You, My Loved One.*

24. Such sentiments have been evoked and examined in recent studies of late Qing and early Republican history and culture. Because of an ideological orientation in the development of this trend, recent studies hold such sentiments to be more complex and less radical and one-dimensional than those produced by what is now termed the May Fourth movement. The irony is that when such sentiments reappear in contemporary Chinese culture mixed with additional historical and cultural legacies, they may not be seen as the real heir of that early middle-brow literature.

25. With regard to why certain television dramas become popular, one should be aware of possible deals involved in generating media hype. Recent court cases against some officials at the Chinese Central Television Station (CCTV) who were accused of receiving bribes for the broadcasting rights of certain television dramas are a reminder of such possibilities. When it comes to the Hai Yan phenomenon, additionally, it is not unlikely that the formula and content of his stories were fine-tuned by more than just the writer himself before they were brought to the television screen. Back-room manipulation (*cao zuo*) may well be part of the game. Nevertheless, these factors are not sufficient to explain the popularity of Hai Yan's dramas (and other dramas identified, sometimes falsely, with his name). Within the context of the rapid social and economic transformations brought about by the market reforms in which questions of value, virtue, and what it means to be "good," "real," and "sincere" seem to have been pushed aside, Hai Yan dramas, their ideological clichés notwithstanding, appear to have touched a cultural nerve by bringing these seemingly outdated issues back. One is compelled to wonder about the structural implications in the representations in Hai Yan's dramas and between this dramatic world and the everyday reality of the viewers who seem to be drawn to that imagined world.

26. For discussions in English of the late-twentieth-century and early-twenty-first-century Chinese "urban generation" cinema, see Zhen Zhang, ed., *The Urban Generation: Chinese Cinema and Society at the Turn of the Twenty-First Century.*

27. Rey Chow, *Sentimental Fabulations, Contemporary Chinese Films.*

28. Many of Wang Shuo's stories portray so-called *da yuan* youngsters (1) who were "military brats," (2) who were a few years younger than the Red Guard generation, (3)

who went to middle and high school during the Cultural Revolution, and (4) many of whom also went to the countryside toward the later part of the Cultural Revolution. One of his novellas, *Dongwu xiongmeng*, was adapted as *Yangguang canlan de rizi* (In the heat of the sun, 1996), a film about Mao era youth.

29. "字词解释：血色浪漫—1）残酷而又激越的青春，2）发自人的本心的纯真浪漫，3）带着探险式的浪漫，4）被烙上革命和战争时代的青春岁月" (http://baike.baidu.com/view/82329.htm).

30. "我们浪费掉了太多的青春，那是一段如此自以为是、又如此狼狈不堪的青春岁月，有欢笑，也有泪水；有朝气，也有颓废；有甜蜜，也有荒唐；有自信，也有迷茫。我们敏感，我们偏执，我们顽固到底地故作坚强；我们轻易的伤害别人，也轻易的被别人所伤，我们追逐于颓废的快乐，陶醉于寂寞的美丽；我们坚信自己与众不 同，坚信世界会因我而改变；我们觉醒其实我们已经不再年轻，我们前途或许也不再是无限的，其实它又何曾是无限的？曾经在某一瞬间，我们都以为自己长大了。但是有一天，我们终于发现，长大的含义除了欲望，还有勇气、责任、坚强以及某种必须的牺牲。在生活面前我们还都是孩子，其实我们从未长大，还不懂爱和被爱。"

31. Wendy Larson offers an interesting discussion on Lei Feng that is closely related to this point. In her somewhat imbalanced discussion pairing Lei Feng with Ah Q in Chinese revolutionary discourse, she seems to downplay the role of *lixiang*, or idealism—also a part of the "revolutionary spirit"—which is related to but goes beyond the "Lei Feng spirit." See Wendy Larson, "Revolutionary Discourse and the Spirit: From Ah Q to Lei Feng," in *From Ah Q to Lei Feng*, 77–113.

32. Ever since the first appearances of "positive" remembrances by former educated youth, critics have dismissed them as nostalgia. See Qiu Xinmu, "'Zhishi qingnian shangshan xiaxiang' yanjiu zongshu" (A summary of the research on the rustication movement of educated youth).

33. It is interesting to note that 2008 was the fortieth anniversary of the rustication movement, but, unlike in 1998, this anniversary was hardly mentioned in the media in China.

34. Larson, *From Ah Q to Lei Feng*, 111.

35. *Shibing tuji*, scripted by Lan Xiaolong (based on his 2003 novel of the same title) and directed by Kang Honglei, was a 2006 production aired in 2007.

36. *Shibing tuji* literally means "soldiers make a sudden attack."

37. On the Internet there are sites where words, phrases, or sentences uttered by Xu Sanduo are listed by enthusiastic fans. Among them perhaps by now his most famous expression is *bu paoqi, bu fangqi*, or never give up and never give in. This slogan was picked up and took on a life its own during the rescue and recovery operation immediately after the Wenchuan earthquake in 2008.

38. "Xu Sanduo: xiandai shenghuo de renwen huigui" (Xu Sanduo: the return of humanism in contemporary life), *Baidu shouye renwu* (Person on the cover page of Baidu), no. 11 (2007) (http://renwu.baidu.com/0711/index.html).

39. The quote comes from http://baike.baidu.com/view/764555.htm.

40. Wang was born into a peasant family in Hebei Province in 1984. Between the ages of eight and fourteen, he lived at the Shaolin Temple. He went to Beijing after his years at the temple and worked as an extra and a small-time actor. At the age of sixteen, he

was discovered by Li Yang, who placed him in *Blind Shaft* (*Mang jing*). The success of this film won Wang notoriety, and he has since appeared in some well-known films and television dramas. It was not, however, until his portrayal of Xu Sanduo that Wang Baoqiang became a household name. For more information, see http://baike.baidu.com/view/764555.htm.

41. Each of these individuals came from different times in the communist revolutionary period: Lei Feng (1940–1962) died during the Mao era; Huang Jiguang (1930–1952) died during the Korean War; Dong Cunrui (1929–1948) died during the Second Civil War (1945–1949); Zhang Side (1915–1944) died in Yan'an. During the Mao era, they became known as "revolutionary heroes."

**Chapter Five: Also beyond Romance**

1. Gesa Zinn, "Melodrama and Women," 316.

2. Ibid.

3. For additional discussions on melodrama and women, see Christine Gledhill, ed., *Home Is Where the Heart Is;* Patrice Petro, *Joyless Streets;* Ken K. Ito, *An Age of Melodrama;* Susan Zlotnick, *Women, Writing, and the Industrial Revolution;* E. Ann Kaplan, *Motherhood and Representations;* Jackie Byars, *All That Hollywood Allows;* Nancy Abelmann, *The Melodrama of Mobility;* Gabrielle Hyslop, "Deviant and Dangerous Behavior"; Kathleen Anne McHugh, *American Domesticity;* and Cavell, *Contesting Tears.*

4. Xie Jin (1923–2008) studied drama and directing during the 1940s. He started directing films in the late 1940s and became a film director stationed in Shanghai after 1949. After the success of *Nülan wuhao* (Woman basketball player number five) in 1957, he went on to make three more films in the 1960s. He resumed filmmaking in 1974 and made three films during the Cultural Revolution and thirteen more films after the Cultural Revolution. Despite the popularity of his films, Xie Jin's melodramatic style drew criticism from critics. Examples include Zhu Dake, "The drawback of Xie Jin's Model," and Li Jie, "Xie Jin's Era Should End."

5. These three women writers began to write in the 1980s but became household names in the 1990s when their subject matter—women's personal experiences in conjunction with the rapid changes in their everyday and materially oriented lives—attracted popular interest.

6. There are many discussions on the *yin sheng yang shuai* issue both in English and in Chinese. To name just a few, see Yuejin Wang, "*Red Sorghum:* Mixing Memory and Desire"; Ling Zhu, "A Brave New World? On the Construction of 'Masculinity' and 'Femininity' in *The Red Sorghum Family*"; and Xueping Zhong, *Masculinity Besieged?*

7. Studies and discussions on women's and men's identities in conjunction with the Communist Party–led women's liberation movement and the Mao era's gender policies began to appear after the late 1970s, both in the West and in China. See Judith Stacey, *Patriarchy and Socialist Revolution in China;* Margery Wolf, *Revolution Postponed: Women in Contemporary China;* Christina K. Gilmartin, Gail Hershatter, Lisa Rofel, and Tyrene White, eds., *Engendering China: Women, Culture, and The State;* Tani Barlow, ed., *Gender Politics in Modern China;* Angela Zito and Tani Barlow, eds., *Body, Subject and Power in China;* and Tani Barlow, *The Question of Women in Chinese Feminism.*

8. In critiquing the Communist Party's gender-blind gender-equality policies, many critics went so far as to negate the revolutionary—and, by extension, the social—component in the formation of women's self-identity in socialist China. The call for restoring women's "femininity" by many critics was accompanied by an unquestioned acceptance of the separation of "the social" from "female identity."

9. I have argued elsewhere that the narrowing of the meaning of "womanhood" can be traced through women's literature in the three decades since the late 1970s, when Chinese women writers, in their critique of the shortcomings of the Communist Party–led women's liberation, turned to what is essentially a bourgeois imaginary of womanhood for "women's essence." See Xueping Zhong, "Who Is a Feminist? Understanding the Ambivalence towards *Shanghai Baby*, 'Body Writing,' and Feminism in Post–Women's Liberation China."

10. Chi Li is a Wuhan-based writer who began to publish in the 1980s but did not become known until the 1990s. The story that secured her name in the contemporary Chinese literary scene is "Fannao rensheng" (Vexed everyday life, 1987) in which the male protagonist Yin Jiahou is portrayed as being trapped by his everyday activities at home and at the factory, which, the story appears to imply, keep a man from being able to do more important things (that a man should be doing). It is interesting to note that, when *Comings and Goings* begins, the figure of Yin Jiahou can be found in Kang Weiye, the male protagonist in this drama, and Kang's story is almost like a sequel in that it is about how, after Kang becomes a successful businessman, he faces new possibilities and new vexations that Yin Jiahou would not have dreamed of.

11. The reference to the Fulian here reveals several gender-politics-related issues. First, it betrays the author Chi Li's bias against the organization, a bias shared by many intellectuals, men and women. It is a bias based on two by-now-familiar views: the Fulian is an official organization and as such it mainly answers to the state's gender policies, and the Fulian is responsible for repressing expressions of "femininity." As a result, when representing Fulian-related issues, including portraying those who work for it, women writers like Chi Li tend to resort to a set of stereotypes. Duan Lina and her colleagues embody such stereotypes. For information on the Fulian, see Ellen Judd, *The Chinese Women's Movement between the State and Market*, and Hongmei Shen, "All-China Women's Federation: A Party Representative or Feminist Organization?"

12. Here, the original author Chi Li and the drama both echo the view that the party-led women's liberation movement was a top-down movement in which women's sexual differences were neglected and rendered subservient to male-centered revolutionary causes and nation-building endeavors. For reexaminations of this view, see Lin Chun, *The Transformations of Chinese Socialism;* Xueping Zhong, "Women Can Hold Up Half the Sky: A 'Fourth-Told' Tale."

13. Wang Hailing is best known for writing about marriage and its problems in contemporary China. Her representative works include *Qian shou* (Holding hands, 1999), *Zhongguo shi lihun* (Divorce Chinese style, 2004), *Xin jiehun shidai* (Marriage in the new era, 2006), and *Daxiao de nüer* (Senior colonel's daughter, 2007), all of which have been adapted into television dramas.

14. See, for example, "Wang Hailing: wo dui hunyin hen jiji" (Wang Hailing: I am positive about marriage) (http://yule.sohu.com/20040913/n222005209.shtml). This

interview took place when *Divorce Chinese Style* first appeared and some critics questioned Wang for blaming women for the failure of their marriages. Wang responds to that criticism in this interview. Also see "Wang Hailing bu fu zhuanjia tiaoci, wei 'li hun' bianjie" (Wang Hailing does not agree with critics and defends *Divorce Chinese Style*) (http://ent.sina.com.cn/2004-10-7/0704524349.html).

15. When *Yearnings* first appeared, it generated much critical response from Chinese women intellectuals, especially with regard to the portrayal of Liu Huifang, the female protagonist of the drama.

16. "Guanyu *kong fangzi* de zhengyi" (Controversy about Empty House) (http://www.yntv.cn/yntv_web/category/30201/2005/11/30/2005-11-30_296523_30201.shtml).

17. http://women.sohu.com/20041021/n222599384.shtml.

18. "Wang Hailing: zuo quanzhi taitai bushi fengxian" (Wang Hailing: being a housewife is not a selfless sacrifice), *Meizhou shibao* (Boston Chinese report), October 8–14, 2004, A6.

**Chapter Six: Listening to Popular Poetics**

1. For writings on contemporary Chinese popular music, see Andrew Jones, *Like a Knife: Ideology and Genre in Contemporary Chinese Popular Music;* Andrew Jones, "The Politics of Popular Music in Post Tiananmen China"; Gregory Lee, *Troubadours, Trumpeters, Trouble Makers: Lyricism, Nationalism, and Hybridity in China and Its Others;* and Nimrod Baranovitch, *China's New Voices: Popular Music, Ethnicity, Gender, and Politics, 1978–1997.*

2. During the celebration of the 2009 Chinese New Year, Channel 3 of CCTV aired a concert in which the thirty most popularly selected songs from television drama were performed.

3. Jonathan Culler, *Literary Theory: A Very Short Introduction,* 71.

4. Ibid., 73–74.

5. Ibid., 77.

6. Ibid., 70–71.

7. Michael Herzfeld, *Cultural Intimacy: Social Poetics in the Nation-State,* 24, 26.

8. Culler, *Literary Theory,* 77.

9. The best-known example is probably "Yiyongjun jinxingqu" (The march of the volunteers), composed for the film *Fengyun ernü* (Children of the storm, 1935), which is now the national anthem of the People's Republic of China. "Siji ge" (Four seasons), sung by Zhou Xuan in *Malu tianshi* (Street angel, 1937), has remained popular in mainland China, Taiwan, and Hong Kong.

10. The music for "The March of the Volunteers" was composed by the well-known composer Nie Er and the lyrics by Tian Han, a well-known left-wing playwright of the 1930s. For a discussion in English on this song, see Robert Chi, "The March of the Volunteers: From Movie Theme Song to National Anthem."

11. For discussion of the songs from *Yellow Earth,* see Rey Chow, *Primitive Passions: Visuality, Sexuality, Ethnography, and Contemporary Chinese Cinema.*

12. It must be noted that films like *Yellow Earth* (dir. Chen Kaige, 1984) and *Beijing Bastards* (dir. Zhang Yuan, 1993) use songs or music as a major part of their narratives. Nevertheless, none of the songs (other than the ones by Cui Jian in *Beijing Bastards* that

were already known before the film) has been performed or has lived on beyond the film. This largely has to do with the fact that *Yellow Earth* did not have a widespread viewership, and *Beijing Bastards* was not publicly distributed in China.

13. The change in the rise of one cultural form (television drama) and the decline of another (film) in mainstream culture is directly related to the structural changes in the two industries and to the role of the market. At the same time, the shift involves both a continuation in the practice of composing songs for visual narratives and a difference in how songs are used and how they are written, composed, and sung. An obvious difference is that in television dramas most of the songs are placed at the ends of an episode (as *piantou ge*, or opening songs, and *pianwei ge*, or closing songs), as opposed to somewhere in the middle of a film (in which case they are generally known as *dianying chaqu*, or songs that occur in the middle of a film). Increasingly, given the need to shorten the opening, many dramas only have an ending song to accompany the credits at the end of each episode. The placement of songs reflects the different ways these two forms of visual narratives are produced and consumed. As such, song placement is also part of the meaning-making mechanism in these visual narratives, something that affects what gets expressed in a song and how that expression is composed not only through lyrics but also through music.

14. For information on the importation of foreign programs, see Junhao Hong, *The Internationalization of Television in China: The Evolution of Ideology, Society, and Media since the Reform*.

15. A term originally associated with *Yearnings*, *daxing shinei ju* was a Chinese phrase coined at the time in reference to the model of American daytime "soap opera." This identification was later dropped, perhaps because most dramas have not been shot in the way American daytime dramas are made.

16. Within the modern context (since the late nineteenth century), there has occurred what can be identified as the elite's (or intellectuals') appropriation of "popular culture" especially in terms of cultural forms ranging from popular fiction, theater, film, music, and television. Depending on the prevailing academic trends or what ideological persuasions prevail, scholars of China in the West have offered varied evaluations of the political implications of various Chinese elite appropriations that have occurred in different modern historical periods.

17. In recent years intellectuals in China have started reexamining the "culture fever" movement of the 1980s and the "modernization" imaginary manifested in this movement. Many have argued that the marketism of the 1990s was in essence "logically" connected with the intellectual discourse of the 1980s. It is because of this connection that intellectuals themselves actively supported, participated in, and benefited from the developmentalism-oriented market reforms. See, for example, Zha Jianying, *Bashi niandai fangtanlu* (Interviews about the 1980s); Gan Yang, *Bashi niandai wenhua yishi* (Cultural consciousness of the 1980s); Wang Hui, "'Xin ziyou zhuyi' de lishi genyuan jiqi pipan—zai lun dangdai Zhongguo dalu de sixiang zhuangkuang yu xiandaixing wenti" (Critiquing the historical resources of "neoliberalism").

18. The last four lines in the opening song, "Bless Good-Hearted People" ("好人一生平安"): "谁能与我同醉，相识年年岁岁，咫尺天涯皆有缘，此情温暖人间."

19. From the middle of "Long Ago Years" ("悠悠岁月"): 漫漫人生路，上下求索，心中渴望真诚的生活，谁能告诉我，是对还是错，问询南来北往的客。恩怨忘却，留下真情从头说. It is not easy to convey the meaning of the title of this song in English. The word "悠" (*you*) refers to the distant past with a touch of nostalgia but nevertheless also suggests that the past always consisted of both good and bad. Music by Lei Lei; lyrics by Yi Ming.

20. Translation from the English subtitles of the VCD version of the drama that is both English- and Chinese-subtitle-ready. The Chinese original goes as follows: 滚滚长江东逝去，浪花淘尽英雄 / 是非成败转空头，青山依旧在 / 几度夕阳红，白发鱼樵江渚上 / 惯看球越春风，一壶浊酒喜相逢 / 古今多少事，都付笑谈中. Music by Gu Jianfen; lyrics by Wang Jian.

21. The Chinese original is as follows: 看不尽，繁华万里/转瞬间落日残烟/图昌盛，百年一梦/看兴衰，弹指挥间. Music by Zhang Qianyi; lyrics by Zhao Daming.

22. The Chinese original is as follows: 数英雄，论成败 / 古今谁能说明白 / 千秋功罪任评说 / 海雨天风独往来 / 一心要江山图治垂青史 / 也难说身后骂名滚滚来 / 有道是人间万苦人最苦 / 终不悔九死落尘埃 / 有道是得民心者得天下 / 看江山由谁来主宰. Music by Xu Peidong; lyrics by Liang Guohua.

23. The Chinese original is as follows: 在滔滔的长河中，你是一朵浪花 / 在绵绵的山脉中，你是一座奇峰 / 你把寂寞藏进乌云的缝隙 / 你把梦想写在蓝天草原 / 你燃烧自己，温暖大地，任自己成为灰烬 / 让一缕缕火焰翩翩起舞，那就是你最后的倾诉. Music by Zhang Hongguang; lyrics by Gegen Tana.

24. Marshall Berman, *All That Is Solid Melts into Air: The Experience of Modernity.*

25. Some scholars, in their examination of Western "historiography," have pointed out that, at least in North America, the study of Chinese history was traditionally relegated to departments other than history departments and was identified as part of the study of "Chinese civilization." For more information, see Q. Edward Wang and George G. Iggers, eds., *Turning Points in Historiography: A Cross-Cultural Perspective;* Lin Chun, "Introduction: Modernity and the Study of China."

26. Given the structural changes in cultural production in the decades after the 1980s, many of these songs function in a public way, more than other cultural forms such as literature, experimental arts, film, and theater, in expressing sentiments that are in effect paradoxically socially critical of the age of roaring economic development.

27. Opening song of *Heroes Have No Regrets* (英雄无悔). The original is as follows: 除了真情，我还能给你什么 / 除了善良，我还能爱你什么 / 除了勇气，我还能留住什么 / 除了伤痛，我还能忘记什么 / 梦想让我们一次次选择 / 又让我们一次次错过 / 真心把我们紧紧连在一起 / 除了误会，我们还能对它，能对它说什么. Music by Cheng Dazhao; lyrics by Li Meng.

28. From *Good Cops and Bad Cops* (刑警本色). Chinese original: 黎明已带我上路，我不能停下脚步 / 善良的人在为我祝福，黄昏落下了帷幕 / 其实我并不孤独，再多地苦我愿意付出 / 我在风雨中追逐，寻找那前面的路 / 我要把这黑暗征服，所以我不能输 / 我要把这黑暗征服，所以我不能哭. Music by Wang Xiaofeng; lyrics by Jiang Mu.

29. Walter Benjamin, *Illuminations*, 256.

30. From *Jade Goddess of Mercy* (玉观音). Chinese original: 请记住冬夜里我的叮咛 / 请留下月光中我的希望 / 请让我亲吻着你的名字 / 请让我铭记着你的善良 / 我仰望苍天群星闪烁 / 我面对苍天呼唤你的出现. Music by Ye Xiaogang; lyrics by Hai Yan.

31. Su Xiaoming became a household name in 1980 after she sang "Jungang zhiye" (As night falls on a naval port) in a nontraditional way. At the time, she was a singer from the Navy Performance Troupe (Haizheng Wengongtuan). Her singing style generated much debate, but today she is known as the mainland Chinese singer who introduced *tongsu changfa:* singing in a "pop manner."

32. Deng Lijun (1953–1995) was a legendary singer originally from Taiwan whose singing style and whose songs became widely (and wildly) popular in Taiwan, Hong Kong, and the Chinese communities in Southeast Asia in the 1970s and 1980s. She was introduced and popularized in China at the time when Deng Xiaoping became the top leader in the Chinese Communist Party and when he promoted the open-door and reform policies. People jokingly referred to them as "Xiao Deng" (the young Deng) and "Lao Deng" (the old Deng), with the former being listened to at night (Deng Lijun) and the other during the day (Deng Xiaoping).

33. From *The Police Chief* (公安局长). Chinese original: 还有没有，一段往事能回首 / 记忆注定伤痛的心让那岁月穿透 / 还有没有，一段往事能挥走 / 沉默教会孤独的你找到忘记的借口 / 还有没有，可以信任的朋友 / 真诚铸就最初的爱让那时光倒流 / 还有没有，可以感受的温柔 / 善良相信诺言还在那是铭记的理由 / 无怨无悔，真情不变 / 诚伴一生 / 哪怕荆棘挡住前路看不清是迷雾 / 未来的手牵着你，你还要走 / 没有尽头不能停留，一生别无所求. Music by Xiao Zhe; lyrics by Liu Yunlong.

## Epilogue

1. In Chinese, *xue* refers to *xueshu,* which usually means scholarship. In this case, however, it refers to the academy, specifically the structural and ideological changes that have taken place in universities and the fact that higher education as an institution has become part of the power establishment.

2. *He shang,* or *River Elegy* (1987), is a six-episode televisual essay originated by a group of scholars, including Su Xiaokang and Wang Luxiang, who criticized "traditional Chinese culture" allegorically and celebrated "Western civilization" (*xifang wenming*). In many ways, this television show is representative of the mind-set of Chinese intellectuals of the 1980s, who imagined and directly argued that the West was the answer to China's problems. For scholarly responses to this televisual text, see, for example, Su Xiaokang and Wang Luxing, *Deathsong of the River,* and Jing Wang "*He Shang* and the Paradoxes of Chinese Enlightenment."

3. Among the earliest challengers of the "modernization" and "modernity" imaginary are He Qinglian's *Xiandaihua de xianjin* (Pitfalls of modernization, 1998), and Wang Hui's "Dangdai Zhongguo de sixiang zhuangkuang yu xiandaixing" (Contemporary Chinese thought and the question of modernity). Both articles help mark the beginning of the late-twentieth-century intellectual debates in China.

4. In recent years, Western scholars have begun to notice post-1980 intellectual debates in China. See Ted Huters' introduction to Wang Hui, *China's New Order,* 2–39; Kang Liu, "Is There an Alternative to (Capitalist) Globalization? The Debate about Modernity, Postmodernity, and Postcoloniality," in *Globalization and Cultural Trends in China,* 23–45; Xudong Zhang, ed., *Wither China?;* Xudong Zhang, *Postsocialism and Cultural Politics;* Sujian Guo and Baogang Guo, eds., *China in Search of a Harmonious Society;*

Edward Gu and Merle Goldman, eds., *Chinese Intellectuals between State and Market;* Min Lin with Maria Galikowski, *The Search for Modernity: Chinese Intellectuals and Cultural Discourse in the Post-Mao Era;* Chaohua Wang, ed., *One China, Many Paths.*

5. These debates are most active and intense on the Internet. Websites representing different ideological persuasions among intellectuals (mostly writers, critics, and academics) and ordinary netizens is an ongoing reality in today's China. Such websites include www.xschina.org, www.wyzxsx.com, www.eduww.com, and www.tecn.cn, representing various positions and perspectives.

# Glossary

"Ai, shi buneng wangji de" 爱，是不能忘记的
Ban Gu 班固
*Beijing dianying xueyuan xuebao* 北京电影学院学报
*Beijingren zai Niuyue* 北京人在纽约
*Bianyi jingcha* 便衣警察
bianzi ju 辫子剧
*Biele, Wengehua* 别了，温哥华
*Cangtian zai shang* 苍天在上
*Chen Zhen* 陈真
Chi Li 池莉
*Cuotuo suiyue* 蹉跎岁月
*Da ming gongci* 大明宫词
*Dangdai dianshi* 当代电视
*Daxiao de nüer* 大校的女儿
daxing shinei ju 大型室内剧
*Daxue wuheng* 大雪无痕
Deng Lijun 邓丽君
deng xia hei 灯下黑
dianshiju 电视剧
*Dianshiju chuangzuo yishu* 电视剧创作艺术
*Dianshiju meixue* 电视剧美学
*Dianshiju shenmei tezheng tansuo* 电视剧审美特征探索
*Dianshi juzuo yishu* 电视剧作艺术
*Dianshi yishulun* 电视艺术论
diwang ju 帝王剧
Dong Cunrui 董存瑞
*Dongbian richu xibian yu* 东边日出西边雨
*Dongwu xiongmeng* 动物凶猛
*Ermo* 二嫫
Eryuehe/Ling Jiefang 二月河/凌解放
fanfu ju 反腐剧
*Fannao rensheng* 烦恼人生
fazhi (rule by law) 法制
fazhi (rule of law) 法治
*Fen dou* 奋斗
fenghua xueyue ju 风花雪月剧
*Fengliu caizi Ji Xiaolan* 风流才子纪晓岚
Fulian 妇联
Gao Xixi 高希希
gaobie geming 告别革命
geming lishi ju 革命历史剧
*Gongan juzhang* 公安局长
guan, mei, chan, xue 官、媒、产、学
*Guo ba ying* 过把瘾
*Guojia gongsu* 国家公诉
guzhuang ju/xi 古装剧/戏
Hai Yan/Si Haiyan 海岩/佀海岩
Han ju 韩剧
*Han shu* 汉书
*Han wu da di* 汉武大帝
*Haoren yisheng ping'an* 好人一生平安
*He shang* 河殇
*Hei bing* 黑冰
*Hei dong* 黑洞
*Hei fen* 黑粉
*Hei jin* 黑金
*Hei qiang* 黑枪
*Hei wu* 黑雾
hexie shehui 和谐社会
*Honglou meng* 红楼梦
hongse jingdian ju 红色经典剧

*Hongse kangnaixin* 红色康乃馨
Hu Mei 胡玫
Huang Jiguang 黄继光
huangdi ju 皇帝剧
*Huanzhu gege* 还珠格格
hunyin wenti ju 婚姻问题剧
*Huo Yuanjia* 霍元甲
Jia Zhangke 贾樟柯
jiating hunyin ju 家庭婚姻剧
jiating lunli ju 家庭伦理剧
*Jidushan bojue* 基督山伯爵
*Jidushan enchou ji* 基督山恩仇记
jingfei ju/pian 警匪剧/片
*Jinye you baofengxue* 今夜有暴风雪
*Juedui quanli* 绝对权力
*Juzi hongle* 橘子红了
*Kangxi dadi* 康熙大帝
*Kangxi wangchao* 康熙王朝
*Kangxi weifu sifang ji* 康熙微服私访
Ke Yunlu 柯云路
*Kewang* 渴望
*Kong fangzi* 空房子
*Kong jingzi* 空镜子
*Kong xiangzi* 空巷子
*Lailai wangwang* 来来往往
*Lanse matilian* 蓝色马蹄莲
laobaixing 老百姓
Lei Feng 雷锋
Liang Xiaosheng 梁晓声
Lu Tianming 陆天明
*Na shenme zhengjiu ni, wode airen* 拿什么拯救你，我的爱人
nüxing jiating hunyin ju 女性家庭婚姻剧
nüxing wenti ju 女性问题剧
Ozaki Fumiaki 尾崎文昭
*Pingdan shenghuo* 平淡生活
*Qianlong huangdi* 乾隆皇帝
*Qianlong wangchao* 乾隆王朝
*Qian shou* 牵手
*Qin Shi Huang* 秦始皇
qingchun ju 青春剧
qingchun ouxiang ju 青春偶像剧
Qiong Yao 琼瑶
quanli (power) 权力
quanli (rights) 权利
*Ren xiaoyao* 任逍遥
Ri ju 日剧
rushang ju 儒商剧
*Sanguo yanyi* 三国演义
*Sanxia haoren* 三峡好人
*Shanghai tan* 上海滩
shean ju 涉案剧
shenghuo ju 生活剧
*Shi ji* 史记
*Shibing tuji* 士兵突击
*Shuihu zhuan* 水浒传
Sima Qian 司马迁
*Sishi tongtang* 四世同堂
*Tiechi tongya Ji Xiaolan* 铁齿铜牙纪晓岚
Wan Fang 万方
Wang Baoqiang 王宝强
Wang Hailing 王海翎
Wang Shuo 王朔
wenyi wei gongnongbing fuwu 文艺为工农兵服务
*Wu Zetian* 武则天
wuxia ju 武侠剧
*Xiang wu xiang yu you xiang feng* 像雾像雨又像风
*Xiao Wu* 小武
*Xiaozhuang mishi* 孝庄秘史
Xie Jin 谢晋
*Xin jiehun shidai* 新结婚时代
*Xingjing bense* 刑警本色
Xiongnu 匈奴
*Xishuo Qianlong* 戏说乾隆
*Xiyou ji* 西游记
Xu Sanduo 许三多
*Xuese langman* 血色浪漫
*Xue yi* 血疑
*Yangguang canlan de rizi* 阳光灿烂的日子
*Yangniu zai Beijing* 洋妞在北京
yasu gongshang 雅俗共赏
Yin Hong 尹鸿
*Yingshi yishu* 影视艺术
*Yingxiong wuhui* 英雄无悔
*Yiyongjun jinxingqu* 义勇军进行曲

*Yong bu mingmu* 永不瞑目
*Yongzheng huangdi* 雍正皇帝
*Yongzheng wangchao* 雍正王朝
*Youyou suiyue* 悠悠岁月
*Yu guanyin* 玉观音
yu guoji jiegui 与国际接轨
yu shi jujin 与时俱进
*Zaixiang Liu Luoguo* 宰相刘罗锅
Zhang Chenggong 张成功
Zhang Jie 张洁
Zhang Ping 张平
Zhang Side 张思德
Zhang Xinxin 张辛欣
Zhang Yiwu 张颐武
*Zhantai* 站台
Zhao Baogang 赵宝刚
*Zhenqing niandai* 真情年代
zhibo fenli 制播分离
*Zhigao liyi* 至高利益
*Zhongcheng* 忠诚
*Zhongguo dianshi* 中国电视
*Zhongguo dianshi hongpishu* 中国电视红皮书
*Zhongguo guangbo yingshi* 中国广播影视
*Zhongguo shi lihun* 中国式离婚
*Zhongguo zhizao* 中国制造
Zhou Meisen 周梅森
Zhou Xiaowen 周晓文
zhuxuanlü 主旋律
*Zouxiang gonghe* 走向共和
zuoan 左岸

# Filmography

This filmography lists most dramas mentioned in the book under their English titles. Recognizing the difference between film and television production in China, I credit script writers as well as directors. Although there tends to be more than one production company for each serial, given limited space, I list only one such entity for each drama. I use pinyin to identify these companies so that they can be easily identified by other researchers.

Entry style: English title (pinyin) Chinese characters (script writer[s]; director[s]); production company, year). No. of episodes.

*Absolute Power* (*Juedui quanli*) 绝对权力 (Zhou Meisen, Sun Xinyue; Cheng Hao and Jiao Shaohua; Hunan Dianguang Chuanmei Gufen Youxian Gongsi Jiemu Fengongsi et al., 2003). 27 episodes.

*Age of True Feelings* (*Zhenqing niandai*) 真情年代 (Li Ming, Zhang Ruizheng, Gao Shan; Gao Xixi; Zhongyang Dianshitai Wenyi Zhongxin Yingshibu et al., 2005). 31 episodes.

*As Tangerines Turn Red* (*Juzi hongle*) 橘子红了 (Qi Jun; Li Shaohong; Zhongguo Guojidianshi Zong Gongsi, 2002). 25 episodes.

*Black Fog* (*Hei wu*) 黑雾 (Zhang Chenggong; Pang Hao; Nanjing Dianshitai, 2003). 24 episodes.

*Black Guns* (*Hei qiang*) 黑枪 (Fu Jingsheng; Jiuzhou Yingshi Wenhua Jiaoliu Youxian Gongsi et al., 2004). 32 episodes.

*Black Hole* (*Hei dong*) 黑洞 (Lu Chuan, Zhang Chenggong; Guan Hu; Beijing Dianying Zhipianchang et al., 2000). 31 episodes.

*Black Ice* (*Hei bing*) 黑冰 (Zhang Chenggong; Wang Jixing; Shanghai Dongfang Dianshitai et al., 2001). 20 episodes.

*Black Money* (*Hei jin*) 黑金 (Jiang Dian; Liu Xin; Shanhai Dianying Jituan Gongsi Dianshiju Zhizuo Zhongxin et al., 2002). 20 episodes.

*Black Powder* (*Hei fen*) 黑粉 (Zhang Yongshen; Dong Zhiqiang; Tianjin Dianshitai Dianshiju Zhizuo Zhongxin et al., 2000). 20 episodes.

*Blue Lilies* (*Lanse matilian*) 蓝色马蹄莲 (Chen Xinhao; Wang Wenjie; Shanghai Wenguang Xinwen Chuanmei Jituan et al., 2002). 20 episodes.

*Clever-and-Sharp-Mouthed Ji Xiaolan* I, II, III, IV (*Tiechi tongya Ji Xiaolan*) 铁齿铜牙纪晓岚 (Chen Wengui; Liu Jiacheng, Luo Changan; Beijing Yahuan Yingshi Zhizuo Youxian Gongsi et al., 2000–2009). 165 episodes.

*Comings and Goings* (*Lailai wangwang*) 来来往往 (Zhang Junan, Ma Xiaoyin, Fu Jingsheng; Tian Di; Beijing Zhongbo Xiandai Touzi Zixun Youxian Zeren Gongsi et al., 1998). 18 episodes.

*Divorce Chinese Style* (*Zhongguo shi lihun*) 中国式离婚 (Wang Hailing; Shen Yan; Chunzhen Niandai Wenhua Chuanbo Youxian Gongsi et al., 2004). 23 episodes.

*East Sunshine, West Rain* (*Dongbian richu xibianyu*) 东边日出西边雨 (Li Xiaoming; Zhao Baogang; Beijing Chengxiang Yingshi Zhizuo Gongsi et al., 1995). 20 episodes.

*Emperor Kangxi Traveling Undercover* I (*Kangxi weifu sifang ji*) 康熙微服私访记 I (Zou Jingzhi; Zhang Zien; Guangdong Juxing Yingye Youxian Gongsi, 1997). 30 episodes.

*Emperor Kangxi Traveling Undercover* II (*Kangxi weifu sifang ji*) 康熙微服私访记 II (Zou Jingshi; Zhang Guoli; Guangdong Juxing Yingye Youxian Gongsi, 1999). 30 episodes.

*Emperor Kangxi Traveling Undercover* III (*Kangxi weifu sifang ji*) 康熙微服私访记 III (Zou Jingzhi; Zhang Guoli; Guangdong Juxing Yingye Youxian Gongsi, 2001). 26 episodes.

*Emperor Wu of the Han Dynasty* (*Han wu da di*) 汉武大帝 (Jiang Qitao; Hu Mei; Zhongguo Dianying Jituan Gongsi et al., 2004). 64 episodes.

*Empress Wu Zetian* (*Wu Zetian*) 武则天 (Zhang Tianmin, Ran Ping, Ke Zhanghe; Chen Jialin; Zhongguo Guoji Dianshi Zong Gongsi, 1995). 30 episodes.

*Empty Alleyway* (*Kong xiangzi*) 空巷子 (Xiao Yu, Zheng Kainan; Wang Xiaoming; Wanke Yingshi Youxian Gongsi et al., 2007). 30 episodes.

*Empty House* (*Kong fangzi*) 空房子 (Wan Fang, Cheng Shijian; Chen Guoxing; Wanke Yingshi Youxian Gongsi et al., 2004). 19 episodes.

*Eyes Forever Open* (*Yong bu mingmu*) 永不瞑目 (Hai Yan; Zhao Baogang; Hairun Guoji Guanggao Youxian Gongsi et al., 1999). 27 episodes.

*Four Generations under One Roof* (*Sishi tongtang*) 四世同堂 (Lin Ruwei, Li Xiang, Niu Xingli; Lin Ruwei; Beijing Dianshi Zhipian Chang, 1985). 28 episodes.

*Good-bye, Vancouver* (*Biele, Wengehua*) 别了，温哥华 (Gao Xuan, Ren Baoru; Zhao Baogang; Zhongguo Dianying Jituan Gongsi et al., 2003). 22 episodes.

*Good Cops and Bad Cops* (*Xingjing bense*) 刑警本色 (Zhang Chengong, Yang Haibo; Zhang Jiandong; Nanfang Zhengquan Beijing Siyu Guanggao Gongsi et al., 1999). 22 episodes.

*Heavens Above* (*Cangtian zai shang*) 苍天在上 (Lu Tianmin; Zhou Huan; Zhongguo Dianshiju Zhongxin, 1995). 17 episodes.

*Heroes Have No Regrets* (*Yingxiong wuhui*) 英雄无悔 (Deng Yuan et al.; He Mengfan et al.; Guangdong Dianshitai et al., 1995). 39 episodes.

*Holding Hands* (*Qian shou*) 牵手 (Wang Hailing; Yang Yang; Zhongguo Guoji Dianshi Zong Gongsi et al., 1999). 18 episodes.

*Huo Yuanjia* (*Huo Yuanjia*) 霍元甲 (Zhang Huabiao; Xu Xiaoming; Xianggang Lidi Dianshi, 1981). 20 episodes.

*In the Name of the Highest Principle* (*Zhigao liyi*) 至高利益 (Zhou Meisen; Ba Te Er; Zhongguo Dianshitai Zhongguo Guoji Dianshi Zong Gongsi et al., 2001). 20 episodes.

*Jade Goddess of Mercy* (*Yu Guanyin*) 玉观音 (Hai Yan; Ding Hei; Hairun Yingshi Zhizuo Youxian Gongsi et al., 2003). 27 episodes.

*Ji Xiaolan, the Gifted Talent* (*Fengliu caizi Ji Xiaolan*) 风流才子纪晓岚 (Ding Shanxi, Sun Shupei; Wu Song; Guangdong Juxing Yingye Youxian Gongsi et al., 2001). 25 episodes.

*Journey to the West* (*Xiyou ji*) 西游记 (Yang Jie; Zhongguo Dianshiju Zhizuo Zhongxin et al., 1982–1988). 25 episodes.

*The Kangxi Court* (*Kangxi wangchao*) 康熙王朝 (Zhu Sujin, Hu Jianxin; Chen Jialin, Liu Dayin; Zhongguo Guoji Dianshi Zong Gongsi, 2001). 50 episodes.

*Like Fog, Like Rain, Also Like Wind* (*Xiang wu xiang yu you xiang feng*) 像雾像雨又像风 (Zhang Baochen; Zhao Baogang;, Beijing Dianying Zhipianchang Dianshi Jimu Zhizuo Zhongxin et al., 2001). 30 episodes.

*Loyalty* (*Zhongcheng*) 忠诚 (Zhou Meisen; Hu Mei; Shanghai Shiwei Xuanchuanbu et al., 2001). 20 episodes.

*Marching towards the Republic* (*Zouxiang gonghe*) 走向共和 (Sheng Heyu, Zhang Jianwei; Zhang Li; Zhongguo Guoji Dianshi Zong Gongsi et al., 2003). 59 episodes.

*Marriage in the New Era* (*Xin jiehun shidai*) 新结婚时代 (Wang Hailing; Yan Bo; Zhongguo Hu Yingshi Zhizuo Gongsi et al., 2006). 25 episodes.

*Nothing in the Mirror* (*Kong jingzi*) 空镜子 (Wan Fang; Yang Yazhou; Zhongguo Guoji Dianshi Zong Gongsi et al., 2001). 20 episodes.

*Ordinary Life* (*Pingdan shenghuo*) 平淡生活 (Hai Yan; Ding Hei; Hairun Yingshi Zhizuo Youxian Gongsi, 2004). 24 episodes.

*Outlaws of the Marsh* (*Shuihu zhuan*) 水浒传 (Yang Zhengguang, Ran Ping; Zhang Shaolin; Zhongguo Dianshiju Zhizuo Zhongxin, 1997). 43 episodes.

*Palace of Desire* (*Daming gongci*) 大明宫词 (Zheng Zhong, Wang Yao; Li Shaohong and Zeng Nianping; Zhongyang Dianshitai et al., 1999). 40 episodes.

*Plain-Clothed Cops* (*Bianyi jingcha*) 便衣警察 (Hai Yan; Lin Ruwei and Cai Fade; Bejing Dianshi Yishu Zhongxin, 1987). 12 episodes.

*Playfully Told Tales of Emperor Qianlong* (*Xishuo Qianlong*) 戏说乾隆 (Song Xiangru; Fan Xiuming; Beijing Dianying Zhipianchang Dianshi Bu and Taiwan Feiteng Dianying Gongsi, 1991). 41 episodes.

*The Police Chief* (*Gongan juzhang*) 公安局长 (Wei Ren; Zhang Guoqing; Gonganbu Yingshi Wenhua Zhongxin et al., 2002). 21 episodes.

*Prime Minister Liu Luoguo* (*Zaixiang Liu Luoguo*) 宰相刘罗锅 (Shi Ling et al.; Zhang Zien; Beijing Chengxiang Yingshi Zhizuo Gongsi et al., 1994). 40 episodes.

*Princess Huanzhu* I (*Huanzhu gege*) 还珠格格 I (Qiong Yao; Sun Shupei; Hunan Jingji Dianshitai, 1997). 24 episodes.

*Princess Huanzhu* II (*Huanzhu gege*) 还珠格格 II (Qiong Yao; Sun Shupei; Hunan Jingji Dianshitai, 1999). 48 episodes.

*Princess Huanzhu* III (*Huanzhu gege*) 还珠格格 III (Qiong Yao; Ling Ping, Ding Yangguo; Hunan Dianshitai, 2003). 40 episodes.

*The Qianlong Court* (*Qianlong wangchao*) 乾隆王朝 (Chen Yasheng, Shui Yunxian, Yao Yuan; Ma Xiao, Zhao Lei; Hunan Dianguang Chuanmei Gufen Youxian Gongsi et al., 2002). 40 episodes.

*Red Carnations* (*Hongse kangnaixin*) 红色康乃馨 (Chen Xinhao; Bao Fuming; Zhongguo Guoji Dianshi Zong Gongsi et al., 2000). 22 episodes.

*Romance of Three Kingdoms* (*Sanguo yanyi*) 三国演义 (Du Jiafu et al.; Wang Fulin; Zhongguo Dianshiju Zhizuo Zhongxin, 1994). 84 episodes.

*Romantic Life in Brilliant Red* (*Xuese langman*) 血色浪漫 (Du Liang; Teng Wenji; Runya Yingshi Chuanbo Youxian Gongsi et al., 2004). 33 episodes.

*Senior Colonel's Daughter* (*Daxiao de nüer*) 大校的女儿 (Wang Hailing; Zhang Jinzhan; Zhongyang Dianshitai Yingshibu et al., 2007). 20 episodes.

*Snow-Covered Traces* (*Daxue wuhen*) 大雪无痕 (Lu Tianming; Lei Xianhe; Zhongguo Dianshiju Zhizuo Zhongxin et al., 2000). 20 episodes.

*Soldiers, Be Ready* (*Shibing tuji*) 士兵突击 (Lan Xiaolong; Kang Honglei; Bayi Dianying Zhipian Chang et al., 2006). 30 episodes.

*Sued by the State* (*Guojia gongsu*) 国家公诉 (Zhou Meisen, Sun Xinyue; Jiang Shaohua; Shanghai Dongfang Dianying Pingdao et al., 2003). 35 episodes.

*There's a Snow Storm Tonight* (*jinye you baofengxue*) 今夜有暴风雪 (Li Deshun, Sun Zhou; Sun Zhou; Shandong Dianshitai, 1984). 4 episodes.

*Time Idled Away* (*Cuotuo suiyue*) 蹉跎岁月 (Ye Xin; Cai Xiaoqing; Zhongyang Dianshitai, 1982). 4 episodes.

*Unknown Life of Empress Xiaozhuang* (*Xiaozhuang mishi*) 孝庄秘史 (Yang Haiwei; You Xiaogang, Liu Dekai; Beijing Dingdu Shiji Wenhua Fazhan Youxian Gongsi, et al., 2000). 38 episodes.

*With What to Save You, My Loved One* (*Na shenme zhengjiu ni, wode airen*) 拿什么拯救你，我的爱人 (Hai Yan; Zhao Baogang; Hairun Yingshi Zhizuo Gongsi et al., 2002). 23 episodes.

*Yearnings* (*Kewang*) 渴望 (Li Xiaoming; Lu Xiaowei; Beijing Dianshi Yishu Zhongxin, 1990). 50 episodes.

*The Yongzheng Court* (*Yongzheng wangchao*) 雍正王朝 (Liu Heping, Luo Qinglie; Hu Mei; Zhongguo Dianshitai Yingshibu et al., 1998). 44 episodes.

# Bibliography


Abelmann, Nancy. *The Melodrama of Mobility: Women, Talk, and Class in Contemporary South Korea.* Honolulu: University of Hawai'i Press, 2003.

Ai Zhisheng. "Jinyibu duanzheng chuangzuo fangxiang, fanrong dianshiju yishu" (Continue to follow the correction direction in the flourishing art of television drama). *Zhongguo renmin daxue shubao ziliao zhongxin fuying baokan ziliao* (Archives of newspaper and magazine materials at the Publication Information Center at Renmin University) 7 (1990): 82–86.

Allen, Robert. "On Reading Soaps." In E. Ann Kaplan, ed., *Regarding Television: Critical Approaches,* 97–108. Los Angeles: The American Film Institute/University Publications of America, 1983.

Bai, Ruoyun. "'Clean Officials,' Emotional Moral Community, and Anti-Corruption Television Drama." In Ying Zhu, Michael Keane, and Ruoyun Bai, eds., *TV Drama in China,* 47–60. Hong Kong: Hong Kong University Press, 2008.

———. "Media Commercialization, Entertainment, and the Party-State: The Political Economy of Contemporary Chinese Television Culture." *Global Media Journal* 4.6 (Spring 2005): article no. 12 (http://lass.calumet.purdue.edu/cca/gmj/submitted documents/spring2005).

Baranovitch, Nimrod. *China's New Voices: Popular Music, Ethnicity, Gender, and Politics, 1978–1997.* Berkeley: University of California Press, 2003.

Barlow, Tani, ed. *Gender Politics in Modern China: Writing and Feminism.* Durham, NC, and London: Duke University Press, 1993.

———. *The Question of Women in Chinese Feminism.* Durham, NC, and London: Duke University Press, 2004.

Barthes, Roland. "Rhetoric of the Image" (1964). In *The Responsibility of Forms: Critical Essays on Music, Art and Representation,* trans. Richard Howard, 32–51. Berkeley: University of California Press, 1991.

Bauman, Zygmunt. *Culture as Praxis.* London, Boson: Routledge and K. Paul, 1973.

Benjamin, Walter. *Illuminations.* New York: Schocken Books, 1969.

Berman, Marshall. *All That Is Solid Melts into Air: The Experience of Modernity.* New York: Simon and Schuster, 1982.

Berry, Chris, ed. *Perspectives on Chinese Cinema.* London: BFI Publishing, 1991.

Bratton, Jacky, Jim Cook, and Christine Gledhill, eds. *Melodrama: Stage Picture Screen.* London: BFI Publishing, 1994.

Brooks, Peter. *The Melodramatic Imagination: Balzac, Henry James, Melodrama, and the Mode of* Excess. New Haven: Yale University Press, 1995.

Byars, Jackie. *All That Hollywood Allows: Re-reading Gender in 1950s Melodrama.* Chapel Hill: University of North Carolina Press, 1991.

Cai, Rong. "Carnivalesque Pleasure: The Audio-Visual Market and the Consumption of Television Drama." In Ying Zhu, Michael Keane, and Ruoyun Bai, eds., *TV Drama in China,* 129–145. Hong Kong: Hong Kong University Press, 2008.

"Caifang Lu Tianming" (Interview with Lu Tianming) (http://www.hunantv.com/newspaper/20061024/news.2.htm).

Cavell, Stanley. *Contesting Tears: The Hollywood Melodrama of the Unknown Woman.* Chicago: University of Chicago Press, 1996.

Chen Mo. "Qingtingju jiazhi daoxiang toushi" (An examination of value guidance in the Qing court drama). *Dianshi yishu* (Television art) 3 (2002): 26–28.

Chen, Y., and X. Hao. "Conflict Resolution in Love Triangles: Perspectives Offered by Chinese TV Dramas." *Intercultural Communication Studies* 7 (1997–1998): 133–148.

Chen Zhiang. "'Zhuxuan lü' yijie" (One interpretation of "main melody"). *Zhongguo guangbo dianshi xuekan* (Journal of Chinese radio and television) 4 (1991): 9–13.

Cheng Wei . *Zhongchan jieji de haizimen* (Children of the middle class). Beijing: Sanlian Shudian, 2006.

Cheng, Yinghong. "Che Guevara: Dramatizing China's Divided Intelligentsia at the Turn of the Century." *Modern Chinese Literature and Culture* 5.2 (Fall 2003): 1–44.

Chi Li. "Fannao rensheng" (Vexed everyday life). *Shanghai wenxue* (Shanghai literature) 8 (1987): 4–22.

Chi, Robert. "The March of the Volunteers: From Movie Theme Song to National Anthem." In Ching Kwan Lee and Guobin Yang, eds., *Re-envisioning the Chinese Revolution: The Politics and Poetics of Collective Memories in Reform China,* 217–244. Washington, DC: Woodrow Wilson Center Press; Stanford, CA: Stanford University Press, 2007.

Chiang, Lydia. *Collecting the Self: Body and Identity in Strange Tale Collections of Late Imperial China.* Leiden and Boston: Brill, 2005.

Chinoy, Mike. *China Live: People Power and the Television Revolution.* Lanham, MD: Rowan and Littlefield, 1999.

Chow, Rey. *Primitive Passions: Visuality, Sexuality, Ethnography, and Contemporary Chinese Cinema.* New York: Columbia University Press, 1995.

———. *Sentimental Fabulations, Contemporary Chinese Films.* New York: Columbia University Press, 2007.

Ciecko, Anne T., and Sheldon H. Lu, "*Ermo:* Televisuality, Capital and the Global Village." *Jump Cut* 42 (December 1998): 77–83.

Conceison, Claire A. "The Main Melody Campaign in Chinese Spoken Drama." *Asian Theatre Journal* 11.2 (Fall 1994): 190–212.

Cui, Shuqin. "Negotiating In-Between: On New-Generation Filmmaking and Jia Zhangke's Films." *Journal of Modern Chinese Literature and Culture* 18.2 (Fall 2006): 98–130.

———. "Screening China: National Allegories and International Receptions." *Women through the Lens,* 99–126. Honolulu: University of Hawai'i Press, 2003.

Culler, Jonathan. *Literary Theory: A Very Short Introduction.* Oxford and New York: Oxford University Press, 1997.

Curtin, Michael. *Playing to the World's Biggest Audience: The Globalization of Chinese Film and TV.* Berkeley, Los Angeles, and London: University of California Press, 2007.

De Gennaro, Angelo A. *The Philosophy of Benedetto Croce: An Introduction.* New York: Greenwood Press, Publishers, 1968.

Dikotter, Frank. *Sex, Culture and Modernity in China.* Honolulu: University of Hawai'i Press, 1995.

Du Qingchun. "Zouxiang wenhua shengchan de jingdian wenben zai shengchan" (The popular cultural industry's reproduction of classics). *Beijing dianying xueyuan xuebao* (Journal of the Beijing Film Academy) 1 (2001): 11–17.

Erwin, Kathleen. "White Women, Male Desires: A Televisual Fantasy of the Transnational Family." In Mayfair Mei Hui Yang, ed., *Spaces of Their Own: Women's Public Sphere in Transnational China,* 232–257. Minneapolis and London: University of Minnesota Press, 1999.

Fairbank, John. *China: A New History.* Cambridge, MA: Belknap Press of Harvard University Press, 1992.

"Fanfu zuojia Lu Tianming: wo jiushi yao xie zhege shidai de shiqing" (Anticorruption writer Lu Tianming: I insist on writing about things that happen in our own times) (http://blog.sina.com.cn/s/blog_46d54ecd0100004w.html).

Farrer, James. *Opening Up: Youth Sex Culture and Market Reform in Shanghai.* Chicago: University of Chicago Press, 2002.

Fewsmith, Joseph. *China since Tiananmen: From Deng Xiaoping to Hu Jintao.* New York: Cambridge University Press, 2008.

Frank, Thomas. *The Conquest of Cool: Business Culture, Counterculture, and the Rise of Hip Consumerism.* Chicago: University of Chicago Press, 1997.

Freccero, Carla. "Chapter One." *Popular Culture: An Introduction,* 1–12. New York: New York University Press, 1999.

Fu, Ping. "*Ermo:* (Tele)Visualising Urban/Rural Transformation." In Chris Berry, ed., *Chinese Films in Focus: 25 New Takes,* 73–80. London: BFI Publishing, 2003.

Gan Yang. *Bashi niandai wenhua yishi* (Cultural consciousness of the 1980s). Shanghai: Shanghai Renmin Chubanshe, 2006.

Gao, Mobo Changfan. "The Rise of Neo-Nationalism and the New Left." In Leong H. Liew and Shaoguang Wang, eds., *Nationalism, Democracy and National Integration in China,* 44–62. London and New York: RoutledgeCurzon, 2004.

Gerould, Daniel, and Jeanine Parisier Plottel, eds. *Melodrama.* New York: New York Literary Forum, 1980.

Gilmartin, Christina K., Gail Hershatter, Lisa Rofel, and Tyrene White, eds. *Engendering China: Women, Culture, and The State.* Cambridge, MA, and London, England: Harvard University Press, 1994.

Gladwell, Malcolm. "The Coolhunt" (originally printed in *The New Yorker,* March 17, 1997). http://www.gladwell.com/1997/1997_03_17_a_cool.htm.

Gledhill, Christine, ed. *Home Is Where the Heart Is: Studies in Melodrama and the Women's Film.* London: BFI Publishing, 1987.

Gu, Edward, and Merle Goldman, eds. *Chinese Intellectuals between State and Market.* London and New York: RoutledgeCurzon, 2004.

"Guanyu *Kong fangzi* de zhengyi" (Controversies about *Empty House*). http://www.yntv.cn/yntv_web/category/30201/2005/11/30/2005-11-30_296523_30201.shtml.

Guo, Sujian, and Baogang Guo, eds. *China in Search of a Harmonious Society.* Lanham, MD: Lexington Books, 2008.

Han Shaogong. "Lengzhan hou: wenxue yu xiezuo xin de chujing" (After the Cold War: new context for literature and creative writing). *Dangdai zuojia pinglun* (Review of contemporary writers) 3 (2003): 26–39.

Hansen, Miriam. *Babel and Babylon: Spectatorship in American Silent Film.* Cambridge, MA: Harvard University Press, 1991.

Hays, Michael, and Anastasia Nikolopoulou, eds. *Melodrama: The Cultural Emergence of a Genre.* New York: St. Martin's Press, 1996.

He Qinglian. *Xiandaihua de xianjin* (Pitfalls of modernization). Beijing: Jinri Zhongguo Chubanshe, 1998.

He Xiaobing. "Dianshiju 'bian zi xian xiang' guan kui" (A close look at the "phenomenon of pigtails" in television drama). *Dianshi yishu* (Television art) 2 (2001): 22–26.

Herzfeld, Michael. *Cultural Intimacy: Social Poetics in the Nation-State.* New York: Routledge, 2005.

Hong, Junhao. "China's TV Program Import 1958–1988: Towards the Internationalization of Television?" *Gazette* 52 (1993): 1–23.

———. *The Internationalization of Television in China: The Evolution of Ideology, Society, and Media since the Reform.* Westport, CT: Praeger, 1998.

———. "Penetration and Interaction of Mass Media between Taiwan, Hong Kong and the Mainland China: Trends and Implications." In Bin Yu and Tsungting Chung, eds., *Dynamics and Dilemma: Mainland, Taiwan and Hong Kong in a Changing World,* 185–208. New York: Nova Science Publishers, 1996.

Huang Qing. "Weihe jingpingju chongbo yu yan yu lie?" (Why is there an increasing interest in reruns of television drama classics?). *People's Daily* (overseas edition), December 23, 2002.

Huang, Ya-chien. "Pink Dramas: Reconciling Consumer Modernity and Confucian Womanhood." In Ying Zhu, Michael Keane, and Ruoyun Bai, eds., *TV Drama in China,* 103–114. Hong Kong: Hong Kong University Press, 2008.

Huang, Yasheng. *Selling China: Foreign Direct Investment during the Reform Era.* New York: Cambridge University Press, 2003.

Hyslop, Gabrielle. "Deviant and Dangerous Behavior: Women in Melodrama." *The Journal of Public Culture* 19.3 (March 2004): 65–78.

Ito, Ken K. *An Age of Melodrama: Family, Gender, and Social Hierarchy in the Turn-of-the-Century Japanese Novel.* Stanford, CA: Stanford University Press, 2008.

Jones, Andrew. *Like a Knife: Ideology and Genre in Contemporary Chinese Popular Music.* Ithaca, NY: East Asian Program, Cornell University, 1992.

———. "The Politics of Popular Music in Post Tiananmen China." In Susan D. Blum and Lionel M. Jensen, eds., *China Off Center: Mapping Margins of the Middle Kingdom,* 291–308. Honolulu: University of Hawai'i Press, 2002.

Judd, Ellen. *The Chinese Women's Movement between the State and Market.* Stanford, CA: Stanford University Press, 2002.

Kaplan, E. Ann. *Motherhood and Representations: The Mother in Popular Culture and Melodrama.* New York: Routledge, 1992.

Keane, Michael. "By the Way, FUCK YOU! Feng Xiaogang's Disturbing Television Dramas." *Media, Culture and Society* 23 (2001): 176–202.

———. "Television Drama in China: Engineering Souls for the Market." In Richard King and Timothy Craig, eds., *Global Goes Local: Popular Culture in Asia,* 176–202. Honolulu: University of Hawai'i Press, 2003.

Kinkley, Jeffrey C. *Chinese Justice, the Fiction: Law and Literature in Modern China.* Stanford, CA: Stanford University Press, 2000.

———. *Corruption and Realism in Late Socialist China: The Return of the Political Novel.* Stanford, CA: Stanford University Press, 2007.

———. "The Trendsetter: Lu Tianming's *Heaven Above.*" In *Corruption and Realism in Late Socialist China: The Return of the Political Novel,* 22–46. Stanford, CA: Stanford University Press, 2007.

Knight, Sabina. *The Heart of Time: Moral Agency in Twentieth-Century Chinese Fiction.* Cambridge, MA, and London: Harvard University Asia Center, 2006.

Kraicer, Shelly. "Chinese Wasteland: Jia Zhangke's Still Life." *Cinema Scope* 29 (http://www.cinema-scope.com/cs29/feat_kraicer/still.html).

Lang, Miriam. "San Mao and Qiong Yao, a 'Popular' Pair." *Modern Chinese Literature and Culture* 15.2 (Fall 2003): 76–120.

Larson, Wendy. *From Ah Q to Lei Feng: Freud and Revolutionary Spirit in Twentieth-Century China.* Stanford, CA: Stanford University Press, 2009.

Lee, Dennis. "Jia Zhangke's Portraits of China's Convulsive Change." *International Herald Tribune,* January 22, 2008 (http://www.iht.com/articles/2008/1/22/arts/chinfilm.php).

Lee, Gregory. *Troubadours, Trumpeters, Trouble Makers: Lyricism, Nationalism, and Hybridity in China and Its Other.* Durham, NC: Duke University Press, 1996.

Lee, Haiyan. "Nannies for Foreigners: The Enchantment of Chinese Womanhood in the Age of Millennial Capitalism." *Public Culture* 18.3 (Fall 2006): 507–529.

———. *Revolution of the Heart: A Genealogy of Love in China: 1900–1950.* Stanford, CA: Stanford University Press, 2007.

Lee, Kevin. "Jia Zhangke." *Senses of Cinema* (http://www.sensesofcinema.com/contents/directors/03/jia.html).

Leonard, Mark. "China's New Intellegentsia." *Prospect,* March 2008 (http://www.prospect-magazine.co.uk/article_details.php?id=10078).

Li Jie. "Xie Jin's Era Should End." In George S. Semsel, Xia Hong, and Hou Jianping, eds., *Chinese Film Theory: A Guide to the New Era,* 147–148. New York: Praeger, 1990.

Li Peng. "Guanyu zhibo fenli" (About *zhibo fenli*). *Guangdian zai xian,* November 8, 2001 (http://www.catvshow.com/tech-center/digital_TV/21.htm).

Li Zehou and Liu Zaifu. *Gaobie geming: huiwang ershi shiji zhongguo* (Farewell to revolution: a retrospective on twentieth-century China). Hong Kong: Tiandi Tushu Youxian Gongsi, 1995.

Liang Qichao. *Shaonian Zhongguo shuo* (On a youthful China). 1900. In *Yinbingshi wenji* (Collected writings from the studio of the Ice-Drinker), vol. 2, 7–12. Shanghai: Zhonghua Shuju, 1926.

Liew, Leong H., and Shangguang Wang, eds. *Nationalism, Democracy and National Integration in China.* London and New York: RoutledgeCurzon, 2004.

Lin Chun. "Introduction: Modernity and the Study of China." In Lin Chun, ed., *China*, vol. 1, xi–xxxvii. Aldershot, England: Dartmouth; Burlington, VT: Ashgate Publishing, 2000.

———. *The Transformation of Chinese Socialism.* Durham, NC, and London: Duke University Press, 2006.

Lin, Min, with Maria Galikowski. *The Search for Modernity: Chinese Intellectuals and Cultural Discourse in the Post-Mao Era.* New York: St. Martin's Press, 1999.

Lin, Xiaoping. "Jia Zhangke's Cinematic Trilogy: A Journey across the Ruins of Post- Mao China." In Sheldon H. Lu and Emilie Yueh-yu Yeh, eds., *Chinese-Language Film: Historiography, Poetics, Politics,* 186–209. Honolulu: University of Hawai'i Press, 2005.

Liu, Alan. *The Laws of Cool: Knowledge Work and the Culture of Information.* Chicago: University of Chicago Press, 2004.

Liu, Jianmei. "Conclusion." In *Revolution Plus Love*, 210–216. Honolulu: University of Hawai'i Press, 2003.

———. "Farewell or Remember Revolution?" In *Revolution Plus Love,* 193–209. Honolulu: University of Hawai'i Press, 2003.

Liu, Jin. "The Rhetoric of Local Languages as the Marginal: Chinese Underground and Independent Films by Jia Zhangke and Others." *Modern Chinese Literature and Culture* 18.2 (Fall 2006): 163–205.

Liu, Kang. *Globalization and Cultural Trends in China.* Honolulu: University of Hawai'i Press, 2004.

Liu, Lydia. "*Beijing Sojourners in New York:* Postcolonialism and the Question of Ideology." *positions* 7.3 (1999): 763–797.

Liu Ping. "Zai lishi yu xianshi de qihedian shang" (Between history and reality). *Zhongguo dianshi* (Chinese television) 5 (2001): 30–33.

Liu Rixin. "Guoyou qiye de guoqu, xianzai he jianglai" (SOEs' past, present, and future). http://www.wyzxsx.com/Article/Class4?200801/3108.html.

Liu Xiliang. "Hongyang zhuxuan lü, tichang duoyang hua" (Promote main melody and encourage variation). *Zhongguo dianshi* (Chinese television) 5 (1994): 7–13.

Liu Yan. "*Yongzheng wangchao:* lishi wenben de wenhua chanshi" (The Yongzheng Court: a cultural interpretation of a text of history). *Zhongguo dianshi* (Chinese television) 5 (1999): 33–36.

Liu Yan and He Ru. "Dianshiju bianpai celüe yu guanzhong manyidu" (Television drama programming and viewers' satisfaction). *Nanfang dianshi xuekan* (Journal of southern television) 4 (2001): 82–86.

Lu Di, ed. *Jiexi Zhongguo mingying dianshi* (Analyzing China's private television industry). Shanghai: Fudan Daxue Chubanshe, 2005.

Lu Haibo. *Dianshiju meixue* (Aesthetics of television drama). Nanjing: Jiangsu Wenyi Chubanshe, 1989.

Lu, Sheldon. *China, Transnational Visuality, Global Postmodernity.* Stanford, CA: Stanford University Press, 2001.

———. "Soap Opera in China: The Transnational Politics of Visuality, Sexuality, and Masculinity." *Cinema Journal* 40:1 (2000): 25–47.

———, ed. *Transnational Chinese Cinemas: Identity, Nationhood, Gender.* Honolulu: University of Hawai'i Press, 1997.

Lu Xun. *Zhongguo xiaoshuo shilüe* (Brief history of Chinese fiction). In *Lu Xun quanji* (Complete works of Lu Xun), vol. 9, 291–305. Beijing: Remin Wenxue Chubanshe, 2005.

Lull, James. *China Turned On: Television, Reform, and Resistance.* London: Routledge, 1991.

MacAdams, Lewis. *Birth of the Cool: Beat, Bebop, and the American Avant Garde.* New York: Simon and Schuster, 2001.

Mao Zedong. "Qilü: he Guo Muoruo tongzhi" (Qilü: a reply to comrade Guo Muoruo). *Mao Zedong shici* (Mao Zedong's poems). Beijing: Renmin Wenxue Chubanshe, 1963.

———. "Yanan wenyi zuotanhui shang de jianghua" (Talks at the Yan'an forum on art and literature). In *Mao Zedong xuanji* (The selected works of Mao Zedong), vol. 3, 847–879. Beijing: Renmin Chubanshe, 1991.

McDougall, Bonnie S. *Fictional Authors, Imaginary Audiences: Modern Chinese Literature in the Twentieth Century.* Hong Kong: The Chinese University Press, 2003.

McGrath, Jason. "The Independent Cinema of Jia Zhangke: From Postsocialist Realism to a Transnational Aesthetic." In Zhang Zhen, ed., *The Urban Generation: Chinese Cinema and Society at the Turn of the Twentieth-first Century,* 81–114. Durham, NC, and London: Duke University Press, 2007.

McHugh, Kathleen Anne. *American Domesticity: From How-to Manual to Hollywood Melodrama.* New York: Oxford University Press, 1999.

Mercer, Hon, and Martin Shingler. *Melodrama: Genre, Style, Sensibility.* London and New York: Wallflower, 2004.

Müller, Gotelind. *Representing History in Chinese Media: The TV Drama Zou Xiang Gonghe (Towards the Republic).* Berlin: LIT, 2007.

Ni Xueli and Zhang Cui. "Gan'ga de Zhongguo qingchun ouxiang ju" (The embarrassing Chinese youth-idol drama). *Yingshi yishu* (Art of film and television) 6 (2001): 81–83.

Ouyang Fenqiang. *Jiyi honglou* (Remembering *honglou*). Shanghai: Shanghai Wenyi Chubanzongshe, 2008.

Pan Xiao. "Rensheng de lu a, zenme yuezou yuezhai" (Why life's path is becoming narrower and narrower). *Zhongguo qingnian* (Youth of China) 5 (1980): 3–5.

Pearce, Susan M. *Museums, Objects and Collections.* Washington, DC: Smithsonian Institution Press, 1993.

———. *On Collecting: An Investigation into Collecting in the European Tradition.* London and New York: Routledge, 1995.

Petro, Patrice. *Joyless Streets: Women and Melodramatic Representation in Weimar Germany.* Princeton, NJ: Princeton University Press, 1989.

Prendergast, Christopher. *Balzac: Fiction and Melodrama.* New York: Homes and Meier Publishers, Inc., 1978.

Qian Liqun. *Jujue yiwang* (Refuse to forget). Shantou: Shantou Daxue Chubanshe, 1999.

———. *Yu Lu Xun xiangyu* (Encounter Lu Xun). Beijing: Sanlian Chubanshe, 2005.

Qin Hui. "Dividing the Big Family Assets." *New Left Review* 20 (March–April 2003): 83–112.

Qiu Xinmu. "'Zhishi qingnian shangshan xiaxiang' yanjiu zongshu" (A summary of the research on the rustication movement of educated youth). *Dangdai Zhongguo yanjiu* (Research on contemporary China) 4 (2003) (http://www.xsix.com/htm/xssy/xszs/2004-10-25-17550.htm).

Rofel, Lisa. "*Yearnings:* Televisual Love and Melodramatic Politics." In *Desiring China: Experiments in Neoliberalism, Sexuality, and Public Culture*, 31–64. Durham, NC, and London: Duke University Press, 2007.

———. "*Yearnings:* Televisual Love and Melodramatic Politics in China." *American Ethnologist* 21.4 (1994): 700–722.

Shao Qi. *Zhongguo dianshiju daolun* (Introduction to Chinese television drama). Shanghai: Jiaotong Daxue Chubanshe, 2008.

Shen, Hongmei. "All-China Women's Federation: A Party Representative or Feminist Organization?" Paper presented at the annual meeting of the International Communication Association, San Francisco, California, May 23, 2007 (http://www.allacademic.com/meta/p170486_index.html).

Shu Jinyu. "Remen dianshiju: ming zuojia men bu maizhang" (Television drama as big hits: famous writers' cool responses). *Zhongguo guangbo yingshi* (Chinese radio, film, and television) 13 (2000): 38–39.

Silbergeld, Jerome. *China into Film: Frames of Reference in Contemporary Chinese Cinema.* London: Reaktion Books, 1995.

Singer, Ben. *Melodrama and Modernity: Early Sensational Cinema and Its Contexts.* New York: Columbia University Press, 2001.

Song Jialing. *Dianshiju yishu lun* (Theory of the art of television drama). Beijing: Beijing Guangbo Xueyuan Chubanshe, 1988.

Song, Mingwei. *Long Live Youth: National Rejuvenation and the Chinese Bildungsroman, 1900–1958.* Ph.D. diss., Columbia University, 2005 (http://academiccommons.columbia.edu:8080/ac/handle/10022/AC:P:6407).

Spence, Jonathan. *The Search for Modern China.* London: Hutchinson, 1990.

Stacey, Judith. *Patriarchy and Socialist Revolution in China.* Berkeley: University of California Press, 1983.

Su Xiaokang and Wang Luxaing. *Deathsong of the River.* Introduced, translated, and annotated by Richard W. Bodman and Pin P. Wan. Ithaca, NY: East Asia Program, Cornell University, 1991.

Sun, Xiaokang. "A Chinese in the New World: Television Dramas, Global Cities and Travels to Modernity." *Inter-Asia Cultural Studies* 2.1 (April 2001): 81–94.

Wang, Ban. "Epic Narrative, Authenticity, and the Memory of Realism: Reflections on Jia Zhangke's *Platform.*" In Ching Kwan Lee and Guobin Yang, eds., *Re-envisioning the Chinese Revolution: The Politics and Poetics of Collective Memories in Reform China*, 193–216. Washington, DC: Woodrow Wilson Center Press; Stanford, CA: Stanford University Press, 2007.

———. *Illuminations from the Past: Trauma, Memory, and History in Modern China.* Stanford, CA: Stanford University Press, 2004.

———. "Review of *One China, Many Paths,* in *Modern Chinese Literature and Culture.*" MCLC Resource Center Publication, January 2006 (http://mclc.osu.edu/rc/pubs/reviews/wang2.htm).

———. *The Sublime Figure of History: Aesthetics and Politics in Twentieth-Century China.* Stanford, CA: Stanford University Press, 1997.

———. "Tradition, Memory, and Hope: Lu Xun and Critical Historical Consciousness." In *Illuminations from the Past: Trauma, Memory, and History in Modern China*, 17–57. Stanford, CA: Stanford University Press.

Wang Baoqiang. "Wang Baoqiang." http://baike.baidu.com/view/764555.htm.

Wang, Chaohua, ed. *One China, Many Paths.* London and New York: Verso, 2003.

Wang Hailing. "Wang Hailing: wo dui hunyin hen jiji" (Wang Hailing: I am positive about marriage). http://yule.sohu.com/20040913/n222005209.shtml.

———. "Wang Hailing: zuo quanzhi taitai bushi fengxian" (Wang Hailing: being a housewife is not a selfless sacrifice). *Meizhou shibao* (Boston Chinese report) October 8–14 (2004): A6.

———. "Wang Hailing bu fu zhuanjia tiaoci, wei 'li hun' bianjie" (Wang Hailing does not agree with critics and defends *Divorce Chinese Style*). http://ent.sina.com.cn/2004-10-7/0704524349.html.

Wang Hui. *China's New Order: Society, Politics, and Economy in Transition.* Edited by Theodore Huters. Cambridge, MA, and London, England: Harvard University Press, 2003.

———. "Dangdai Zhongguo de sixiang zhuangkuang yu xiandaixing wenti" (Contemporary Chinese thought and the question of modernity). *Tianya* (Frontiers) 5 (1997): 133–150.

———. "Depoliticized Politics: From East to West." *New Left Review* 41 (September–October 2006): 29–45.

———. *Fankang juewang* (Against despair). Shijiazhuang: Hebei Jiaoyu Chubanshe, 1999.

———. *Xiandai Zhongguo sixiang de xingqi* (The rise of modern Chinese thought). Beijing: Sanlian Chubanshe, 2004.

———. "'Xin ziyou zhuyi' de lishi genyuan jiqi pipan—zai lun dangdai Zhongguo dalu de sixiang zhuangkuang yu xiandaixing wenti" (Critiquing the historical resources of "neoliberalism": additional reflection on contemporary Chinese thought and issues of modernity). The first section of the article appears in *Taiwan shehui yanjiu jikan* (Taiwan social research quarterly) 2 (2001) (http://www.tech.cn/data/detail.php?id=12659).

Wang Jinhe. "Fan'an yue fan yue luan: ye tan *yongzheng wangchao*" (Confusion increased: also about *The Yongzheng Court*). *Zhongguo dianshi* (Chinese television) 5 (1999): 28–29.

Wang, Jing. "*He Shang* and the Paradoxes of Chinese Enlightenment," In *High Culture Fever: Politics, Aesthetics, and Ideology in Deng's China*, 118–136. Berkeley, Los Angeles, and London: University of California Press, 1996.

———. "Introduction." *positions* (special issue: Chinese Popular Culture and the State) 9.1 (Spring 2001): 1–27.

———, ed. *Locating China: Space, Place, and Popular Culture.* London and New York: Routledge, 2005.

Wang, Q. Edward, and George G. Iggers, eds. *Turning Points in Historiography: A Cross-Cultural Perspective.* Rochester, NY: University of Rochester Press, 2002.

Wang Wei. "Jiaowang guozheng de Yongzheng xingxiang" (Overly corrected image of Yongzheng). *Zhongguo dianshi* (Chinese television) 5 (1999): 30–32.

Wang Xiaoyu. "Yichang wenhua de guangrong geming" (A glorious revolution of culture). *Dushu* (Reading) 4 (2008): 10–15.

Wang Yichuan. "Wo kan dangqian Zhongguo dianshi de hou lishi ju xianxiang" (Emperors and unofficial history: my view on the posthistory drama phenomenon in contemporary Chinese television), *Dianying yishu* (Film art) 3 (2002): 39–41.

Wang, Yuejing. "Melodrama as Historical Understanding: The Making and Unmaking of Communist History." In Wimal Dissanayake, ed., *Melodrama and Asian Cinema,* 73–100. Cambridge and New York: Cambridge University Press, 1993.

———. "*Red Sorghum:* Mixing Memory and Desire." In Chris Berry, ed., *Perspectives on Chinese Cinema,* 80–103. London: BFI Publishing, 1991.

Williams, Raymond. *Television: Technology and Cultural Form.* Hanover, NH: University Press of New England and Wesleyan University, 1992.

Wittenberg, David. "Introduction: Extreme Mainstream." *Iowa Journal of Cultural Studies* 4 (Spring 2004) (http://www.uiowa.edu/~englgrad/ijcs/mainstream/mainintro.htm).

Wolf, Margery. *Revolution Postponed: Women in Contemporary China.* Stanford, CA: Stanford University Press, 1985.

Wong, John, and Lai Hongyi, eds. *China into the Hu-Wen Era: Policy Initiatives and Challenges.* Singapore: World Scientific Publishing, 2006.

Wu Di and Lisa Pola, eds. *Class and Gender Debates over the Television Soap Opera "Aspirations."* Armonk, NY: M. E. Sharpe, 1995.

Wu Suling. *Zhongguo dianshiju fazhan shigang* (A historical outline of Chinese television drama). Beijing: Bejing Guangbo Xueyuan Chubanshe, 1997.

Xi, Jieying, Yunxiao Sun, and Jing Jian Xiao, eds. *Chinese Youth in Transition.* Aldershot, England, and Burlington, VT: Ashgate Publishing, Ltd., 2006.

Xie Xizhang. "Dianshiju 'Zhang Damin de xingfu shenghuo'de wenhua pingxi" (A cultural analysis of the television drama *Zhang Damin's Happy Life*). *Beijing Dianying Xueyuan xuebao* (Journal of the Beijing Film Academy) 1 (2001): 1–6.

Xu, Ben. *Disenchanted Democracy: Chinese Cultural Criticism of 1989.* Ann Arbor: University of Michigan Press, 1999

Xu Hong. *Dianshiju shenmei tezheng tansuo* (An exploration of the aesthetics of television drama). Jinan: Shandong Wenyi Chubanshe, 1991.

"Xu Sanduo: xiandai shenghuo de renwen huigui" (Xu Sanduo: the return of humanism in contemporary life). *Baidu shouye renwu* (Person on the cover page of *Baidu*) 11 (2007) (http://renwu.baidu.com/0711/index.html).

Yan, Haiping. *Chinese Women Writers and the Feminist Imagination, 1905–1948.* London and New York: Routledge, 2006.

Yang, Guobin, and Ming-Bao Yue, eds. *Collective Memories of the Cultural Revolution. The China Review* (special issue) 5.2 (Fall 2005).

Yang Tiancun. *Dianshi chuangzuo lun* (On creating television drama). Beijing: Beijing Guangbo Xueyuan Chubanshe, 1988.

Yin Hong. "Chongtu yu gongmou—lun Zhongguo dianshiju de wenhua celüe" (Conflicts and collaborations: on the cultural strategies of Chinese television drama). *Yingshi yishu* (Art of film and television) 1 (2002): 8–15.

———. "Meaning, Production, Consumption: The History and Reality of Television Drama in China." In Stephanie Hemelryk Donald, Michael Keane and Yin Hong, eds., *Media in China: Consumption, Content, and Crisis*, 28-40. London and New York: RoutledgeCurzon, 2002.

Yin Hong and Yang Daihui. "Yin Hong and Yang Daihui: Zhongguo dianshiju yishu chuantong) (Yin Hong and Yang Daihui on the artistic tradition of Chinese television drama). http://medial.people.com.cn/GB/5258393.html.

Yu Bing and Wen Ye. "Zhongguo qingchun ouxiang ju weishenme re bu qilai" (Why Chinese youth-idol drama does not attract viewers' interest). *Zhongguo guangbo yingshi* (Chinese radio, film, and television) 6 (2000): 24–27.

Yu Xingzhong. "Qiangshi wenhua, eryuan renshi yu fazhi" (Hegemonic culture, binary-oppositional epistemology, and rule by law). Originally published in *Qinghua fazhi lunhen* (Tsinghua collection of law theory papers), vol. 3 (http://www.lun-wen.cn//legalscience/lawtheory/2007.3/109380.asp?d=12).

Yue Peng. "Qinggong xi zouhong manshuo" (Some thoughts on the popularity of the Qing court drama). *Zhongguo dianshi* (Chinese television) 2 (2000): 36–40.

Zeng Qingrui and Lu Rong. *Zhongguo dianshiju de shenmei yishu* (The aesthetics of Chinese television drama). Beijing: Beijing Guangbo Xueyuan Chubanshe, 1997.

Zha Jianying. *Bashi niandai fangtanlu* (Interviews about the 1980s). Beijing: Sanlian Chubanshe, 2006.

———."Yearnings." In *China Pop: How Soap Operas, Tabloids, and Bestsellers Are Transforming a Culture*, 25–54. New York: New Press, 1995.

Zhang Dexiang. "*Yongzheng wangchao* sanwei" (Three flavors of *The Yongzheng Court*). *Zhongguo dianshi* (Chinese television) 4 (1999): 2–5.

Zhang, Xudong. *Chinese Modernism: Culture Fever, Avant-Garde Fiction, and the New Chinese Cinema.* Durham, NC, and London: Duke University Press, 1997.

———. *Postsocialism and Cultural Politics: China in the Last Decade of the Twentieth Century.* Durham, NC, and London: Duke University Press, 2008.

———. *Whither China? Intellectual Politics in Contemporary China.* Durham, NC: Duke University Press, 2002.

Zhang Yi. "Shashibiya hua yu dianshiju jingping" (Shakespeare-ization and good television drama). *Zhongguo dianshi* (Chinese television) 3 (2000): 56–59.

Zhang Yiwu. "Bei 'zhuanhuan' he bei 'tidai' de xin wenxue" (New literature that has been transformed and replaced). *Wenxue ziyou tan* (Forum for free discussion on literature) 4 (2004): 83–90.

———. "Facts and Flaws Make Up Epic TV Tales." *China Daily*, February 2, 2005 (http://www.chinadaily.com.cn/english/doc/2005-02/content_414251.htm).

Zhang, Zhen. *An Amorous History of the Silver Screen: Shanghai Cinema 1896–1937.* Chicago: University of Chicago Press, 2005.

———. "The 'Rice Bowl of Youth' in Fin de Siècle Urban China." *Public Culture* 2.1 (Winter 2000): 93–113.

———, ed. *The Urban Generation: Chinese Cinema and Society at the Turn of the Twenty-First Century.* Durham, NC, and London: Duke University Press, 2007.

Zhong Chenxiang. "2000 nian Zhongguo dianshiju chuangzuo gaikuang" (A brief summary of Chinese TV drama and its creation in 2000). *Zhongguo dianshi* (Chinese television) 8 (2001): 13-16.

*Zhongguo dianshi guanzhong xianzhuang baogao* ((Reports on the viewership of Chinese television). Beijing: Shehui Kexue Wenxian Chubanshe, 1998.

Zhong, Xueping. "'Long Live Youth' and the Ironies of Youth and Gender in Chinese Films of the 1950s and 1960s." *Modern Chinese Literature and Culture* 11 .2 (Fall 1999): 150–185.

———. *Masculinity Besieged? Issues of Modernity and Male Subjectivity in Chinese Literature of the Late Twentieth Century.* Durham, NC, and London: Duke University Press, 2000.

———. "Multiple Readings and Personal Reconfigurations against the 'Nationalist Grain.'" In Sharon Hom, ed., *Chinese Women Traversing Diaspora,* 103–125. New York: Garland Publishing, 1999.

———. "Who Is a Feminist? Understanding the Ambivalence towards *Shanghai Baby,* 'Body Writing,' and Feminism in Post–Women's Liberation China." In Dorothy Ko and Wang Zheng, eds., *Translating Feminism in China,* 215–246. Malden, MA; Oxford, UK; and Carlton, Australia: Blackwell Publishing, 2007.

———. "Who Is Afraid of Lu Xun? Politics of 'Lu Xun lun zheng' and the Question of His Legacy in the Post-Revolution China." In Lu Jie, ed., *China's Literary and Cultural Scenes at the Turn of the Twenty-First Century,* 81–102. London and New York: Routledge, 2008.

———. "Women Can Hold Up Half the Sky: A 'Fourth-Told' Tale." In Ban Wang, ed., *Words and Their Stories.* Brill, forthcoming.

Zhong, Xueping, Wang Zheng, and Bai Di, eds. *Some of Us: Chinese Women Growing Up in the Mao Era.* New Brunswick, NJ, and London: Rutgers University Press, 2001.

Zhong Yibing. *Zhongguo dianshi yishu fazhanshi* (History of Chinese television art). Hangzhou: Zhejiang Renmin Chubanshe, 1994.

*Zhongguo dianshi hongpishu, 2001* (The red book of Chinese television, 2001). Guilin, Guangxi: Lijiang Chubanshe, 2002.

Zhu Dake. "The Drawback of Xie Jin's Model." In George S. Semsel, Xia Hong, and Hou Jianping, eds., *Chinese Film Theory: A Guide to the New Era,* 144–146. New York, Westport, CT, and London: Praeger, 1990.

Zhu Guoliang. "Huangjin shiduan 'fengsha' yinjin ju" (Limiting imported dramas in primetime). *Dianshiju* (Television Drama) 4 (2002): 5–9.

Zhu, Ling. "A Brave New World? On the Construction of 'Masculinity' and 'Femininity' in *The Red Sorghum Family.*" In Tonglin Lu, ed., *Gender and Sexuality in Twentieth-Century Chinese Literature and Society,* 121–134. Albany: State University of New York Press, 1993.

Zhu, Ying. *Television in Post-Reform China: Serial Dramas, Confucian Leadership and the Global Television Market.* London and New York: Routledge, 2008.

———. "Transnational Circulation of Chinese-Language Television Dramas." In Ying Zhu and Chris Berry, eds., *TV China*, 221–242. Bloomington and Indianapolis: Indiana University Press, 2009.

———. "*Yongzheng Dynasty* and Chinese Primetime Television Drama." *Cinema Journal* 44.4 (2005): 3–17.

———. "*Yongzheng Dynasty* and Totalitarian Nostalgia." In Ying Zhu, Michael Keane, and Ruoyun Bai, eds., *TV Drama in China*, 21–32. Hong Kong: Hong Kong University Press, 2008.

Zhu, Ying, Michael Keane, and Ruoyun Bai, eds. *TV Drama in China*. Hong Kong: Hong Kong University Press, 2008.

Zhu, Ying, and Chris Berry, eds. *TV China*. Bloomington and Indianapolis: Indiana University Press, 2009.

Zinn, Gesa. "Melodrama and Women." In Friederike Eigler and Susanne Kord, eds., *The Feminist Encyclopedia of German Literature*, 316–317. Westport, Conn.: Greenwood Press, 1997.

Zizek, Slavoj. "Introduction." In Slavoj Zizek, ed., *Mapping Ideology*, 1–33. London and New York: Verso, 1994.

Zito, Angela, and Tani Barlow, eds. *Body, Subject and Power in China*. Chicago: University of Chicago Press, 1994.

Zlotnick, Susan. *Women, Writing, and the Industrial Revolution*. Baltimore, MD: Johns Hopkins University Press, 1998.

# Index

## About the Author

ZHONG XUEPING is associate professor of Chinese literature and culture at Tufts University and the author of *Masculinity Beseiged? Issues of Modernity and Male Subjectivity in Chinese Literature of the Late Twentieth Century* (2000).

Production Notes for Zhong / *Mainstream Culture Refocused*

Jacket design by Wilson Angel

Text design by University of Hawai'i Press production staff
with text in Minion Pro and display in Myriad Pro

Composition by Lucille C. Aono

Printing and binding by The Maple-Vail Book
Manufacturing Group

Printed on 60# Maple Recycled Opaque, 408 ppi